Ethnic Conflict and International Security

Ethnic Conflict and International Security

Michael E. Brown, Editor

Princeton University Press
Princeton, New Jersey

Published by Princeton University Press, 41 William Street, Princeton, New Jersey 08540

In the United Kingdom: Princeton University Press, Chichester, West Sussex

Library of Congress Cataloging-in-Publication Data
Ethnic conflict and international security / Michael E. Brown, editor.
p.   cm.
    Articles reprinted from various issues of Survival.
    Includes bibliographical references and index.
    ISBN 0-691-03368-4
    ISBN 0-691-00068-9 (pbk.)
    1. Ethnic relations.   2. Conflict management.   3. Security, International.   4. Mediation, International.   I. Brown, Michael E. (Michael Edward), 1954–   .
GN496.E838   1993
305.8—dc20   93-2175

This book has been composed in Times New Roman. It was copyedited by Christine Zibas and typeset by Clare Wilkes

Princeton University Press books are printed on acid-free paper and meet the guidelines for permanence and durability of the Committee on Production Guidelines for Book Longevity of the Council on Library Resources

Printed in the United States of America

10 9 8 7 6 5 4 3 2

Contents

Preface

Until recently, international relations theorists and strategic studies analysts paid comparatively little attention to the causes, effects, and international implications of ethnic and other forms of communal conflict. There are three main reasons for this. First, for most of the postwar era, authoritarian rule dampened ethnic problems and stifled national aspirations in Eastern Europe and the Soviet Union, as well as parts of Central and East Asia and Africa. This stabilized large parts of the world in a highly effective, if noxious, way. Second, the most serious threat to international security during the Cold War was the possibility that an East–West confrontation would lead to nuclear war. Many scholars and analysts, not unnaturally, focused their intellectual energies on this issue. Third, moves toward economic and political integration in Europe, in conjunction with growing economic interdependence internationally, led many to think that ethnic and national identifications—and the prospects for ethnic conflict—were fading.

Disregard for the importance of ethnic issues in world affairs, always misguided as far as the developing world was concerned, has been overtaken, in stunning fashion, by events from Abkhazia to Zaire. Our understanding of these issues, however, is still in a formative stage.

Journalistic accounts of the ethnic conflicts now under way in the former Yugoslavia and the former Soviet Union, for example, generally argue that these conflicts are taking place because the collapse of authoritarian rule has made them possible: The "lid" on ancient rivalries, it is said, has been taken off. If this simple explanation is true, then why has open warfare broken out in some places, but not others? Can we be more precise in identifying the conditions under which conflict is most likely? Can we identify the conditions under which conflicts are likely to be particularly intense? Similarly, our understanding of the immediate effects and international implications of ethnic and communal disputes is inadequate. What kinds of problems will different types of ethnic disputes pose for the international community? What, if anything, can the international community do to minimize the potential for ethnic and communal conflict?

This volume tries to shed some light on these questions. In an introductory chapter, I analyze alternative explanations of the causes of ethnic conflict and discuss the implications of different kinds of ethnic conflict for the international community. Drawing on an array of historical and contemporary illustrations, Anthony Smith examines the nature of ethnicity and the ethnic roots of nationalism and nationalistic conflicts. David Welsh analyzes the domestic political roots of ethnic conflicts, as well as possible political, institutional, and constitutional solutions to such conflicts. Renée de Nevers examines the interrelationship between democratization and ethnic conflict, identifying conditions under which democratization makes ethnic conflict more likely. Jack Snyder develops several sets of hypotheses about the sources of nationalism and the conditions under which nationalistic conflicts are likely to break out and escalate. Along the way, he examines the current situation in Russia, in particular. Barry Posen argues that security dilemmas are especially acute in certain kinds of ethnic relationships, which helps explain why conflict breaks out and escalates in some cases, but not others. He draws on these insights to explain why conflict has broken out between Serbia and Croatia, but not Russia and Ukraine. Pierre Hassner ponders the fact that both integration and disintegration are major forces in world politics today. Kathleen Newland examines the impact that ethnic conflicts are having on population movements and refugee problems, concluding with an appraisal of international actions designed to address these problems. Jenonne Walker analyzes the roles of individuals, outside powers, and international institutions in the mediation of ethnic disputes, arguing that one must distinguish among different kinds of mediation efforts. Robert Cooper and Mats Berdal begin with an assessment of outside interventions in the conflicts in Sri Lanka, Lebanon, Cyprus, and Bangladesh, before going on to discuss the conditions most propitious for successful interventions. Adam Roberts challenges the commonly held view that the United Nations will play a leading role in resolving ethnic conflicts and promoting international security in the near future. Finally, in a wide-ranging and thought-provoking essay, John Chipman analyzes the options available for managing what he calls "the politics of parochialism."

Except for my introductory essay, these chapters were originally published in the Spring and Summer 1993 issues of *Survival*, the quarterly journal of the International Institute for Strategic Studies, which I edit. I organized these articles along thematic, rather than regional lines, thinking that heavily descriptive studies of current disputes would soon be overtaken by events. In choosing authors, I made a concerted effort to bring different professional and national perspectives to bear on the problems at hand. As a result, the authors of these pieces are distinguished academics (from the fields of political science, sociology, and history), policy analysts, and policymakers from the United States, Canada, Britain, France, Norway, and South Africa. All are internationally recognized experts in their fields.

Friends and colleagues were tremendously helpful in identifying key issues and potential authors. In particular, I would like to express my gratitude to Philip Bobbit, John Chipman, Ivo Daalder, Chris Demchak, Renée de Nevers, Lori Gronich, Helga Haftendorn, Don Horowitz, Bo Huldt, Sam Huntington, Jo Husbands, Kenneth Jensen, Joe Joffee, Charles Kupchan, Arend Lijphart, Rob Litwak, James Mayall, John Mearsheimer, Robert O'Neill, George Quester, Richard Rosecrance, Gerry Segal, Jack Snyder, Paul Stern, Sven Tägil, and Steve Van Evera.

Chris Zibas, the Assistant Editor of *Survival*, spent long hours (and many weekends) helping me edit manuscripts and getting them ready for publication in London. Chris played the leading role in preparing these articles for publication in the United States, changing English spelling and punctuation into their proper American counterparts. Clare Wilkes, the journal's Production Supervisor, displayed considerable wizardry in turning heavily edited manuscripts into pristine, camera-ready copy. Vicky Fisher and Rachel Neaman helped with proofreading and production at various stages. Sheelagh Urbanoviez helped me prepare the bibliography, and in many other ways too numerous to mention. Chris, Rachel, Sheelagh, and Clare helped me prepare the index; their efforts were above and beyond the call of duty and are greatly appreciated. My sincere thanks to one and all.

Finally, I would like to thank Walter Lippincott, the Director of Princeton University Press; Malcolm DeBevoise, the Law and Political Science Editor at Princeton; and Jennifer Mathews, who coordinated our transatlantic enterprise, for their support of this project and their efforts in bringing it to fruition.

This volume represents neither the first nor the final word on this misunderstood and complex subject, but I believe it advances our understanding of the causes of ethnic and communal conflict, the regional and international implications of such conflicts, and what the international community can do to minimize the potential for instability and violence. I hope it makes a difference.

Michael E. Brown
London, May 1993

Contributors

Mats Berdal is a Research Associate at the International Institute for Strategic Studies in London.

Michael E. Brown is Senior Fellow in U.S. Security Policy and Editor of *Survival* at the International Institute for Strategic Studies in London.

John Chipman is Director of Studies at the International Institute for Strategic Studies in London.

Robert Cooper is Head of Chancery at the British Embassy, Bonn.

Renée de Nevers is a Research Associate at the International Institute for Strategic Studies in London.

Pierre Hassner is Research Director at the Centre d'Etudes et de Recherches Internationales (CERI), and Professor of Political Science, Paris.

Kathleen Newland is a consultant to the UN High Commissioner for Refugees.

Barry R. Posen is a Professor in the Political Science Department of the Massachusetts Institute of Technology.

Adam Roberts is Montague Burton Professor of International Relations at the University of Oxford and a Fellow of Balliol College.

Anthony D. Smith is a Professor in the Department of Sociology at the London School of Economics.

Jack Snyder is Professor of Political Science at Columbia University.

Jenonne Walker is Special Assistant to President Clinton and Senior Director for Europe on the National Security Council Staff.

David Welsh is Professor of Southern African Studies in the Political Studies Department at the University of Cape Town.

Ethnic Conflict and International Security

Chapter 1

Causes and Implications of Ethnic Conflict
Michael E. Brown

Expectations were too high. The Cold War generated great tension, but also exceptional stability—at least as far as Europe was concerned. When the Cold War ended, many people assumed that international tensions would be reduced, but that stability would be retained—perhaps even extended to previously troubled parts of the world. Learned commentators spoke of "the end of history." Presidents suggested that the great powers would work together to create a "New World Order." Many people expected, inferring too much from the international community's response to the Iraqi invasion of Kuwait, that effective international action would be taken in the future to prevent conflicts from breaking out and to resolve those that did. Many people seemed to think that the end of the Cold War marked the advent of the millenium.

These great expectations—which could only have been generated by willfully ignoring the many ethnic conflicts around the world that have raged for years, even decades—have been dashed. People have been stunned by both the breadth and depth of the ethnic conflicts that are now taking place in many regions. The war in Bosnia-Herzegovina has received the most attention in the West because of the intense coverage it has received from the Western media, but equally if not more horrific conflicts are under way in Afghanistan, Angola, Armenia, Azerbaijan, Burma, Georgia, India, Indonesia, Liberia, Sri Lanka, Sudan, and Tajikistan. Other trouble spots abound—Bangladesh, Belgium, Bhutan, Burundi, Estonia, Ethiopia, Guatemala, Iraq, Latvia, Lebanon, Mali, Moldova, Niger, Northern Ireland, Pakistan, the Philippines, Romania, Rwanda, South Africa, Spain, and Turkey, for example—and the prospects for ethnic conflict in Russia and China cannot be dismissed.

Expectations about the willingness and ability of outside powers to prevent and resolve ethnic conflicts have also been dampened. European and American leaders have agonized over the conflict in Bosnia, trying to decide if genocidal acts and threats to outside interests have created either moral or strategic imperatives for intervention. Except for providing some small measure of humanitarian assistance, no action was taken as cities were bombed and civilians slaughtered. The possibility that Western powers will intervene in other ethnic conflicts, where their interests are even less engaged and where media attention is less intense, is remote.

This chapter pulls together the main arguments developed in this book about the causes and implications of ethnic conflict, as well as the recommendations that have been put forward to minimize the potential for instability and violence. Its objective is to provide a framework for analyzing the key issues that will be discussed in more detail in subsequent chapters. It begins with a brief discussion of some basic definitional issues, in an effort to sharpen an understanding of the parameters of the term, "ethnic conflict." Second, it examines alternative explanations of the causes of ethnic conflict, focusing in turn on systemic, domestic, and perceptual explanations. Third, it analyzes the regional and international implications of ethnic conflicts, arguing that one must distinguish among the effects of three basic kinds of conflict outcomes: peaceful reconciliation, peaceful separation, and ethnic war. The latter, it is argued, can affect the strategic interests and moral calculations of the outside world in seven important ways. This chapter concludes with a discussion of recommendations that have been developed to prevent or dampen ethnic conflicts, focusing in particular on steps outside powers and the international community could take in this regard.

DEFINITIONS

The term "ethnic conflict" is often used loosely, to describe a wide range of intrastate conflicts that are not, in fact, ethnic in character. The conflict in Somalia, for example, is occasionally referred to as an ethnic conflict even though Somalia is the most ethnically homogenous country in Africa. The conflict in Somalia is not between rival ethnic groups, but between rival gangs, clans, and warlords, all of whom belong to the same ethnic group.

This inquiry consequently begins with some definitions. According to Anthony Smith, an "ethnic community" is "a named human population with a myth of common ancestry, shared memories, and cultural elements; a link with a historic territory or homeland; and a measure of solidarity."[1] Six criteria must be met, therefore, before a group can be called an ethnic community. First, the group must have a name for itself. This is not trivial; a lack of a name reflects an insufficiently developed collective identity. Second, the people in the group must believe in a common ancestry. This is more important than genetic ties, which may exist, but are not essential. Third, the members of the group must share historical memories, often myths or legends passed from generation to generation by word of mouth. Fourth, the group must have a shared culture, generally based on a combination of language, religion, laws, customs, institutions, dress, music, crafts, architecture, even food. Fifth, the group must feel an attachment to a specific piece of territory, which it may or may not actually inhabit. Sixth and last, the people in a group have to think of themselves as a group in order to constitute an ethnic community; that is, they must have a sense of their common ethnicity. The group must be self-aware.[2]

At the risk of stating the obvious, an "ethnic conflict" is a dispute about important political, economic, social, cultural, or territorial issues between two or more ethnic communities. Some ethnic conflicts involve little or no violence. The struggle of French Canadians within Quebec to win more autonomy from the Canadian government is a case in point; Czechoslovakia's "velvet divorce" is another. Tragically, other ethnic conflicts involve full-scale military hostilities and unspeakable levels of savagery, as seen in Angola, Bosnia, the Caucasus, and elsewhere.

Two points should be kept in mind about these definitions. First, although Smith's conception of ethnic communities is a broad one—it would include many groups defined in terms of religious and tribal distinctions—many domestic disputes and civil wars are not ethnic in character. The war between the Sendero Luminoso and the Peruvian government, for example, is primarily political and ideological in nature, as is the continuing struggle between the Khmer Rouge and other factions in Cambodia; Cambodian persecution of ethnic Vietnamese is another matter, however. The problems in Georgia with South Ossetian and Abkhazian separatists are ethnic in nature; the struggle for power in Tblisi among various Georgian factions is not. The Burmese military's repression of Karen, Kachin, Naga, and Rohingya insurgents is an ethnic conflict; its suppression of the democracy movement in the country as a whole has other political motivations.

Second, many ethnic conflicts start out as domestic disputes, but become interstate conflicts when outside powers become involved. In some cases, trouble spills over into neighboring countries. In others, neighboring powers intervene in domestic disputes to protect the interests of their ethnic brethren. Disinterested powers may intervene in ethnic wars, which often involve attacks on civilian populations, for humanitarian reasons. For these and other reasons that will be discussed in more detail below, ethnic conflicts often become internationalized.

CAUSES

The conventional wisdom among journalists and policymakers is that ethnic conflicts have sprung up in Eastern Europe, the former Soviet Union, and elsewhere because the collapse of authoritarian rule has made such conflicts possible. The "lid" on ancient rivalries, it is said, has been taken off, and long-suppressed grievances are now being settled. Scholars generally agree that this conventional wisdom offers an inadequate explanation of the causes of ethnic conflict. It fails to explain why conflicts have broken out in some places, but not others, and it fails to explain why some ethnic disputes are more violent than others. In short, this single-factor explanation cannot account for significant variation in the incidence and intensity of ethnic conflict.[3]

Serious academic studies of the causes of ethnic conflict develop explanations at three main levels of analysis: the systemic level, the domestic level, and the perceptual level.[4]

Systemic Explanations

Systemic explanations of ethnic conflict focus on the nature of the security systems in which ethnic groups operate and the security concerns of these groups. The first and most obvious systemic prerequisite for ethnic conflict is that two or more ethnic groups must reside in close proximity. This condition is met in many parts of the world. As David Welsh observes, "Of the approximately 180 states that exist today, fewer than 20 are ethnically homogenous, in the sense that minorities account for less than 5 percent of the population."[5]

The second systemic prerequisite for ethnic conflict is that national, regional, and international authorities must be too weak to keep groups from fighting and too weak to ensure the security of individual groups. As Barry Posen explains, in systems where there is no sovereign—that is, where anarchy prevails—individual groups have to provide for their own defense.[6] They have to worry about whether neighboring groups pose security threats and whether threats will grow or diminish over time. The problem groups face is that, in taking steps to defend themselves—mobilizing armies and deploying military forces—they often threaten the security of others. This, in turn, can lead neighboring groups to take actions that will diminish the security of the first group. This is the security dilemma. Groups are often unaware of, or insensitive to, the impact their actions will have on others. In other cases, they are aware of this problem, but act anyway because they feel compelled to address what they see as imminent security threats. This, of course, is the situation in Eastern Europe and the former Soviet Union today. Imperial "sovereigns" have disappeared, and individual groups have to provide for their own defense.

According to Posen, instabilities develop when either of two conditions hold. First, when offensive and defensive military forces are hard to distinguish, groups cannot signal their defensive intentions by the kinds of military forces they deploy. Forces deployed for defensive purposes will have offensive capabilities and will therefore be seen as threatening by others. Second, if offensive military operations are more effective than defensive operations, due to the nature of military technology or the kinds of capabilities that are available, groups will adopt offensive military postures, and they will have powerful incentives to launch preemptive attacks in political crises.

Posen argues that these conditions are often generated when empires collapse and ethnic groups suddenly have to provide for their own security. First, under these circumstances, offensive and defensive forces are generally hard to distinguish. The military hardware available to newly independent ethnic groups is often unsophisticated from a technological standpoint, so defenses are based on infantry. Whether or not these forces are effective is essentially a function of the number, cohesiveness, and motivation of the troops in the field. Not surprising, newly independent ethnic groups often have large numbers of highly motivated, like-minded volunteers on which to draw. Cohesive, well-motivated infantries have inherent offensive capabilities against similarly configured forces, however, so they will inevitably be seen as threatening by other newly independent ethnic groups. This, in turn, will serve as a stimulus to military mobilization elsewhere.

Second, Posen argues that when empires break up, ethnic geography frequently creates situations that favor the offense over the defense. In some cases, ethnic groups will effectively surround "islands" of people from other groups. Defending these islands in the event of hostilities is generally quite difficult: All are vulnerable to blockades and sieges, and some are simply indefensible. Often, groups will try to expel pockets of minorities from their territory. The offense has tremendous tactical advantages in these "ethnic cleansing" operations; even small, lightly armed forces can generate tremendous amounts of terror in attacks on civilians. Posen is careful to note that ethnic geography is a variable, not a constant: Some ethnic islands are large, economically autonomous, and militarily defensible; others could be reinforced by nearby brethren. In short, ethnic geography can be stabilizing or destabilizing. In some cases, groups will be able to defend themselves and their brethren. In many cases, however, the offense will have the upper hand, and stability will be tenuous.

Posen identifies two other factors that have to be taken into account in analyses of the prospects for ethnic stability. First, windows of opportunity and vulnerability will be created because newly independent groups will develop state structures at different rates. Groups that are further along in developing states and deploying military forces will have powerful incentives to go on the offensive—expelling minorities, rescuing islands of brethren, launching preventive attacks against potential adversaries—before rival groups are able to defend themselves or launch offensives of their own. Second, the presence of nuclear weapons will affect stability in important ways: Nuclear weapons make infantries less important, they make defense easier, and they can prevent windows of vulnerability from opening up. In the hands of a status quo power, nuclear weapons could enhance stability.

Domestic Explanations

Other explanations of ethnic conflict focus on factors that operate primarily at the domestic level: the effectiveness of states in addressing the concerns of their constituents, the impact of nationalism on inter-ethnic relations, and the impact of democratization on inter-ethnic relations.

Jack Snyder argues that people look to states to provide security and promote economic prosperity.[7] Nationalism, he maintains, reflects the need to establish states capable of achieving these goals. Thus, it is not surprising that nationalism has flared up in parts of Eastern Europe and the former Soviet Union, where state structures have weakened or collapsed altogether. New state structures have been, or are in the process of being, established, but in many cases they are not yet able to provide for the security and well-being of their constituents. In some cases, ethnic minorities feel persecuted by the new states in which they find themselves. More generally, many in Eastern Europe and the former Soviet Union feel that they are not being adequately protected from unregulated markets. Inflation and unemployment are high, and economic prospects are often grim. Ethnic minorities frequently find themselves being blamed for these economic difficulties.

These problems are compounded by the fact that, when state structures are weak, nationalism is likely to be based on ethnic distinctions, rather than the idea that everyone who lives in a country is entitled to the same rights and privileges. As Snyder explains: "By its nature, nationalism based on equal and universal citizenship rights within a territory depends on a framework of laws to guarantee those rights, as well as effective institutions to allow citizens to give voice to their views. Ethnic nationalism, in contrast, depends not on institutions, but on culture."[8] It is not surprising, therefore, that there are strong currents of ethnic nationalism in Eastern Europe and the former Soviet Union, where state structures and political institutions have diminished capacities, and in those parts of the developing world where state structures and political institutions are inherently fragile.

The emergence of ethnic nationalism makes some form of ethnic conflict almost inevitable. The rise of ethnic nationalism in one group will be seen as threatening by others and will lead to the development of similar sentiments elsewhere. This will sharpen distinctions between groups, make it more likely that minority groups will be persecuted and more likely that ethnic minorities will demand states of their own. Secessionist crusades might be launched—and opposed. Ethnic nationalism will also make it easier for groups to field large, highly motivated armies. This will lead others to be more vigilant and to build up their own military forces. This, in turn, can make preemptive attacks or preventive war between neighboring groups more likely.

Other scholars—such as Donald Horowitz, Arend Lijphart, Renée de Nevers, and David Welsh—have examined the impact that democratization and other domestic political factors have on the prospects for ethnic conflict.[9] Democratization, scholars agree, is particularly problematic in multiethnic societies. It often exacerbates existing ethnic problems.

Much depends on the level of ethnic tension when the democratization process begins, according to de Nevers.[10] If the old regime was an extension of a minority ethnic group that suppressed demographically larger groups, then ethnic problems will complicate negotiations over new political arrangements from the very beginning. If the old regime exacerbated ethnic problems by engaging in forced assimilation, forced relocation, ethnic expulsion, or extermination campaigns, then the democratization process is likely to be both highly problematic and emotionally charged; many ethnic problems will be on the agenda. If, on the other hand, the old regime drew from all major ethnic groups in a fairly representative way and pursued comparatively benign policies toward the ethnic groups under its sway, ethnic issues will probably play a less prominent role in negotiations over new arrangements. These negotiations, in turn, will be more likely to resolve those ethnic problems that do exist.

A second factor in the equation, de Nevers argues, is the relative size of the ethnic groups in the country. If one group is substantially larger than the others, then it is more likely that the majority group will be able to dominate discussions about new political arrangements and that minority interests will be neglected. If negotiations are between two or more groups of roughly equal size, however, it is more likely that all groups' core concerns will be addressed. Third, if the opposition to the old regime was led by only one or two groups and if the old regime itself was an extension of another, the country's political system could easily fragment along ethnic lines as the democratization process unfolds. Ethnic tensions would intensify correspondingly. If, on the other hand, the opposition to the old regime emanated from all major ethnic groups in that society, these groups will have a cooperative foundation on which to build when they begin their discussions on new political arrangements. Fourth, if the military is loyal to a single ethnic group, rather than the state, then the prospects for managing ethnic conflict are not good. If the military is loyal to the state, however, the prospects are substantially better.

Finally, de Nevers points out that different kinds of democratization processes pose different problems for the management of ethnic conflict. If the fall of the old regime comes about suddenly, negotiations on new political arrangements will be conducted in great haste. Ethnic problems are more likely to be ignored, and power struggles, perhaps along ethnic lines, are more likely to take place. The euphoria experienced as the old regime passes from the scene might produce a moment of national unity, but this moment will not endure if underlying problems are neglected. If the demise of the old regime takes place over a period of months or even years, opposition leaders will have more time to address ethnic problems when they go about devising new political institutions and processes. They will also have more of an opportunity to develop a broad-based political alliance, and ethnic leaders will have a stronger cooperative foundation on which to build. One of the keys to minimizing ethnic conflict during democratic transitions, de Nevers maintains, is addressing ethnic problems early in the transition process. If ethnic grievances can be anticipated and dealt with early, ethnic conflicts are more likely to be prevented or at least mitigated.

A number of other domestic factors also affect the prospects for ethnic conflict. One problem, as Horowitz and Welsh point out, is the tendency in multiethnic societies for political parties to be organized along ethnic lines.[11] When this happens, party affiliations are a reflection of ethnic identity rather than political conviction. Political systems organized along these lines contain few independent voters, individuals who might cast votes for different parties in different elections. Under these circumstances, elections are mere censuses, and minority parties have no chance of winning power. In countries where parties are organized along ethnic lines and where winner-take-all elections are conducted—not uncommon in many parts of the world—democratic forms might be observed, but minorities remain essentially powerless, victims of a "tyranny of the majority."[12]

A related problem is the tendency in multiethnic societies for opportunistic politicians to appeal to communal, ethnic, and nationalistic impulses. This is often an effective way of mobilizing support and winning elections. Along the way, ethnic minorities are often blamed for many of society's ills; ethnic bashing and scapegoating are common features of electoral politics in many parts of the world. In many multiethnic societies, especially those coming out from under years or decades of authoritarian rule, political accommodation and compromise are alien principles. This, along with a lack of familiarity with and interest in coalition-building, undermines the prospects for ethnic rapprochement and the development of broad-based political communities. The mass media are often used for partisan and propagandistic purposes in ways that further damage inter-ethnic relations.

Finally, many countries have inadequate constitutional safeguards for minority rights. Even in places where minority rights guarantees exist on paper, they are often inadequately enforced. In short, constitutional and political reforms are needed in many places to address important ethnic grievances.

Perceptual Explanations

Some explanations of ethnic conflict focus on the false histories that many ethnic groups have of themselves and others. As Posen and Snyder point out, these histories are not subjected to dispassionate, scholarly scrutiny because they are usually passed from generation to generation by word of mouth.[13] These stories become part of a group's lore. They tend to be highly selective in their coverage of events and not unbiased in their interpretation of these events. Distorted and exaggerated with time, these histories present one's own group as heroic, while other groups are demonized. Grievances are enshrined, and other groups are portrayed as inherently vicious and aggressive. Group members typically treat these ethnic myths as received wisdom.

It is not surprising, therefore, that the oral histories of groups involved in an intense rivalry tend to be mirror images of each other. Serbs, for example, see themselves as heroic defenders of Europe and they see Croats as belligerent thugs; Croats see themselves as valiant victims of oppression and Serbs as congenital aggressors. Under such circumstances, the slightest provocation on either side simply confirms deeply held systems of beliefs and provides the justification for a retaliatory response. Incendiary perceptions such as these, especially when they are held by both parties in a rivalry—which is generally the case—make conflict hard to avoid and even harder to limit. These kinds of beliefs and perceptions create tremendous escalatory pressures. The fact that opportunistic politicians use, propagate, and embellish these myths compounds the problem.

These problems are particularly pronounced in countries that have experienced long stretches of authoritarian rule. Authoritarian regimes invariably suppress ethnic histories and, in an effort to create their own political myths, manipulate historical facts to suit their own purposes. Furthermore, authoritarian regimes fail to promote objective historical inquiry or scholarly standards of evidence in political discourse. Therefore, it is no surprise that the pernicious effects of ethnic mythology are especially pronounced today in Eastern Europe and the former Soviet Union.

Explaining the Causes of Ethnic Conflict

If political science was as advanced as the physical sciences, it might be possible to integrate these systemic, domestic, and perceptual factors in an overarching theory of the causes of ethnic conflict. Sadly, that is not possible. It is not yet clear what conditions are necessary and sufficient for the initiation of ethnic hostilities, nor is there a rigorous understanding of why some conflicts are more intense than others. Perhaps this is because, as Albert Einstein once remarked, politics is like physics, only harder.

However, it is possible to delineate some systemic conditions that are *necessary* for ethnic conflict to occur. First, two or more ethnic groups must reside in close proximity. Second, national, regional, and international authorities must be too weak to keep groups from fighting and too weak to ensure the security of individual groups. It is far from clear, however, that the presence of these and other systemic factors by themselves will be *sufficient* for ethnic conflict to break out. It seems more likely that systemic conditions will make conflict possible—and some of the systemic factors analyzed by Posen might even make it highly probable—but in most cases factors operating at the domestic and perceptual levels will have to be taken into account as well. More effort needs to be put into integrating explanations across these levels of analysis, as Posen and Snyder have begun to do. Equally important, more effort needs to be put into developing testable propositions about the incidence and intensity of ethnic conflict, as Posen, Snyder, Welsh, de Nevers, and others have done.

IMPLICATIONS

What are the implications of ethnic conflicts for outside powers and the international community in general? The answer to this question depends on the type of conflict and its course. Three broad types of ethnic conflict outcomes can be identified: peaceful reconciliation, peaceful separation, and war. In other words, groups might agree to live together, agree to live apart, or fight for control of the situation.

Ethnic Reconciliation

In some cases, the ethnic groups involved in a dispute may stay associated with each other under some sort of overarching political and legal framework, although they may devise new constitutional arrangements to address specific concerns and grievances. Often, more local autonomy and more explicit minority rights guarantees will be incorporated into new schemas. Austria, Belgium, and Switzerland operate under federal arrangements of various kinds that have been altered in various ways without recourse to violence.[14] The onset of democratization provided the occasion for negotiations on more autonomy for Catalans, Galicians, and Basques in Spain. Disputes between the Indian government, on the one hand, and Naga, Mizo, and Gharo separatists, on the other, were resolved when internal statehood was granted to the latter.[15] Negotiations between Quebec and the other Canadian provinces about Quebec's constitutional status have been continuing for years; whether new, mutually acceptable constitutional arrangements can be devised remains an unresolved issue, however.[16]

When ethnic groups are able to resolve their differences peacefully, ethnic conflicts pose comparatively few problems for outside powers because the international status quo is, by and large, maintained. In cases in which negotiations are the main conduit for conflict resolution, the international community may be able to help mediate disputes, devise minority rights guarantees, and suggest possible constitutional changes. When these internal negotiations are completed, outside powers may have to devise new trading arrangements with newly autonomous regional actors, but little else would change as far as the outside world is concerned.

Ethnic Separation

In other cases, groups may be unable to devise new constitutional arrangements that are satisfactory to all concerned. They may consequently decide to dissolve existing legal ties. In some cases—the breakup of the Soviet Union and the separation of Czechoslovakia into separate, independent republics—this process might involve comparatively little bloodshed. Velvet divorces are likely to be rare, however, because ethnic geography is generally complicated and because many groups will see fragmentation as a threat to their identity, their regional influence, and their place in world affairs.

Be that as it may, cases such as these pose several problems for the international community. Specifically, cases such as these disrupt the international status quo in at least six respects. First, what were previously internal borders will have to be accepted and respected as international borders.[17] Second, outside powers will have to decide if and when to extend diplomatic recognition to the new political entities. If diplomatic recognition is extended, outside powers will have to decide how to go about establishing and exchanging diplomatic missions with the new states. Third, outside powers will have to decide if and when to extend membership in regional and international organizations—such as the Conference on Security and Cooperation in Europe (CSCE), the Organization of African Unity (OAU), the Council of Europe (COE), the European Community (EC), the International Monetary Fund (IMF), the General Agreement on Tariffs and Trade (GATT), and the United Nations (UN).

Fourth, international treaties signed by the defunct state will have to be reformulated. For example, the first Strategic Arms Reduction Treaty (START I), signed by the United States and the Soviet Union in July 1991, had to be revised in 1992 to take into account the demise of the Soviet Union; Soviet strategic nuclear weapons were deployed in four republics—Russia, Ukraine, Kazakhstan, and Belarus—each of which had to be made a party to the agreement. In general, outside powers will want to receive assurances from new states that they will uphold the treaties and commitments undertaken by the defunct state, with reasonable allowances for the political and economic circumstances in which the new states find themselves. Fifth, new commercial and financial relationships will have to be developed with the new states. Decisions will have to be made about granting most favored nation trading status to new states and about providing economic, financial, and technical assistance to these states. Sixth, outside powers will have to assess the implications of these developments for regional stability and the international balance of power. These implications could be momentous indeed, as they were in the case of the breakup of the Soviet Union. At a practical level, outside powers will have to decide how these developments will affect their defense postures and alliance commitments, and how they will respond to requests from new states for security guarantees and membership in existing military alliances. Several Eastern European states and several republics of the former Soviet Union have expressed an interest in joining the North Atlantic Treaty Organization (NATO), for example.

Many of these issues will come up before negotiations between the disputing groups have been completed. Outside powers, therefore, will be under great pressure to make the right decisions at the right time. If they fail to do so, they may find that they have disrupted the negotiating process and made war more likely.

The breakup of the Russian Federation, a possibility that cannot be ruled out, would present special problems for the international community. Although Russia's future is particularly murky, it is at least conceivable that economic collapse and ethnically based secessionist movements could lead to the disintegration of the Russian Federation. Bashkortostan, Chechnia, Kalmyk, Tatarstan, Tyumen, and Yakutsia (now Sakha) have been lobbying for—and some have already received—substantial amounts of autonomy from Moscow. Should this process lead to the fragmentation of Russia and the collapse of the Russian military, effective control of Russia's 25,000 strategic and tactical nuclear weapons and 40,000 agent tons of chemical weapons could be lost, along with control of Russia's extensive nuclear weapons establishment. Should this occur, international efforts to control the transfer of assembled nuclear weapons, nuclear weapon components, nuclear weapon technology, fissile material, technical expertise, and chemical weapon stockpiles would suffer a cataclysmic setback. National and international security policies would have to be radically overhauled as a result.

Ethnic War

In many cases, antagonistic ethnic groups will not be able to agree on new constitutional arrangements or a peaceful separation. Many ethnic disputes consequently become violent, some escalating into all-out interethnic wars. The objectives of the combatants will of course vary from case to case. A minority group might insist on seceding and establishing an independent state of its own; it might demand an independent state within a confederation of states; it might insist on an independent political entity within a new federal structure; it might want more political, economic, cultural, or administrative autonomy within existing institutional arrangements; or it might be satisfied with democratic reforms aimed the implementation of a consociational democracy, ethnic power-sharing, or simply more equitable representation.[18] Groups of roughly equal size and power might fight about similar issues or control of the state. Majority groups might fight to retain or extend their influence and position in the rest of the country.

In some cases, those seeking more autonomy are defeated, and central authorities are successful in imposing their own conception of order on the vanquished, as in the case of Tibet. Cases such as these have few direct effects on the international community because the international status quo is unchanged. The issue that is added to the international agenda is whether or not outside powers want to exert pressure on the winner to respect the rights of the loser. In other cases, secessionist groups are successful in breaking away and establishing states of their own, as in Bangladesh, Eritrea, and Slovenia, for example. Once this process is completed, the implications for the international community are similar to those for peaceful separation, with the added complication that outside assistance will probably be needed to help the combatants recover from the effects of war. In still other cases, neither party is able to win on the battlefield, and the conflict degenerates into a stalemate. This is the situation today in Angola, Cyprus, Kashmir, Lebanon, and Sri Lanka, for example, where neither political nor military solutions are in sight. It is not yet clear how other conflicts—in Afghanistan, Bosnia, the Caucasus, Liberia, and Tajikistan, for example—will eventually play out.

Why should outside powers care about ethnic wars? Why should they even think about intervening in these potential quagmires? The short answer to these questions is that some ethnic conflicts create moral imperatives for intervention, and some threaten the strategic interests of outside powers and the international community as a whole. Specifically, ethnic wars can affect the outside world in seven respects.

Ethnic Wars and Civilian Slaughter

Ethnic wars almost always involve deliberate, systematic attacks on civilians. Why is this so? First, ethnic conflicts are rarely high-technology affairs. They are usually fought by recently formed or recently augmented militias composed of ordinary citizens. A group's civilian population, therefore, is the wellspring of its military power; it is the group's main source of military manpower and an essential source of economic and logistical support. Civilian populations are attacked to weaken the military resources on which adversaries can draw. Second, militarily weak groups will have strong incentives to conduct guerrilla campaigns and launch terrorist attacks against soft, high-value targets—cities, towns, and villages—in an attempt to force powerful adversaries into acquiescence. Third, the civilian populations of warring groups are often intermingled. When battle lines exist, they often cut through cities, towns, even neighborhoods. Civilians are inevitably killed under such circumstances. Fourth, ethnic conflicts are often fought for control of particular pieces of territory. To secure complete territorial control, militias seek to drive out civilians from other groups: intimidating, threatening, evicting, assassinating, raping, massacring, and commiting genocide along the way. Many ethnic conflicts involve forced expulsions and systematic slaughter of civilians, now known as ethnic cleansing.[19]

Why should outside powers care about civilian slaughter in distant lands? One reason is that it poses a direct challenge to important international norms of behavior, the maintenance and promotion of which is in the interest of the international community a whole. The international community has tried to distinguish between combatants and noncombatants in formulating rules and laws about the conduct of war; it will find its distinctions and norms hard to sustain in the long run if it allows them to be trampled in ethnic conflicts, in which civilians are attacked not just indiscriminately, but deliberately and systematically. Another reason for caring about—and taking action against—civilian slaughter is that tolerating it is morally diminishing. The savagery in Bosnia, it could be argued, has been proscribed by the Genocide Convention. If so, the international community has a moral obligation—as well as a legal right—to intervene.

Ethnic Wars and Refugees

Ethnic conflicts often generate staggering numbers of refugees, precisely because they typically involve systematic attacks on civilian populations. It has been estimated, for example, that 100,000 Hindus have fled their homes because of the war in Kashmir, and an equal number of South Ossetians have become refugees as a result of their conflict with Georgia. The war between Armenia and Azerbaijan has generated an estimated 500,000 refugees, and 600,000 people—roughly one-quarter of the total population—have been displaced by the war in Liberia. Conflict in the former Yugoslavia has uprooted an estimated 3 million people, 600,000 of whom have fled the Balkans altogether. In addition, huge numbers of refugees have been generated by the ethnic conflicts in Bhutan, Burma, Cambodia, Ethiopia, Iraq, Sri Lanka, Sudan, and Tajikistan.[20]

Refugee problems, especially of this magnitude, affect the outside world in several ways.[21] First, offering sanctuary to refugees can invite military reprisal, thereby drawing the host country into the conflict. Often, fighters mingle with refugee populations, using refugee camps for rest, recuperation, and recruitment. Second, if refugees flee to neighboring countries where large numbers of their ethnic brethren live, their plight can lead their compatriots to become more involved in the original conflict, thereby widening the war. Third, refugees impose tremendous economic costs on host states. Large numbers of impoverished people have to be housed and fed for long and sometimes indefinite periods of time. Fourth, refugees can be seen as potential threats to the cultural identity of host states, especially when refugee communities are large and when they establish their own schools, newspapers, cultural organizations, and places of worship. Fifth, refugees can become political forces in host countries, particularly regarding foreign policy issues relating to their homeland. Some host governments worry that refugee communities will turn against them if they pursue uncongenial policies. Sixth and last, when refugee problems pose threats to "international peace and security," as they often do, the United Nations has a right, if not an obligation, to consider intervening in the crisis.

Ethnic Wars and Weapons of Mass Destruction

The proliferation of nuclear weapons and other weapons of mass destruction has added a new dimension to ethnic conflicts: the possibility, however remote, that these weapons could be used in interstate or intrastate ethnic wars. Both India and Pakistan have nuclear and chemical weapon capabilities, and tensions between the two have risen to high levels on more than one occasion in recent years.[22] One of the main sources of tension between the two is India's claim that Pakistan is supporting Kashmiri separatists and Pakistan's claim that India is supporting Sindh insurgents. India and Pakistan are also involved in a prolonged, bitter battle over the Siachen Glacier and their northern border. Russia and Ukraine both have nuclear weapons stationed on their territory, although the latter does not yet have operational control of the weapons on its soil. Although military hostilities between the two are unlikely at present, they cannot be ruled out for the future.

Another possibility is that central authorities could use weapons of mass destruction against would-be secessionists in desperate attempts to maintain the integrity of their states. China has both nuclear and chemical weapon capabilities, and the current regime in Beijing would presumably use every means at its disposal to prevent Tibet, Xinxiang, or Inner Mongolia from seceding, which many in these nominally autonomous regions would like to do. Iran has chemical weapon capabilities and is trying to develop or acquire nuclear weapon capabilities. One suspects that Tehran would not rule out using harsh measures to keep Azeris in northwestern Iran from seceding, should they become inclined to push this course of action. It is not inconceivable that Russian, Indian, and Pakistani leaders could be persuaded to take similar steps in the face of national collapse.

Use of nuclear or chemical weapons in any of these situations would undermine international taboos about the use of weapons of mass destruction and, thus, would be detrimental to international nonproliferation efforts, as well as international security in general. Although the possibility that a state would use weapons of mass destruction against its citizens might appear remote, it cannot be dismissed altogether: The Iraqi government used chemical weapons in attacks on Kurdish civilians in the 1980s.

Ethnic Wars and Chain Reaction Effects

Ethnic conflicts can spread in a number of ways. If a multiethnic state begins to fragment and allows some ethnic groups to secede, other groups will inevitably press for more autonomy, if not total independence. This is happening in the former Soviet Union, where 14 republics successfully broke away from Moscow. Now, other groups want to redefine their relationships with the Russian Federation; as noted earlier, Bashkortostan, Chechnia, Kalmyk, Tatarstan, Tyumen, and Yakutsia (now Sakha) have been lobbying for—and some have already received—substantial amounts of autonomy from Moscow. India is fighting tenaciously to retain control of Kashmir because it fears that Kashmiri secession would be the first step in a process that would lead to disintegration of perhaps the most heterogenous state in the world. The view in Delhi, a view not unsupported by logic and history, is that fragmentation is easier to prevent than control.

Other problems are created when state A fragments, allowing B to secede and form its own state. A minority group in B might attempt to secede from B. If it has ethnic ties to A, it might prefer to be associated with its brethren in A. When Croatia seceded from Yugoslavia, for example, Serbs in Croatia attempted to secede from Croatia to maintain ties with Serbs in what was left of Yugoslavia. Similarly, when Georgia seceded from the Soviet Union, South Ossetians attempted to secede from Georgia and pressed for union with their Ossetian brethren in Russia. Other problems are created when the minority group in question has a distinct ethnic identity. It might want its own state, C, either because it fears persecution or simply because establishing an independent state appears to be within the realm of the possible. When Moldova seceded from the Soviet Union, for example, the Gagauz attempted to secede from Moldova and form their own state.

Many of these chain reactions have been accompanied by extremely high levels of violence. This has important international implications and not just because fragmentation and violence can combine to create chaos. The more worrisome prospect, at least from the West's perspective, is that fragmentation, violence, and chaos in and around Russia could provide a useful pretext for hard-liners in Moscow to seize power. A hard-line regime might then deploy large numbers of troops in unstable parts of Russia. This, in turn, might lead Moscow to attempt to reassert control over unstable neighboring states. This would inevitably lead to interstate war, and it would constitute a breach of Moscow's pledge not to use military force to resolve international disputes. Developments of this kind, were they to take place, would have profound implications for Moscow's relations with the West and for international security in general, for all the obvious reasons.

Another kind of chain reaction effect is more indirect: Successful secessions in one part of the world could inspire secessionist movements in others. The growth of international telecommunications capabilities and international media networks makes these "demonstration effects" increasingly potent.[23]

Ethnic Wars and Neighboring Powers

Neighboring powers can become involved in ethnic wars in a variety of ways. First, if state A fragments, allowing B to secede and form its own state, a minority group in B might attempt to secede from B and join with its brethren in C. When Azerbaijan seceded from the Soviet Union, for example, Armenians in Nagorno-Karabakh pushed forward with their demand to secede from Azerbaijan and join Armenia.

Second, when minority groups are persecuted, their brethren in neighboring states might come to their defense. If Serbia took steps to drive ethnic Albanians from Kosovo, for example, Albania might try to defend them. The war in the Balkans could consequently spread. Many in Moscow argue that Russia should come to the aid of ethnic Russians who are being denied their political and economic rights in Estonia and Latvia. In many cases, of course, those who come to the defense of their brethren have ulterior motives in mind—absorption and expansion. Many believe that Belgrade's assistance to Serbs in Croatia and Bosnia, for example, is part of a blatant campaign to create a "Greater Serbia." Similarly, Delhi believes that Pakistani support for Kashmiri insurgents in India reflects Islamabad's desire to control more of Kashmir.

Third, the establishment of new, ethnically defined states might create pressures in neighboring states for more autonomy or outright independence. As John Chipman points out, the creation of an independent Azerbaijani state has worried Iran, which has a large Azeri population. Similarly, the creation of an independent Kazakhstan has troubled China: China fears that Kazakhs in China's Xinxiang Province might try to develop ties with their newly independent brethren or agitate for more autonomy. Similarly, India feared that a federal solution to the conflict in Sri Lanka would give more autonomy to Tamils there than India was willing to grant to Tamils living in the Indian state of Tamil Nadu.[24]

Fourth, if an ethnic group spread over two (or more) states is persecuted in one, the group as a whole could become more nationalistic and militant. This, in turn, could lead to trouble with central authorities in other states. Iraqi persecution of its Kurdish population, for example, has intensified Kurdish sensitivities and, along with the creation of large numbers of Kurdish refugees, has led to increased agitation in Turkey.

Finally, in some cases, states might take advantage of ethnic troubles in neighboring states to further their own strategic and political ends. Indian support for Sindh separatists in Pakistan, for example, is at least in part motivated by a desire to weaken a regional rival and create another lever in Indian-Pakistani relations.

Ethnic Wars and Distant Interests

In some cases, the interests of distant powers will be affected by ethnic conflicts. In 1990, for example, the United States sent military forces into Liberia to rescue US citizens trapped and endangered by the conflict there. France and Belgium sent forces into Rwanda in 1990 for the same reason. In other cases, states intervene to protect or promote broader strategic and political interests. Saudi Arabia, for example, has tried to contain Iranian influence by opposing Shi'a factions and the Persian-speaking Tajiks in the Afghan civil war; it has thrown its weight behind fundamentalist Pashtuns instead.[25] Although unlikely at the moment, it is possible that intensified ethnic warfare in Iraq in the future could lead Western powers to intervene in an effort to safeguard the Kirkuk oil fields in the north, on Kurdish lands, and the Rumaila oil fields in the south, where large numbers of Shi'a live.

Ethnic Wars and International Organizations

Finally, ethnic wars affect outside powers because they can undermine the credibility of regional and international security organizations. Among its functions, the CSCE is supposed to help European powers anticipate, prevent, and resolve European conflicts. One of the reasons for preserving NATO, it is often said, is that it helps maintain stability in Europe. Neither of these organizations has played an effective role in the Yugoslav crisis, which can only diminish their viability and long-term prospects. Similarly, Bosnian Serb defiance of UN Security Council resolutions and UN humanitarian initiatives, a prominent feature of the Yugoslav crisis, will inevitably impede the development of the United Nations' peacemaking and peacekeeping capabilities. This, in turn, will have an impact on the prospect for ethnic violence and international conflict in general: Just as effective intervention would bolster the credibility of international action and possibly have a deterrent effect elsewhere, ineffective intervention has a demonstration effect of its own.

More generally, casual defiance of international norms of behavior—with respect to minority rights and the use of force, for example—will undercut principles that the international community would do well to maintain and extend. In short, ethnic wars can undermine the long-term ability of outside powers to preserve international order.

RECOMMENDATIONS

What, if anything, can outside powers do to minimize the potential for ethnic violence? The conventional wisdom among many journalists and policymakers is that there is little outsiders can do because these conflicts are driven by implacable ancient hatred. Their implicit policy recommendation, as Snyder points out, is to steer clear and let conflicts play themselves out.[26] In fact, the causes of ethnic conflict are complex. A number of variables affect the probability and intensity of ethnic conflict, and some of these variables are manipulatable; that is, they can be influenced by outside powers.

Jenonne Walker argues persuasively that the best course of action is to address ethnic problems early, before concrete disputes materialize and violence erupts. If ethnic conflicts are easier to prevent than resolve, then the first question to be considered should be: What can outside powers usefully do to ease tensions between and among potentially hostile ethnic groups?[27]

At the systemic level, as Posen argues, groups worry about immediate, imminent, and potential security threats. One of the keys to dampening the potential for ethnic violence, therefore, is to address these security concerns. This will not be easy, however. Providing arms to a group, thus enhancing its ability to protect itself, will often increase its offensive military capacities. This, in turn, will be seen as threatening by others. Providing arms to several rival groups in an attempt to establish a balance of power will be problematic as well. Vague security commitments from outsiders who do not have much at stake will not be particularly credible. Security commitments will be more credible—and, therefore, more effective—if an ethnic war would have important security implications for powerful outside actors.[28]

At the domestic level, three main avenues are open. First, as Snyder suggests, outside powers should help groups develop effective states. This will dampen nationalism in general and ethnic nationalism in particular. Therefore, international economic initiatives should be framed with these overriding political objectives in mind; imposing harsh economic medicine on groups already in turmoil could weaken fragile state structures and trigger a nationalistic backlash. Similarly, outside powers should be careful not to bully groups in turmoil, as this could also weaken already fragile states.[29]

Second, outside powers can help groups develop more representative political institutions. Welsh explains: "No salient group should be prohibited from a share of effective power. Political institutions should be designed to ensure that minorities are proportionately represented in parliaments and bureaucracies and that their interests—political, cultural, and economic—are heeded."[30] Ideally, governments would be based on broad coalitions. To achieve this, winner-take-all elections should be proscribed.[31] In addition to playing an advisory role, outside powers can help shape political institutions and processes in troubled countries by withholding diplomatic recognition and economic assistance from those who retain or advance unrepresentative schemas.

Third, outside powers should insist that cultural diversity be respected, even nourished, in multiethnic states.[32] At a minimum, outside powers should insist that discrimination against minorities be prohibited. All ethnic groups should be equal before the law. All should have the same political and economic rights and opportunities. All should be entitled to worship as they see fit. As far as possible, ethnic groups should be allowed to use their own languages in schools, bureaucracies, parliaments, and courts. Legal mechanisms for redress of grievances should be established if they do not already exist.

In December 1992, the UN General Assembly passed a Declaration on the Rights of Persons Belonging to National or Ethnic, Religious, and Linguistic Minorities that outlined the international community's views on these issues. However, as Kathleen Newland points out, this declaration, like other UN human rights instruments, contains no implementation or enforcement provisions. On the whole, Newland maintains, the UN human rights regime is weak.[33] To improve the situation, outside powers and the United Nations should do more to help states draft effective minority rights safeguards. They should develop more effective capabilities to detect minority rights violations and be more aggressive in deploying monitors in potentially troubled areas. Indeed, deploying monitors might help deter violations in the first place. In addition, outside powers should withhold diplomatic recognition, economic assistance, and membership in regional and international organizations from new states until they develop effective minority rights safeguards. Trial memberships in regional and international institutions should be granted in cases in which the prospects for minorities are uncertain. Finally, outside powers should impose sanctions—diplomatic, economic, even military— on states that fail to grant and protect these rights. In short, outside powers should do more to help develop and enforce minority rights standards and utilize more effectively the considerable leverage they all too often squander.

At the perceptual level, outside powers should try to help ethnic groups develop better histories of each other. Posen suggests that oral histories should be openly discussed with other groups and assessed by disinterested parties. Where possible, competing versions of events should be reconciled. This process should involve outsiders, including academics and representatives from nongovernmental organizations. Obviously, as Posen points out, a few conferences will not undo "generations of hateful, politicized history, bolstered by reams of more recent propaganda."[34] However, these exercises would cost little and, therefore, should be tried.

What should outside powers do if preventive measures fail, violence erupts, and an ethnic war breaks out? Under what conditions should outside powers intervene in such a war? Drawing on the arguments developed by Robert Cooper and Mats Berdal, five conditions should be met before action is taken.[35] First, there should be either a strategic or moral imperative for action. Second, those contemplating intervention should have clear political objectives. If military forces are to be used, political objectives must be translatable into clear military objectives. Third, one must have options—diplomatic, political, economic, military—that will lead to the attainment of one's objectives. Fourth, one must be willing and able to persevere in the face of adversity. Ethnic wars tend to be both long-lasting and intense: Warring groups are highly motivated because, in many cases, they believe their existence is on the line. If outsiders are to impose their will on such combatants, they will have to be determined. Multinational or international efforts, therefore, must be based on a strong, sustainable political consensus; legitimization in the form of strong backing from the UN Security Council is extremely important in this regard. Fifth, before one intervenes in an ethnic war, one should identify the circumstances that would lead one to withdraw. These are general guidelines, to be sure, but policymakers need to keep such considerations in mind when they contemplate intervening in ethnic wars. Discrete decisions should be made one way or the other; otherwise, leaders run the risk of gradually becoming involved in conflicts about which they care little and can do less.

In contemplating intervention in ethnic wars, it is important to note that diplomatic efforts are unlikely to be successful unless they are backed by the threat of economic and military sanctions. It is also important to note that military operations will be more effective at keeping combatants apart than bringing people together. Military interventions, by themselves, will not resolve the underlying strategic, political, and perceptual problems that propel ethnic conflicts. The key to true conflict resolution is the development of civil societies in genuine political communities. That, however, is something about which the international community still has much to learn—and not just in conjunction with ethnic conflict.[36]

Notes

1 Anthony Smith, "The Ethnic Sources of Nationalism," chapter 2 in this volume, pp. 28–29.

2 This discussion is based on Ibid., pp. 28–31.

3 See Jack Snyder, "Nationalism and the Crisis of the Post-Soviet State," chapter 5 in this volume; Barry Posen, "The Security Dilemma and Ethnic Conflict," chapter 6 in this volume; Kathleen Newland, "Ethnic Conflict and Refugees," chapter 8 in this volume; Smith, "Ethnic Sources."

4 For an erudite exposition on levels of analysis and the study of international politics, see Kenneth N. Waltz, *Man, the State, and War: A Theoretical Analysis* (New York: Columbia University Press, 1959).

5 David Welsh, "Domestic Politics and Ethnic Conflict," chapter 3 in this volume, p. 45.

6 The discussion that follows is based on the account in Posen, "Security Dilemma," pp. 104–111. See also Kenneth Waltz, *Theory of International Politics* (Reading, Mass.: Addison Wesley, 1979), chapters 6 and 8; Robert Jervis, "Cooperation under the Security Dilemma," *World Politics*, vol. 30, no. 2, January 1978, pp. 167–213; Robert Jervis, *Perception and Misperception in International Politics* (Princeton, N.J.: Princeton University Press, 1976), chapter 3.

7 The discussion that follows is drawn from Snyder, "Nationalism," passim.

8 Snyder, "Nationalism," p. 86.

9 See Donald Horowitz, *Ethnic Groups in Conflict* (Berkeley, Calif.: University of California Press, 1985), especially chapters 7–10, 15; Arend Lijphart, "The Power-Sharing Approach," in Joseph V. Montville, ed., *Conflict and Peacemaking in Multiethnic Societies* (Lexington, Mass.: Lexington Books, 1990), pp. 491–509; Renée de Nevers, "Democratization and Ethnic Conflict," chapter 4 in this volume; Welsh, "Domestic Politics."

10 See de Nevers, "Democratization," passim.

11 See Horowitz, *Ethnic Groups*, chapters 2, 7–10; Welsh, "Domestic Politics," passim.

12 Welsh, "Domestic Politics," p. 48.

13 See Posen, "Security Dilemma," p. 107; Snyder, "Nationalism," pp. 92–93. For a thorough discussion of perceptual issues and how people learn from history, see Jervis, *Perception and Misperception*, especially chapters 4–7.

14 This is not to say that internal Austrian, Belgian, and Swiss relations have been relentlessly amicable, only that some political and constitutional adjustments have been implemented at various times without recourse to violence.

15 It is important to note that Indian military superiority cast a long shadow over these negotiations.

16 For more discussion of this general issue and more details on these cases, see Horowitz, *Ethnic Groups*, pp. 601–628; Welsh, "Domestic Politics," passim.

17 For more discussion of the implications of border changes, see Daniel Franklin, "International Boundaries: Ex-Soviet Union and Eastern Europe," *The World Today*, vol. 48, no. 3, March 1992, pp. 38–40; James Eberle, "International Boundaries: The Security Angle," *The World Today*, vol. 48, no. 4, April 1992, pp. 68–71.

18 See International Institute for Strategic Studies (IISS), *Strategic Survey, 1992–1993* (London: Brassey's for the IISS, 1993), pp. 16–23.

19 Ethnic cleansing was a prominent feature of the early stages of the India–Pakistan and Arab–Israeli conflicts in the 1940s, for example. It is currently being practiced, inter alia, in Bhutan, Cambodia, the Caucasus, Kashmir, Tajikistan, and Tibet. For more discus-

sion, see Paul A. Goble, "Some Russians Now Talk of 'Cleansing'," *International Herald Tribune*, August 14, 1992, p. 4; Kunda Dixit, "'Cleansing': The Agony of Bhutan," *International Herald Tribune*, September 17, 1992, p. 4; A.M. Rosenthal, "A Model: Cleansing in Tibet," *International Herald Tribune*, April 28, 1993, p. 6.

[20] For more details and discussion, see Newland, "Ethnic Conflict and Refugees," passim.

[21] This discussion is based on Gil Loescher, *Refugee Movements and International Security*, Adelphi Paper 268 (London: Brassey's for the IISS, Summer 1992), pp. 46–51.

[22] International experts generally agree that India and Pakistan have the ability to assemble nuclear weapons on short notice, although neither claims to have (or admits to having) fully assembled, ready-to-use weapons in its military arsenal. It is believed that India has to capacity to field 15–50 weapons and Pakistan, 5–20.

[23] See IISS, *Strategic Survey, 1992–1993*, pp. 22–23.

[24] See John Chipman, "Managing the Politics of Parochialism," chapter 12 in this volume, pp. 246–253.

[25] See IISS, *Strategic Survey, 1992–1993*, pp. 178–179.

[26] Snyder, "Nationalism," pp. 79–81, 94–98.

[27] See Jenonne Walker, "International Mediation of Ethnic Disputes," chapter 9 in this volume, p. 168.

[28] See Posen, "Security Dilemma," pp. 119–121.

[29] See Snyder, "Nationalism," pp. 94–98.

[30] Welsh, "Domestic Politics," p. 56.

[31] See Ibid., passim; Lijphart, "Power-Sharing Approach," passim; Horowitz, *Ethnic Groups*, chapter 15.

[32] See Newland, "Ethnic Conflict and Refugees," pp. 154–161; Jonathan Eyal, "Eastern Europe: What About the Minorities?" *The World Today*, vol. 45, no. 12, December 1989, pp. 205–208; L. Michael Hager, "To Get More Peace, Try More Justice," *International Herald Tribune*, July 30, 1992, p. 6.

[33] Newland, "Ethnic Conflict and Refugees," p. 155.

[34] Posen, "Security Dilemma," p. 120.

[35] See Robert Cooper and Mats Berdal, "Outside Intervention in Ethnic Conflicts," chapter 10 in this volume, pp. 197–203.

[36] See Walker, "International Mediation," pp. 168, 177–180; Cooper and Berdal, "Outside Intervention," pp. 200–203; Chipman, "Managing the Politics of Parochialism," pp. 253–259.

Chapter 2

The Ethnic Sources of Nationalism
Anthony D. Smith

For more than 40 years following the World War II, few new states were created through ethnic secession. From Iceland's independence to the secession of the Baltic states, only two new ethnic states emerged: Singapore and Bangladesh. Of course, the world saw the creation of many new states in Africa and Asia through decolonization. Yet, ethnicity was not the decisive factor in their formation (with the exception of Israel). In the past two years, however, more than 10 ethnically defined states have emerged. Others may follow.

Is there anything peculiar about this sudden resurgence of ethnicity and its use as a criterion for statehood? Can it be explained simply as the result of the abrupt removal of a "totalitarian lid," which kept smoldering ethnic tensions in check? Would the same phenomenon not be occurring elsewhere, but for the ability of states in other regions to contain the aspirations and demands of their ethnically heterogeneous populations? Did not the Kurdish and Shi'a revolts in Iraq portend the dissolution of that state? Is it not the superior force of the Indian and Sri Lankan governments that has prevented the secession of their Sikh, Naga, Kashmiri, and Tamil populations? Is not the same true for the Kurds in Iran, the Moro in the Philippines, and the Uigurs and Tibetans in China? In Africa, apart from Ethiopia, Sudan, and Angola, are there not other ethnic candidates for autonomy and secession?

Because only a few ethnic communities—out of the many that could (and may) demand autonomy and independence—have obtained states of their own, a more discriminating analysis of the causes of ethnic separatism is required. This analysis must take into account a range of variables—geopolitical, socioeconomic, and historical–cultural. This article will focus on the historical and cultural factors in the resurgence of ethnic nationalism. This is not to deny the importance of strategic, economic, and political factors in providing conditions for ethnic conflict and secession and of the uses to which such conflicts may be put by elite manipulation. However, these conflicts are also the product of demands for political recognition that owe much to the ideologies of nationalism. Nationalism, in turn, derives its force not only from the "demonstration effect" of other successful examples, but also from the inner resources of specific ethnic communities, as well as the perceptions and sentiments that they inspire. History and culture are the wellsprings of these inner resources, for they can indicate much about the likelihood of ethnic consciousness developing into ethnic nationalism and, hence, into a secessionist movement.

THE NATURE OF ETHNIC TIES

What are the bases or foundations for ethnic nationalism? What are the collective ties and sentiments that must be aroused and ignited by political, economic, and other forces, if demands for national recognition are to emerge?

Human beings have always lived in a multiplicity of communities and possessed a variety of identifications. These are usually held simultaneously without much difficulty. Individuals identify with families; villages or towns; regions; age and sex groups; classes; and religious, ethnic, and national communities, as well as with humanity as a whole. These affiliations are invoked for different purposes and on different occasions. Only rarely do they come into conflict, and only rarely (for example, in time of war) does one allegiance override others. Identity, in other words, is "situational."[1]

Such an analysis, of course, is centered on the individual and sees collective identities as composed of aggregates of individual identities, or dimensions thereof. However, if the focus is altered to the level of the collective, the dimensions and powers of different collective identities and communities become more important than the dispositions of its particular members. Individuals, although important, are no longer treated as the key to defining and explaining the nature and durability of collectivities. Instead, the properties of collective cultural identities become the center of attention.

The contention here is that, to grasp the nature and power of ethnic nationalism today, one must focus primarily on the collective level of identity and community. The particular collective cultural identity of concern here is the *ethnie*, or ethnic community. It is in the properties of such communities that one can find the key to the explosive power of nationalism and, hence, of many of the conflicts that wrack the interstate system today.

A brief working definition of the *ethnie* is a named human population with a myth of common ancestry, shared memories, and cultural elements; a link with a historic territory or homeland; and a measure of solidarity. There are several points about this definition that need amplification.

First, names are important, not only for self- and other-identification, but also as expressive emblems of the collective "personality." Until a collective cultural identity receives a proper name, it lacks, in an important sense, a recognizable sense of community (both by members and outsiders). Until recently, this was the case with the Muslims of Yugoslavia. It was only in the 1960s that members of this category took the name "Muslim." For their neighbors (and now their adversaries), they were Islamicized Slavs (Serb or Croat). Yet, these individuals increasingly felt themselves to be separate—a different community, whose myth of collective ancestry was traced back to the moment of conversion to Islam.

Second, what is important is the belief or myth of common ancestry and not some genetic heritage. (The two may or may not coincide, but it is the belief that is vital, not the "reality" of physical descent.) Ethnicity is not about blood or genes as such, but about myths and beliefs in common origins. Of course, ethnic nationalists frequently appeal to "common blood" to bolster their case. Metaphors of the family are common currency, and this is not simply a manipulative ploy in the political game. Members of these respective communities respond to such appeals, and an explanation in terms of mere manipulation is inadequate. For the ethnic nationalists and their followers, the *ethnie* is indeed a "superfamily"—extended in space and time to distant relatives over many generations, including the yet unborn.[2]

Third, one must note the importance of historical memories. Of course, such memories are not the relics of historians, the careful inferences that may be drawn from tested documentary sources by supposedly dispassionate historians. They are ethnohistorical memories of the collectivity, sources of moral inspiration to its members, selective traditions (including legends) about their past handed down from earlier generations, in which certain events and personages are remembered and others forgotten. This history becomes a potent and malleable resource for ethnic communities, embellishing kernels of historical "fact" with *exempla virtutis* to create a sense of common history and destiny.[3]

A fourth feature, shared culture, is more variable. These cultural components include dress, food, music, crafts, and architecture, as well as laws, customs, and institutions. By far the most common shared cultural elements are language and religion. In Europe and parts of Asia, language has been the most frequent differentiator of *ethnies*. For some scholars in the tradition of Johann von Herder, with his belief in cultural and linguistic diversity, language is the decisive criterion of ethnicity. As Max

Muller came to realize a century ago, however, it is dangerous and misleading to equate language with ethnic origins (let alone race); there is no proof that related language groups share common ethnic origins. Conversely, broad language areas (Spanish and French, for example) frequently include more than one ethnic community (Spaniards and Mexicans, French and Quebecois).[4]

Neither is religion any longer the key criterion of ethnicity. In premodern eras, many *ethnies* defined themselves by their separate pantheons and rituals, and religion can still be a vital force for ethnic difference and conflict, as in present-day India and the Middle East. Where religion and language are superimposed, the community in question is sharply differentiated from all others. Likewise, one should not assume that ethnoreligious communities are on the decline. Yet, for many communities today, religion, if it is at all relevant, is only one of several differentiating criteria.[5]

Fifth is the attachment to a specific territory; here, too, it is important to emphasize the symbolic nature of such a link. The *ethnie* in question may even be exiled from the homeland, as was the case with most Jews and many Armenians from the time of the Crusades. However, what is vital for ethnicity is the sense of attachment to a particular land, the fervently held belief in a historical connection of this people with that land and the desire to return to its "sacred centers"—those hallowed places where ethnohistory intersects with decisive turning points in the trajectory of the community: birth, liberation, victory or defeat, revelation, sanctification, fulfillment. Hence, what is crucial for ethnicity is not the possession of the homeland, but the sense of mutual belonging, even from afar.[6]

Finally, there is the element of solidarity. Clearly, not all the members of a given *ethnie* feel an equal sense of belonging to the community. Indeed, in premodern times, the majority of a given "ethnic population" often felt little or no sense of ethnic belonging. It was outsiders who categorized them as members of a particular community. Usually, only the upper strata—the landed nobility, officials, and priests—had any sense of shared ethnic origin and heritage. Quite often, these upper strata excluded artisans and peasants from the community, as did the Romanian nobles and clergy until the early nineteenth century. In other cases (usually ethnoreligious communities or city-state amphictyonies), the lower classes did participate in the sense of common ethnicity.

Thus, one must carefully distinguish between ethnic categories and ethnic communities. The former are characterized as a distinct cultural (usually, linguistic) group by outsiders (often scholars, missionaries, travelers, and traders), but possess little or no sense of their common ethnicity. Such was the case of the Ewe tribespeople in present northern

Ghana and Togo, until their language was given a common script by pastors from Bremen, Germany, in the nineteenth century. This was also the case of Slovak valley-dwellers until they acquired a common written language and literature in the late nineteenth century. In contrast, there are ethnic communities that, however scattered their membership, have never lost the sense of common ethnicity, of belonging to an all-embracing *ethnie* wherever they may be. This is obvious in the case of diaspora Chinese, Armenian, Greek, and Jewish communities, but *ethnie* is also found among many expatriate enclaves throughout the world.[7]

The distinction between ethnic category and ethnic community is important for grasping the dynamics of ethnic nationalism. One of the self-appointed tasks of nationalists is to turn ethnic categories into ethnic communities, and ethnic communities into ethnic nations. There are hundreds, if not thousands, of ethnic categories in the world, characterized by external cultural criteria: customs, language, religion, and other components. Yet, only some of these ethnic categories have, to date, been rendered collectively self-aware. Only a proportion of these categories possess, or can be endowed with, the other characteristics of *ethnies*—a proper name, a shared ancestral myth, an ethnohistory, cultural elements, a link with a homeland. Throughout history, there have been countless ethnic categories, but only under certain conditions have the members of these categories coalesced into ethnic communities. Furthermore, even fewer of these managed to survive the pressures of absorption and assimilation throughout the centuries. What is often witnessed is a kaleidoscope of ever-shifting ethnic ties and units, only some of which became firmly crystallized and durable.

What this means is that Jean-Jacques Rousseau's injunction to endow with a national character a unit or population that lacks one, is no simple task. "Inventing" *ethnies*, like creating nations, requires certain preexisting elements and appropriate conditions. Otherwise, the "inventions" will fail to take root among the designated populations. This is the problem faced by every nationalist operating in culturally "inhospitable terrain."[8]

THE CONDITIONS OF ETHNIC CRYSTALLIZATION

What are the conditions for the formation of *ethnies*? How are their members rendered collectively self-aware? Here, it is valuable to distinguish between the conditions that were prevalent in premodern epochs and those in the modern era.

In premodern epochs, the general conditions that favored ethnic crystallization and survival were four. The most obvious was the acquisition (or, later, the loss) of a particular piece of territory, which was felt to "belong" to a people as they belonged to it. This was the "homeland" of the people. Here, the seasonal rhythms of folk life and culture were played out, as village communities were embedded in wider trading and cultural networks. If the people, or a significant proportion of them, were exiled from the homeland, they may still have retained a yearning to return. Frequently, the ideal of restoration became central to the spiritual aspirations of the people, as it became for diaspora Armenians and Jews. The homeland became a symbol of redemption because it was seen as the cradle of the people.[9]

A second condition was the vicissitudes of struggle with an array of enemies. Prolonged warfare, usually between states, tended to mobilize populations every year in the summer season and nourish a sense of community. A tradition of struggle and warfare was often maintained and served to inspire in later generations a belief in a common fate, provided that defeats were balanced by victories and that specialists in oral or written communication emerged to record the chronicles of the ethnic past. In such cases, the myths and symbols of heroes, battles, and their sacred sites became an essential part of the ethnic fabric.

The third condition is closely linked to the foregoing. Some form of organized religion was vital for producing specialists in communications and record-keeping, as well as for generating the rituals and traditions that formed the channels of continuity for ethnic communities. Priesthoods, sacred texts, and rituals often sustained the emergent sense of common ethnicity among peoples throughout the world, and these facets of organized religion remain powerful forces today in some areas. It is arguable that the conservatism of organized religion has been the most effective force in preserving ethnic myths, symbols, and memories.[10]

Finally, and dependent upon the other conditions, the proximate cause of ethnic durability and survival was the rise and power of a myth of "ethnic chosenness." Wherever such a myth occurs, the *ethnie* in question seems assured of a long life. The popular sense of "chosenness," religious in origin and nature, has proven to be a vital inner resource in the tribulations that many *ethnies*, particularly ethnic minorities, have faced. In one sense, a myth of ethnic election is a vital dimension of ethnic crystallization and survival. In another sense, given that *ethnies* can emerge, although not survive for long without such a myth, one must treat such myths as an element that helps to ensure ethnic longevity.

In the modern era, the number of conditions that can foster a sense of common ethnicity has greatly increased. In addition to association with a homeland, warfare, and organized religion, there also exists a series of factors stemming from the activities of the modern state, of the secular intelligentsia, and of external agencies, including the example of other *ethnies*. Perhaps the most potent have been the cultural and civic activities of the modern state and the ideologies of ethnic nationalism.

As the modern state extended the scope of its activities and agencies, it increasingly tended to incorporate and homogenize populations and impart to them a sense of civic solidarity. In some cases, these activities have had the effect of breaking down barriers between ethnic categories and communities, and gradually submerging and attenuating any sense of separate culture and heritage. This appears to be the case in Mauritius, Eritrea, and Indonesia (with some exceptions). Here, the colonial state proved to be stronger than the preexisting ethnic differences; thus, the postcolonial state (or movement, in the Eritrean case) has succeeded in fostering a sense of national identity defined by the territory of the previous colonial state.[11]

In contrast, in cases in which members of an ethnic community retained a vivid sense of community, often in the face of persecution, or in which it was sustained by the imperial or colonial regime, then the growing interventionism of the modern state simply reinforced ethnic solidarity and exacerbated ethnic differences. The introduction of mass civic education systems was particularly effective in stirring up the latent sentiments of different *ethnies* or even of implanting a sense of ethnic identity among populations that were categorized by the majority as different. This was very much the case with Bretons under the Third French Republic (and earlier) and Jews in Tsarist Russia or with Sikhs and Tamils in British India and Ceylon. The existing sense of ethnic difference among minority populations was sharpened: in the first case, by the attempted cultural homogenization of populations within the territories of a civic or imperial state and, in the second case, by cultural categorization on the part of that state. In both cases, the extension of state powers and intervention in social life created new ethnic communities out of preexisting ethnic categories or reinforced ethnic differences and identities.[12]

Equally important have been the activities of intellectuals and intelligentsias. If intellectuals proposed new *ethnies* and nations, the professional intelligentsia was often the main conduit and beneficiary of their dissemination. Lawyers, doctors, architects, engineers, technicians, journalists, and especially teachers were active in promoting the idea of the ethnic nation, especially for communities incorporated within an imperial or colonial state. Their cultural, economic, and social activities created new networks for members of minority ethnic categories or communities who were subject to the often-contradictory forces of state assimilation and discrimination. These networks formed the microcosm of a new community, and they imparted to members a sense of activism and self-assertion that stood in stark contrast to the compliance required by state authorities.[13]

Perhaps the most decisive of the new factors in the creation of modern *ethnies* has been the ideology of nationalism or, rather, the ideology of ethnic nationalism. For, unlike the territorial and civic versions of nationalism, ethnic nationalism conceives of the nation as a genealogical and vernacular cultural community. Whereas civic and territorial conceptions of the nation regard it as a community of shared culture, common laws, and territorial citizenship, ethnic concepts of the nation focus on the genealogy of its members, however fictive; on popular mobilization of "the folk"; on native history and customs; and on the vernacular culture. As a vernacular community of genealogical descent, the ethnic nation seeks to create itself in the image of an ancestral *ethnie*. In so doing, it often helps to recreate that *ethnie*.

In other words, the rise of ethnic nationalism has meant a telescoping of the former pattern by which modernization, and notably the modern state, helped to create nations on the basis of preexisting *ethnies*. The civic and territorial pattern largely prevailed in the West—in Britain, France, Spain, Holland, and Sweden. In the East, however—in Eastern Europe and Russia, the Middle East, and much of southern and eastern Asia—the ethnic, genealogical conception of the nation prevailed, and ethnic nationalism aimed at forging nations on the basis of preexisting *ethnies*, while often crystallizing the *ethnie* itself out of a preexisting ethnic category—as with the Slovaks, the Ukrainians, the Turks, the Azeris, Tadzhiks, Sikhs, and Tamils.[14]

Ethnic nationalism has had an advantage over territorial and civic nationalism—that of building the nation, as it were, out of preexisting ethnic ties. Thus, it does not necessarily entail the kind of revolution that the rise of civic nations brought about in the West. The nation appears as a natural continuation of a preexisting *ethnie*. Yet, this appearance is deceptive. The preexisting *ethnie*, even when embodied in a fully fledged community with a vivid sense of solidarity, lacked a number of the attributes of a nation—features also attributed by ethnic nationalists themselves. These include the following: a clearly delimited, compact, and recognized homeland; a mass, public culture; a centralized economy with mobility throughout; and common rights and duties for all conationals, usually to the exclusion of outsiders. These are features that, along with shared myths and memories, define the concept of "nation."[15]

These features, in turn, require a much more inclusive, active participant membership than is to be found in most *ethnies*. Ethnic nationalism implies a revolution in the outlook of its ethnic members. Where before they had seen themselves as passive and quiescent, seeking accommodation with alien rulers, they began to assert themselves, actively participating in shaping their own collective destiny. Where before their heroes were servants of God and his divine plan in the nationalist cosmos, they became leaders and inspirers of the nation, and interpreters of the national will. If, in the past, ancient struggles and golden ages were events and epochs in the epic of the community, in the era of nationalism, they became exemplars and testimonies to the latent powers of national regeneration.

FROM VERNACULAR MOBILIZATION
TO ETHNIC PURIFICATION

By what processes are *ethnies*, crystallized ethnic communities, mobilized by ethnic nationalism? How are they transformed into ethnic nations?

Although there are several variations, three basic processes of ethnonational transformation can be discerned. The first is here termed "vernacular mobilization." This involves a rediscovery by ethnic intellectuals of indigenous traditions, customs, memories, symbols, and, especially, languages and their dissemination to wider strata of the designated population. This is usually the task of the ethnic intelligentsia—the professionals whose status and careers are often bound up with the success of a vernacular culture in a historic homeland. This has been well documented in the Quebecois nationalist movement. In this case, it has been the professional intelligentsia that has been the most active disseminator of an indigenous francophone culture, in opposition to the dominance of the anglophone majority in Canada. It is the intelligentsia's perceptions, status needs, and career interests that have mobilized the francophone population in Quebec to adopt the vernacular language and culture.[16]

The same pattern is also found in Eastern Europe and Russia. Once again, it has been ethnic intellectuals, and the attendant intelligentsia, that have mobilized themselves, and later other strata, through a vernacular culture, elevating a formerly "low" oral culture and language to the status of a "high" literary culture. Through the compilation of dictionaries, grammars, and philological treatises, ethnic elites have modernized and regenerated peasant languages and cultures. The Czech, Finnish, and Ukrainian languages and cultures are examples of initially peripheral and neglected cultures that were to become fully fledged and internationally recognized.[17]

The second concomitant process has been the "cultural politicization" of the vernacular heritage. In previous eras, that heritage was respected by successive generations as the repository of communal wisdom and virtue, but such veneration had few political consequences. Once ethnic nationalism has begun to transform the *ethnie* into a would-be nation, it becomes imperative to treat the community's cultural heritage as a political resource. What were formerly venerated traditions now become weapons in a cultural war waged both against outsiders and against the guardians of the tradition. The nationalists see their task as twofold: to fight against outside enemies, as well as with the "fathers" within. The struggle of the "sons against their fathers" is every bit as vital for ethnic transformation as the battle for territorial independence.

The most clear-cut manifestation of this transformation is in the treatment of the past. In the old ethnic tradition, battles were recorded as the result of royal virtues and dynastic policies. In nationalist historiography, they become examples of the national virtue and will, and barometers of the state of the nation in successive periods. Similarly, the great figures of the past—warriors, saints, or lawgivers—formerly seen as exemplars of a religious or communal tradition, became national leaders, founders of the nation, or prophets of national destiny. Moses, Mohammed, Buddha, Homer, Dante, Luther, even Jesus, were no longer simply servants of God or great epic poets; they became founders, inspirers, and exemplars of the national community and the national will.[18]

Where the politicization of culture is linked to a living ethnic past and where it combines well with an ethnohistorical tradition, there exists an extremely potent and explosive ethnonational energy that is frequently tapped by ethnic nationalists. This is just what Tilak managed to do in his use of the cults of Shivaji, the Marathi hero, and of Kali, the great Hindu goddess of destruction, in the Indian nationalist struggle with the British in the first decade of this century. In both cases, Tilak linked present nationalist concerns to mass sentiments and to the ethnohistorical traditions of large segments of the Hindu population, thus changing the course of middle-class Indian civic nationalism to a lower-class ethnic Hindu nationalism—a legacy that survives to this day in Indian politics.[19]

The third process is an all-too-familiar consequence of the other two: "ethnic purification." It begins with the return to a popular vernacular culture, which is used for political purposes, and injects a belief in the sanctity of that culture. The ethnic culture is believed to consist of irreplaceable cultural values. To preserve the culture, to guard against alien and contaminating influences, it must be kept unadulterated—indeed, it must be purged and purified. Its adherents, too, must be kept away from these undesirable influences through the relegation, segregation, expulsion, deportation, and even extermination of aliens. Ethnic purification is part of the logic of a genealogical ethnic nationalism, even when people do not act out its precepts.[20]

It is important to draw out this logic because commentators frequently stigmatize ethnic purification as an expression of an ethnic inferiority complex and an exaggerated ethnic defensiveness. This psychologism misses the cultural and social logic of the processes outlined here. This logic is common to all ethnic nationalisms, whether of small, struggling communities or large, dominant ethnic nations. Whether this logic will be fully acted upon depends on a variety of circumstances—the relative size of different *ethnies*, their strategic location, their cultural skills and institutions, the ethnohistory of their ethnic relations, the nature of the organizations that espouse ethnic nationalism, and so on. These factors will determine the exact nature and intensity of ethnic purification, as well as the severity of the actions that are based upon these premises. What is constant, however, is the propensity and drive of all ethnic nationalism toward some form and degree of ethnic purification. The potential for explosive and radical collective action derives from the resources unfolded by the three processes of vernacular mobilization, cultural politicization, and ethnic purification.

NATIONAL SELF-DETERMINATION AND ITS CONSEQUENCES

To summarize the argument, among the various sources of past and current ethnic conflicts, the various forms of ethnic nationalism occupy pride of place. Ethnic nationalism, in turn, is derived from a variety of factors, but two of them, by definition, figure most prominently: first, the features of ethnicity and their crystallization into ethnic communities and, second, the impact of nationalist ideology. Neither of these, by themselves, can explain the resurgence of ethnic conflict and ethnic nationalism. It is their conjunction that furnishes the spark for the great conflagrations that burst with such intensity and apparent unpredictability.

As a doctrine, nationalism can be fairly securely dated to the last quarter of the eighteenth century—in the United States, England, France, Italy, and Poland, with nationalist ideologies springing up immediately thereafter in Spain, Germany, Switzerland, Greece, Serbia, and Russia, as well as among the Creole elite of Latin America.[21]

On the whole, the first forms of nationalism were civic and territorial in conception, although an ethnic element was always present, if only through the identification of the nation with the ideal of popular sovereignty. This meant that residence and political participation in a public culture tended to determine citizenship and membership of the nation. However, as the nineteenth century progressed, ethnic nationalism came to the fore—in Germany and Eastern Europe, in Ireland and Scandinavia, and, later, in the Middle East and India. Even in the early nineteenth century, the idea of national self-determination was applied to ethnic communities such as the Greeks, Italians, Serbs, Poles, and Germans. The problematic nature of the "self" exercising determination was theoretically solved, at least to the satisfaction of ethnic nationalists, by attributing collective identity to the popular nation—that is, the nation defined as a "people"—and identifying the people with the chosen *ethnie*, or historical–cultural community.[22]

In practice, however, this attribution posed several major problems. These included determining the degree to which a given population formed a clear-cut *ethnie*, defining exactly the extent and composition of each *ethnie*, and deciding how to separate and territorialize *ethnies* whose members resided in ethnically mixed areas. If the self-determination of territorially defined civic nations has sometimes posed problems for the interstate order—as with Belgium, India, Indonesia, and Nigeria—that of ethnically defined "genealogical" nations has created far more persistent, complex, and bitter conflicts and challenges.[23]

For this impasse to be reached, for ethnic relations to develop into protracted ethnic antagonisms, at least three internal conditions must be met. First, an ethnic category must evolve or become transformed into an ethnic community, or *ethnie*. Second, varieties of ethnic nationalism must have spread to the relevant area of the globe. Third, the *ethnie* in question must have produced a stratum of ethnic intellectuals and an intelligentsia that will apply the ideals of national self-determination to the *ethnie* in question and disseminate those ideals to its members. Historically, these conditions have been met in a variety of ways—through war, revolution, and migration, as well as by state action—with or without the example of other *ethnies*. The main point about these conditions, however, is that they represent processes that exist among *ethnies* that emerge at different times in different areas. Thus, to understand ethnic conflict, one must study the conditions in each case that help to retard or hasten these processes. Scholars and others are far from identifying in any detail the factors that can ignite ethnic differences and transform them into conflicts between self-aware and self-identifying *ethnies* intent on national self-determination.

What this means for international strategies and policy initiatives is far from clear. The means to predict with any degree of certainty the location, extent, intensity, and durability of ethnic conflict does not currently exist, nor can politicians be sure that the "solutions" to earlier conflicts will remain pertinent. That, at least, is a lesson that can be drawn from the recent history of the Balkans. Hence, any attempt to draw out policy implications from the preceding analysis must be extremely tentative.

Two things, however, are relatively certain. The first is the immense power and unpredictability of ethnic nationalism. There is always the danger of reifying ideologies and collective myths and sentiments, but it is nevertheless difficult to gainsay the huge appeal of ethnic nationalism for so many men and women in so many lands. Some reasons that derive from ethnic sources have been suggested here. The other sources of ethnic nationalism's appeal are all too apparent, including its use for elite manipulation, its involvement in situations of threat and defense, its relationship to relative economic deprivation, and the interstate rivalries that feed on ethnic secession and irredentism for their own ends. The fact that all these sources feed into a single set of ideologies and sentiments underlines the centrality and power of nationalism today.[24]

The second apparent certainty is the impossibility of envisaging a realistic alternative to a world of nations—increasingly, a world of ethnic nations. The collapse of Czechoslovakia, Yugoslavia, the Soviet Union, and Ethiopia, although not sealing the fate of the multiethnic state, has certainly encouraged many more *ethnies* to take their chances in a world of interstate politics. Kashmiris, Sikhs, Tamils, Nagas, Moros, Uigurs, Tibetans, Karen, Shan, Kurds, Shi'a, Palestinians, Maronites, as well as southern Sudanese, Kikuyu, Shona, Ovimbundu, Zulu, and many others, may flex their ethnic muscles once again in anticipation of a more favorable international climate. Even in the affluent and democratic West, with its constitutional outlets for ethnic grievances and economic palliatives for ethnic discontent, the strength of the ethnic past should not be underestimated. Although there are many signs of a lowering of ethnic barriers, and a greater sense of European and Western solidarity, especially among younger generations, the rise of racism and anti-Semitism, and the anxieties of smaller ethnic nations vis-à-vis a "European identity," should create a wariness about any illusions of a "world without nationalism." There is a long march ahead for those who are sanguine enough to believe in an early supersession of nationalism, and many a bitter conflict to be fought.

The underlying reason for such pessimism, or realism, is not simply the result of the shock of resurgent ethnic conflict. After all, since the beginning of the nineteenth century, even the most cursory historical inspection will reveal the resilience of ethnic nationalism in every part of the globe, as well as its ability to serve as the mainspring and banner of social discontent and cultural alienation. Even when its proponents fail to deliver on their promises, ethnic nationalism offers a vision that appears at once more vibrant and sharply focused for those whom it elevates into "the chosen" than any of the other ideologies on offer. One reason for this enhanced power of the ethnic vision is the nationalist ability to harness popular ties, myths, and sentiments of ethnic chosenness, which are much older, deeper, and denser, and more closely attuned to popular perceptions and needs, than are other ideologies.

Thus, wherever an *ethnie* has formed itself, on whatever grounds, wherever it produces the intellectuals and professionals to mobilize "the people" into an ethnic nation, wherever ethnic nationalism has taken hold of populations, there one may expect to find powerful assertions of national self-determination that, if long opposed, will embroil whole regions in bitter and protracted ethnic conflict. Whether the peace and stability of such regions will be better served in the short term by measures of containment, federation, mediation, or even partition, in the long run, there can be little escape from the many conflagrations that the unsatisfied yearnings of ethnic nationalism are likely to kindle.

Notes

[1] J. Okamura, "Situational Ethnicity," *Ethnic and Racial Studies*, vol. 4, no. 4, October 1981, pp. 452–465.

[2] D. Horowitz, *Ethnic Groups in Conflict* (Berkeley, Calif.: University of California Press, 1985), pp. 55–92.

[3] E. Tonkin, M. McDonald, and M. Chapman, eds., *History and Ethnicity*, ASA Monographs 27 (London: Routledge, 1989).

[4] J. Edwards, *Language, Society and Identity* (Oxford: Basil Blackwell, 1985), pp. 23–46.

[5] D.E. Smith, ed., *Religion and Political Modernization* (New Haven, Conn.: Yale University Press, 1974).

[6] J. Armstrong, *Nations Before Nationalism* (Chapel Hill, N.C.: University of North Carolina Press, 1982), pp. 201–240.

[7] G. Sheffer, ed., *Modern Diasporas in International Politics* (London: Croom Helm, 1986).

[8] A. Cobban, *Rousseau and the Modern State*, 2nd ed. (London: Allen and Unwin, 1964); A.D. Smith, "The Nation: Invented, Imagined, Reconstructed?" *Millennium: Journal of International Studies*, vol. 20, no. 3, Winter 1991, pp. 353–368.

[9] Armstrong, *Nations before Nationalism*, pp. 14–53, 201–240.

[10] Ibid., pp. 54–92, 201–240; A.D. Smith, *The Ethnic Origins of Nations* (Oxford: Basil Blackwell, 1986), pp. 92–125.

[11] L. Cliffe, "Forging a Nation: The Eritrean Experience," *Third World Quarterly*, vol. 11, no. 4, October 1989, pp. 131–147; G.McT. Kahin, *Nationalism and Revolution in Indonesia* (Ithaca, N.Y.: Cornell University Press, 1952).

[12] K.M. de Silva, *A History of Sri Lanka* (London: C. Hurst and Co., 1981); S. Citron, *Le Mythe National* (Paris: Presses Ouvrieres, 1988).

[13] See A. Gella, ed., *The Intelligentsia and the Intellectuals* (Beverly Hills, Calif.: Sage Publications, 1976); A. Melucci, *Nomads of the Present: Social Movements and Individual Needs in Contemporary Society* (London: Hutchinson Radius, 1989), pp. 89–92.

[14] H. Kohn, *The Idea of Nationalism*, 2nd ed. (New York: Macmillan, 1967); H. Seton-Watson, *Nations and States* (London: Methuen, 1977), pp. 17–191.

[15] See K. Deutsch, *Nationalism and Social Communication*, 2nd ed. (Cambridge, Mass.: MIT Press, 1966), chapter 1; A.D. Smith, *National Identity* (Harmondsworth, England: Penguin Books, 1991), p. 14.

[16] M. Pinard and R. Hamilton, "The Class Bases of the Quebec Independence Movement: Conjectures and Evidence," *Ethnic and Racial Studies*, vol. 7, no. 1, January 1984, pp. 19–54.

[17] E. Gellner, *Nations and Nationalism* (Oxford: Basil Blackwell, 1983); B. Anderson, *Imagined Communities: Reflections on the Origins and Spread of Nationalism* (London: Verso Books, 1983), pp. 67–79; M. Hroch, *Social Preconditions of National Revival* (Cambridge: Cambridge University Press, 1985).

[18] E. Kedourie, ed., *Nationalism in Asia and Africa* (London: Weidenfeld and Nicolson, 1971), pp. 1–146; J. Hutchinson, *The Dynamics of Cultural Nationalism: The Gaelic Revival and the Creation of the Irish Nation State* (London: Allen and Unwin, 1987), pp. 74–150.

[19] See R.I. Crane, "Problems of Divergent Developments within Indian Nationalism, 1895–1905," and M. Adenwalla, "Hindu Concepts and the Gita in early Indian National Thought," in R. Sakai, ed., *Studies on Asia* (Lincoln, Nebr.: University of Nebraska Press, 1961).

[20] G. Mosse, *The Crisis of German Ideology* (New York: Grosset and Dunlap, 1964); L. Poliakov, *The Aryan Myth* (New York: Basic Books, 1974).

[21] Kohn, *The Idea of Nationalism*; A.D. Smith, *Theories of Nationalism*, 2nd ed. (London: Duckworth, 1983).

[22] J. Breuilly, *Nationalism and the State* (Manchester: Manchester University Press, 1982), pp. 1–41, 352–384.

[23] E. Kedourie, *Nationalism* (London: Hutchinson, 1960); B. Neuberger, *National Self-Determination in Post-Colonial Africa* (Boulder, Colo.: Lynne Rienner Publishers, 1986); E. Hobsbawm, *Nations and Nationalism since 1780* (Cambridge: Cambridge University Press, 1990).

[24] Gellner, *Nations and Nationalism*.

Chapter 3

Domestic Politics and Ethnic Conflict
David Welsh

Since 1945, some 20 million people have been killed in wars, revolutions, liberation struggles, and insurrections. Perhaps as many as an additional 20 million have been made refugees by conflict. It is impossible to say with precision the percentage of these figures that represent victims of ethnic violence, but an estimate of 70 percent would not seem unreasonable. Of the 100 wars fought (or still being fought) since 1945, nearly one-half have involved ethnic conflict, including insurrections against colonial authority.[1]

Ethnic conflicts abound in the developing world: Only a handful of the former colonial states that received independence in the postwar period are ethnically homogeneous, and they are numerically and geographically small. Ethnic problems, however, are not confined to the developing world, as events in Belgium, Canada, and Northern Ireland show. Moreover, with the demise of Marxist–Leninist governments in Eastern Europe and the former Soviet Union, ethnic conflicts that smoldered under the hegemony of communist rule have flared up as that rule has broken down. The situation is, in some respects, similar to the one at the end of World War I, when the Austro-Hungarian, Romanov, and Ottoman Empires were dismantled, and previously subordinate ethnic groups pressed their claims for national self-determination.

The idea of the nation-state was born in the late eighteenth and nineteenth centuries. Its central proposition was that a "nation"—that is, a people welded together by common ties of culture, descent, and territory—should enjoy self-government within the same state. In France and England, absolutist systems created the framework of the modern state and, in the process, leveled many political, economic, and social differences: Legal systems, market systems, currencies, and languages were standardized as much as possible. Even so, the process was limited. Alexis de Tocqueville records that, before the French Revolution of 1789, the apparently homogeneous population of France "was still divided within itself into a great number of watertight compartments, small self-contained units, each of which watched vigilantly over its own interests and took no part in the life of the community at large."[2] Only 50 percent of the population spoke French, local dialects being the language of the ordinary people outside the major cities.[3] In Italy, at the time of unification in 1880, only a minuscule percentage of the population spoke "standard" Italian. As Massimo d'Azeglio observed in a famous comment: "We have made Italy, now we must make Italians!" (For all the centralizing efforts of the new Italian state, Italy's internal differences have stubbornly refused to be erased, even now.)

Of course, not all of the states of Europe were based on putative nationhood: Belgium, established in 1831, consisted of two major language groups; Switzerland, formed in 1291 as a loose alliance of German-speaking cantons, by 1848 also contained French- and Italian-speaking cantons. Similarly, Spain's internal diversity has not been eliminated by the growth of a modern state: As its decentralization in recent times has shown, it remains a country with pronounced regional orientations.

A crucial difference between the nation-building of Western Europe and that of Africa and much of Asia was that the processes in Europe occurred well before the rise of popular demands for democratic rights: Nations already existed as relatively cohesive citizenries.[4] In postcolonial Asia and Africa, on the other hand, nation-building was the first task on the agenda of newly independent colonies, which were suddenly endowed with the full panoply of democratic institutions. As this chapter will argue, democratization and nation-building were to prove antithetical in circumstances of ethnic diversity.

The ideal of the nation-state has proved elusive. Ronald Cohen declares it to have been "one of history's more serious mistakes."[5] Modernization theorists of the 1950s and 1960s assumed that nation-building was a viable option. Parochial or subnational ethnic loyalties would give way, it was believed, under the imperatives of development; statewide loyalties or an overarching sense of national identity would eclipse them. Similarly, a long tradition of Marxist theorists, beginning with Karl Marx himself, viewed ethnicity as an evanescent, retrograde phenomenon that would ultimately be transcended by class solidarity.

Nowhere has either of these two possibilities been realized. "Parochial" ethnic loyalties have proved stubbornly intractable and, although class has become a significant basis of stratification within developing states, nowhere has it eclipsed ethnicity as a basis for political mobilization. More common, in fact, has been the case in which national identity and class solidarity have been subsumed *within* ethnic groups, which are the critical actors. Ethnicity, so to speak, has encapsulated class, providing in the process a basis for especially intense conflict. Nation-building, too, is a project that has failed, except, of course, in those rare states in the developing world that have culturally homogeneous populations. "Melting pots" have not succeeded in creating homogeneity. The best that can be hoped for is that the diverse elements of ethnically mixed societies can reach political accommodation that will permit unity in diversity.

In the 1860s, two eminent British philosophers debated the nature of the nation-state. In his essay on representative government, John Stuart Mill reached the pessimistic conclusion that "it is in general a necessary condition of free institutions that the boundaries of governments should coincide in the main with nationalities."[6] In a response, the historian Lord Acton rejected Mill's views and reaffirmed his faith in the multinational state, declaring that the congruence of political and national boundaries was a recipe for stagnation, whereas the "presence of different nations under the same sovereignty" raised "inferior" races and revitalized "exhausted and decaying nations," while simultaneously establishing barriers to tyranny. The multinational state, he claimed, "provides against the servility which flourishes under the shadow of a single authority, by balancing interests, multiplying associations . . . diversity preserves liberty . . . ."[7]

More than 100 years after these observations were made and with popular democracy enjoying growing legitimacy, one might be tempted to conclude that the evidence supports Mill's views more than Acton's. Democratic government has been exceedingly difficult to sustain in ethnically divided societies. This may be so, but the difficulty with Mill's argument is that it leads, by implication, into the political cul-de-sac of the nation-state model, whose conditions are likely to be satisfied only in a handful of cases—or to appalling alternatives, ranging from genocide, "ethnic cleansing," and apartheid to forced assimilation.

Ethnicity has abundantly demonstrated its durability and its disruptive potential in the domestic politics of numerous states. Ethnic conflict is not a problem that will disappear. Of the approximately 180 states that exist today, fewer than 20 are ethnically homogeneous, in the sense that ethnic minorities account for less than 5 percent of the population. Numerous studies of ethnicity have appeared in recent years, making it one of the most widely studied political phenomena of modern times. However, to borrow and substantially amend Marx's dictum, the problem is not to understand ethnicity, but to learn how to cope with it. The challenge is to develop ways of managing ethnic conflict.

The argument thus far has stressed the ubiquity of ethnic conflict and the inappropriateness of the traditional nation-state as a means of coping with it. The "nation-building" projects initiated by many ex-colonial states in the post-1945 period have enjoyed only scant success largely because democratization unleashes powerful incentives for mobilizing along ethnic lines.

Succeeding sections attempt to demonstrate how this process of ethnic politics has operated in a number of different states and to identify some techniques that have enjoyed at least modest success in reconciling the existence of ethnic conflict with democratic political systems.

ETHNICITY AND THE POLITICAL PROCESS

It is hardly a coincidence that nineteenth-century nationalism over-lapped with the beginnings of democratic enfranchisement in Western Europe or that the extraordinary rise of ethnic consciousness around the world since the 1950s coincided with decolonization. In some respects, ethnicity and democracy are intimately, if not symbiotically, linked. If democracy means "the people shall rule," then who are "the people?" Who are to be considered citizens, entitled to the vote? Thus is opened the way to invidious questions about the status and rights of particular cat-egories of the people. "All men are created equal" proclaimed the US Declaration of Independence in 1776, but did this apply to African-Americans or Native Americans? In 1858, the South African Republic proclaimed itself "an independent and free people" governed by a Volksraad, consisting of representatives of "the people." In Article 9 of its constitution, however, "the people" made it clear that they would permit "no equality between coloured [African] people and the white inhabitants, either in Church or State."

It is not that far a cry from these narrow definitions of "the people" to some contemporary issues: Should Auslanders have civil rights in West-ern European states? Should indigenous Latvians, who constitute slightly more than 50 percent of Latvia's population due to intensive russification policies, cede full political equality to Russians? Should native Fijians be entitled to a permanent parliamentary majority, even if they are now outnumbered by the descendants of Indian indentured laborers?

These random and diverse examples show the intimate connection between ethnicity and power. As a relational concept, ethnicity draws boundaries between "us" and "them." As a political resource, it is a potent rallying cry for politicians—far more potent than, for example, class. For the nascent bourgeoisie, ethnic networks provide ready markets and sources of capital, as Afrikaner nationalists demonstrated in South Africa.

In democratic polities, the scope for ethnic politics is dramatically widened. Previously dominated ethnic groups may have resented their domination, as in the former Soviet Union, but voicing ethnic protest and displaying ethnic symbols was both illegal and dangerous. The lifting of the hegemonic controls and the initiation of liberalization and democratization are like air to a smoldering fire. In such circumstances, the passions ignited could not be contained by the cautious reforms of Mikhail Gorbachev.

Enfranchisement means popular empowerment. To political leaders, who in ethnically riven societies are invariably ethnic leaders, ethnicity becomes the obvious focus of mobilization. The problem that ethnicity causes for democratic political systems is best understood against the theory that underpins the modern democratic state. Briefly, the assumption is that democratic elections determine who shall govern and, in multiparty competitions, that significant parties (that is, excluding "fringe" parties) have a reasonable expectation of winning power or, where a coalition government is normal, a share of power. Parties rotate in power or, alternatively, coalitions are established on a shifting basis. The assumption is that voters are not irrevocably committed to a particular party: Votes (or, at least, some proportion of votes) will shift, and an electoral swing will result in a change of government.

In the ascriptive politics of ethnically divided societies, however, these assumptions either do not operate or operate only in attenuated form. As Donald Horowitz has observed, in ethnically divided societies, parties are often organized and votes are often cast along ethnic lines. If Group A constitutes 60 percent of the population and Group B constitutes 40 percent, then the corresponding ethnic parties of A and B might be expected to win, respectively, about 60 percent and 40 percent of the votes in an election. Horowitz explains:

> If we ask what went wrong with this election, there are at first plausible grounds for saying nothing went wrong. The election was democratically conducted. The results are in conformity with the principle of majority rule. But that is the sticking point. Majority rule in perpetuity is not what we mean by "majority rule." We assume the possibility of shifting majorities, of oppositions becoming governments, of an alterable public opinion. All this is foreclosed by the ascriptive character of the majority that voted for Party A. The election, intended to be a vehicle of choice, was no such thing and will be no such thing in the future; it registered, not choice, but birth [ethnic] affiliation. This was no election—it was a census.[8]

In short, voters in ethnically riven societies are more tightly tied to ethnically based parties than are voters in societies in which the principal basis of party preference is socioeconomic class.

The structure of political conflict will obviously vary with the configuration of ethnic groups in individual states. A common syndrome is the case of the minority that is frozen out of power (or a share of power) over time. Such minorities may be tiny (such as the Sikhs of India, who number only 2 percent of India's population), relatively small (like the Tamils of Sri Lanka, who are, in turn, subdivided into Ceylon and Indian Tamils, comprising 18 percent of the total population), or relatively large (like the Catholics of Northern Ireland who account for 35 percent of the Northern Irish population). Each of these states is putatively democratic, but politicians from these minority groups perceive themselves as the victims of a "tyranny of the majority"—as much a danger to democracy as its antithesis, minority domination.

The case of Northern Ireland has proved to be one of peculiar intractability, exacerbated by the reluctance of its Catholic population and of the Republic of Ireland to countenance the partition of Ireland in 1920–1921 and the resulting substate of Northern Ireland. In the years of Stormont's operation as an elected parliament, from 1920–1921 to 1972, the Protestants used their demographic majority to consolidate their grip on domestic politics. Until 1972, when the British government imposed direct rule, Unionist domination was a seemingly unalterable feature of Ulster politics, and Catholic parties that participated in elections (which, in the formal sense, were "open and fair") were denied any effective leverage in politics. During the 50-year period of Stormont's operation, only once was a Catholic-sponsored bill enacted into law: the Wild Bird Act of 1931, legislation that John Darby notes, "even the most ingenious argument could not make controversial."[9]

Northern Ireland's politics illustrate two additional phenomena that bedevil democratic processes in ethnically divided societies. First, one sees instances of "ethnic outbidding" or "flanking"—the incentive radical ethnic parties have to make political capital out of the efforts by more moderate parties in the same ethnic group to seek an accommodation with parties from rival ethnic groups. In Ulster, even the most tentative moves toward reform cost consecutive prime ministers their jobs and culminated in the destruction of the power-sharing experiment of 1974; strike actions by mobilized Protestant workers, led by the demagogic Reverend Ian Paisley, paralyzed the province.

Second, in ethnically divided societies, inter-ethnic parties that seek to build a moderate center or to mobilize workers on the basis of class in socialist or communist parties generally do not prosper. In Northern Ireland, the Alliance Party's inability to become more than a minor political player illustrates the point; in South Africa, a broadly comparable fate befell the liberal (although preponderantly white and English-speaking) Progressive Federal Party and its successor, the Democratic Party. The principle of "worker solidarity" has been honored more in the breach than in the observance in multiethnic states. A telling example was the bifurcation of the Belgian Communist Party into linguistic divisions as Belgium's language issue became increasingly salient in the 1980s.

One could argue that the Indian National Congress, the ruling party in India for most of the postindependence period, constitutes a major exception to the proposition that inter-ethnic parties do not prosper. Congress is a broad-based, "catchall" party, a coalition that subsumes within its ranks widely disparate linguistic, religious, ideological, and caste forces. A second possible exception is South Africa's African National Congress (ANC), which is without doubt the biggest single political movement in the country. It, too, is a coalition of disparate forces, cobbled together to make common cause against racial discrimination. Although overwhelmingly black African in membership, its leadership stresses commitment to "nonracialism." Notwithstanding the undoubtedly genuine commitment of Nelson Mandela to nonracial democracy, it is not clear that the ANC will win majority support in the coloured ("mixed race") and Indian communities, which have also suffered as victims of apartheid. Its support in the white community is minuscule. In its campaign for support, the ANC faces challenges that typify the politics of divided societies: allegations from the left (notably, the Pan Africanist Congress, a classic flanking party) that in seeking a constitutional settlement with the ruling (overwhelmingly white) National Party, the ANC is preparing for a "sellout," and allegations from the Zulu-dominated Inkatha Freedom Party that the ANC aspires to "Xhosa hegemony."

Another state that illustrates the politics of minority exclusion is Israel. Even disregarding its administration of the territories that were occupied in 1967—pursuing policies that resemble in some respects the South African government's treatment of African homelands—Israel's relationship with its Arab minority, comprising 18 percent of the (pre-1967) population, is a classic case of majority tyranny. In many respects, Israel is a vigorously democratic state, with a multiparty system, a free and lively press, a strong civil society, and, with some exceptions, a strong commitment to the rule of law. With the disintegration of Lebanon after 1975, Israel can validly claim to be the most open and democratic state in the Middle East (even if the competition is not strong).

Israel, however, is fundamentally and intrinsically a Jewish state, created in furtherance of Zionist aims and enshrining Hebrew as its official language. Whatever civil rights Israeli Arabs enjoy—and their voting rights are secure—they are second-class citizens because their political leverage is insufficient to challenge the Jewish nature of the Israeli state.

They are, moreover, subjected to various forms of discrimination, including a virtual prohibition on their service in the Israeli army.

It remains an unspoken rule of Israeli politics, applying as much to Likud as to Labour, that no Arab or Arab-dominated party should be invited to participate in a coalition. As in Northern Ireland, where Protestants tend to assume that the loyalties of Catholics are to the Republic of Ireland, so in Israel there is a common stereotype of Arabs as potential coconspirators with the hostile Arab world that surrounds Israel and threatens its elimination.[10]

A variation on the theme of "majority domination" is provided by Canada, which, notwithstanding the severity of its ethnic problems, has remained an impeccably democratic state. Until the early 1980s, relations between Canada's English-speakers, who account for 62 percent of the total population, and French-speakers, who account for 25 percent, could be described as "less a confrontation of opposing forces than a coexistence of two solitudes."[11] Beginning in the 1960s, Quebec, where more than 82 percent of Canadian French-speakers live, underwent a "quiet revolution"—an emergence from the torpor that had long characterized francophone society. Economic, cultural, and educational advancement went hand in hand with a growing resentment of anglophone domination of Canada and a rising assertion of Quebec ethnic nationalism. Increasingly, people in Quebec began to chafe at the perceived limitations imposed upon the province by the federal system. Extremists resorted to a limited amount of terrorism. A major part of the problem was the widespread indifference of anglophone Canada to Quebec's concerns. Increasingly, francophone Canada regarded Quebec as its political and cultural heartland, in which French and French-Canadian culture could enjoy an exclusive and unchallenged dominance.

In 1976, the separatist, Réné Levesque, became first minister of Quebec. Agitation for sovereignty subsequently increased, culminating in a referendum in Quebec in 1980 in which the separatists were decisively, although not overwhelmingly, beaten. The issue of separatism was by no means dead, however. Throughout the 1980s and into the 1990s, Canada wrestled with the constitutional dimensions of the problem. In 1982, the constitution was patriated (that is, constitutional amendments no longer required enactment by the British Parliament), and further efforts were made to expand Prime Minister Pierre Trudeau's vision of a "pan-Canadianism" based on the acceptance of Canada as a bilingual and bicultural society. A Charter of Rights and Freedom was adopted, the terms of which furthered efforts to promote language equality: English and French were made the official languages in all federal institutions, and, in addition to Quebec where language guarantees had been established earlier, New Brunswick (approximately one-third of whose population is French) was required to adopt French and English as official languages in all of its government institutions.[12] Notwithstanding significant constitutional changes and the explicit recognition of Canada's multicultural heritage, the Quebec provincial government refused to ratify the Constitution Act of 1982, maintaining that the changes failed to recognize Quebec as a "distinct society" within Canada's federal system.

In 1987, all 10 provincial first ministers and the federal prime minister, Brian Mulroney of the Progressive Conservative Party, signed the Meech Lake Accord, which recognized Quebec as a distinct society. It marked an attempt to loosen further Canada's federal ties by according to Quebec increased powers of self-government. The accord required ratification by the Canadian Parliament and by all 10 provincial legislatures within a three-year period that expired in June 1990. Ultimately, the accord foundered on the refusal of Manitoba and Newfoundland to accept it.

The next step in the saga was the signing in August 1992 of the Charlottetown Agreement by the federal prime minister, the 10 provincial premiers, the leaders of the 2 territories, and leaders of various indigenous Indian and Inuit groups. The agreement, like the Meech Lake Accord, had as its core a clause that would recognize Quebec as a distinct society and commit Canadians to "linguistic duality." Moreover, aboriginal rights and a determination that aboriginal governments constitute one of the three orders of government in Canada would also be recognized.

According to the Charlottetown Agreement, Quebec was to be guaranteed a minimum of 25 percent of the seats in the federal House of Commons; three judges of the Supreme Court (from a total of nine) would be drawn from Quebec; and federal bills materially affecting French language or culture would require a "double majority"—a majority of all senators voting and a majority of all francophone senators voting. The Senate was to be reformed by granting it more powers, and the principle of parity of representation among the provinces was to be established and entrenched. Decentralization was to be promoted in the name of replacing "domineering federalism" with a "true partnership based on mutual respect." This implied, for example, that Quebec or any other province could acquire control over labor market development, immigration, and regional development. Amendments to the constitution would require unanimous agreement of all provinces and the federal government.[13]

Despite its being supported by all elected heads of government in Canada, including Quebec's, and by the major opposition parties in the federal parliament and all of the provinces except British Columbia, Manitoba, and Quebec (whose federal and provincial parties opposed it), the Charlottetown Agreement was rejected in a referendum held in October 1992. Clearly, much of anglophone Canada expressed pique at the gains Quebec would have made under the agreement and resentment at seemingly petty efforts by Quebec politicians to restrict the use of English in the province. To Quebec separatists (roughly one-third of the Quebec electorate), rejection of the Charlottetown Agreement meant that anglophone Canada had again dismissed Quebec's claims. Although Canada's constitutional future is unclear, it is by no means certain that a majority of Quebecois will support separation or "sovereignty association."

Canada's dilemma finds echoes in other ethnically divided states that have sought to hold together by federalizing or increasing the extent of federal decentralization. India's recasting of state boundaries along linguistic lines in the 1950s, Belgium's steady retreat from unitary government to federalism, Spain's regionalization, Sri Lanka's (belated) effort to federalize, and Gorbachev's frantic attempts to hold the Soviet Union together on true (as opposed to the former artificial) federal lines, are all variations on the same theme.

In the Canadian case, the existence of an overall anglophone majority is not in doubt. In at least three other cases, however, the question of which group is in the majority has been a bone of contention. Lebanon's rickety consociational democracy, which survived from 1943 to 1975, rested upon a National Pact that, in turn, was based upon the ethnic profile shown by a census taken in 1932; this census showed that Maronites and other Christian sects constituted 51 percent of the total population, the remaining 49 percent consisting of different Muslim groups. The pact revolved around a complex system of power-sharing in which Christians would maintain a parliamentary majority over Muslims, while the president would always be a Maronite Christian, the prime minister a Sunni Muslim, and the speaker of parliament a Shi'a Muslim. Furthermore, careful attention was paid to sectarian considerations in the formation of cabinets, with key ministries being reserved for particular sects.

Although the pact provided mechanisms for continuous intersectarian bargaining, it was always an inherently precarious arrangement. Muslim resentment at their minority status grew, erupting in serious violence in 1958 and flaring up again in the early 1970s, by which time it had become clear even in the absence of a census that Muslims and the Druze accounted for two-thirds of the population. The Maronites, however, refused to concede more than equal parliamentary representation and the abolition of sectarian criteria in civil service appointments. The Muslims rejected this as insufficient. Private militias started to form, and, with the involvement of Syrians, Palestinians, and Israelis, Lebanon was plunged into civil war. Whether Lebanon could have succeeded in reforming its political institutions in the absence of external actors remains a moot question.

The case of Fiji has already been mentioned: Native Fijians and Indians constitute groups that are roughly equal in size, with Indians having a slight numerical edge. In 1987, the Fijian-dominated army staged successive coups after an election in which an alliance between the overwhelmingly Indian National Federation Party and the Fijian-dominated Fiji Labour Party succeeded in defeating the Alliance Party, which represents the majority of Fijians. A new constitution, promulgated in 1990, aims at securing Fijian dominance and, in particular, political control by the chiefs who are the traditional, indigenous leaders of Fiji. It provides for separate or communal representation, weighted heavily in favor of Fijians, and a Senate of Chiefs that will be dominated by the traditional elite. The intention of the framers of the constitution is crystal clear: to exclude Indians from any meaningful share of political power.[14]

Similar demographic and political concerns have been expressed by Malay political organizations in Malaysia, where indigenous Malays make up approximately 53 percent of the population, the economically powerful Chinese approximately 33 percent, and the Indians 10 percent. (Singapore's withdrawal from Malaysia in 1965 strengthened Malay numerical domination in Malaysia because 75 percent of Singapore's 2 million people are Chinese.) The pact on which Malaysia's political system rests states that, in return for recognition of Malay hegemony, including national symbols, language, and religion, the citizenship rights and interests of non-Malays will be recognized. Since independence in 1957 (as Malaya), Malaysia has been governed by a coalition of Malay, Chinese, and Indian ethnic parties. Essentially, though, it has been dominated by one Malay party, whose democratic credentials are suspect.

In each of the cases of ethnically divided states described above, the issue arises as to whether a political community can be said to exist. The term "political community" in this context suggests an inclusive code of political understanding, a shared political culture, commonly respected symbols of statehood, and, most critical, a shared view that the outcomes of the political processes (most notably, elections) are legitimate. Related issues include whether, in spite of ethnic divisions, there exists a transcending bond of national unity. Few multiethnic states have been political communities in this sense.

Switzerland is a major exception: In spite of religious and linguistic divisions that have afflicted other states, the Swiss have managed to maintain an overarching sense of national identity and a democratic political system. Explanations of Switzerland's political stability and its ethnic amity vary, and space considerations do not permit a detailed review of the issues. Four aspects of the Swiss experience, however, deserve brief mention. First, its long tradition of neutrality (dating from the sixteenth century) has ensured that its different linguistic groups have not sought to make common cause with German, French, or Italian colinguals in the great European conflicts. Second, the principal axes of potential conflict—religion and class—cut across each other so that, as a Swiss saying has it, "everyone is part of a minority in some respect." Third, Swiss politics, especially at the federal level, runs along consensual lines. In terms of the "magic formula," a convention adopted in 1959, each of the four major parties enjoys representation in the Federal Council. In addition, care is taken to ensure that a reasonable proportionality of languages and cantons is maintained. Fourth, the highly decentralized nature of Swiss federalism and the salience of cantonal and communal identities inhibits the development of societywide polarization on particular issues.[15]

The United States is a more problematic case, in view of the continuing salience of racial problems there. Yet, its achievement in incorporating millions of European, Asian, and Hispanic immigrants into a common civic culture and the absence of any serious challenge to US political institutions and national symbols suggest that, in spite of its diversity and frequent manifestations of racial antipathy, there exists, often inarticulated, an overarching sense of "being an American." As far as African-Americans are concerned, although the legal barriers to political equality have been removed, residual racism remains a powerful obstacle to full equality. As Charles Hamilton noted in 1989: "It is still the case that most blacks are elected to office mainly when there is a sizable black constituency . . . . For the most part, white voters still prefer white candidates over black candidates. In the realm of analysis, one cannot say that blacks have reached political parity until a black candidate can run in an election in a majority white district and have an equal chance of being elected."[16]

However, disappointment with the operation of the US political system and even a degree of alienation (a partial cause for low African-American voter turnout) should not be confused with a rejection of the system's premises or with the espousal of separatist views. Such views, in various forms, have had their adherents in black political history in the United States, but support for them has never exceeded one-third of the African-American electorate.

MAINTAINING DEMOCRACY IN
DIVIDED SOCIETIES

Establishing and sustaining democratic institutions in ethnically divided societies is a difficult task. Long-established democracies, such as Belgium, Canada, and India, have managed to do so, but in each case the integrity of the state must be a matter of doubt. India's survival as a democracy is a remarkable achievement. India has perhaps the most diverse society on earth, with an electorate of more than 500 million—by far the largest democracy worldwide. India has 4 major religions, 15 major languages, and thousands of castes. Its founders, Mahatma Gandhi and Jawaharlal Nehru, insisted that India be a secular state. Formally it is, but religion, as with language and caste, is highly politicized. One explanation for India's relative success as a democratic state derives from its diversity. As Edward Ross observed, "A society which is riven by a dozen oppositions along lines running in every direction may actually be in less danger of being torn with violence or falling to pieces than one split along just one line."[17] The divisions, "divisive in isolation, are, in fact integrative in India's plural society."[18]

Stable pluralism, however, has also required skilled and prudent management, and most of India's leaders have displayed these qualities. The Congress Party, dominant for all but two brief periods, has shown a remarkable ability to integrate in its "catchall" structure a diverse set of components. At the national level, the careful allocation of important posts has operated on the semiconsociational lines of proportionality, ensuring that major segments of the population are sewn into the system. The federal system, moreover, although more centralized than most other federations, has allowed opposition parties to gain power at the state level, thereby inhibiting potential alienation from the political system.

In recent years, however, India's prospects for continued democratic stability have been threatened by Sikh demands in the Punjab, the unresolved problem of Kashmir, and, even more serious, by the rise of militant Hindu nationalism. At the core of the Hindu demands is a proposal to transform India into a Hindu state, thus terminating its secular tradition. Because Hindus account for 83 percent of India's population, the danger posed by growing militancy is obvious. The political arm of Hindu extremism, the Bharatiya Janata Party (BJP), portrays India as a basically Hindu state, surrounded by a sea of hostile Muslim states. It accuses the ruling Congress Party of pandering to the needs of India's 100 million Muslims, who constitute a little more than 10 percent of the total population. In the 1991 elections, the BJP made further gains, winning 119 of the 546 seats in parliament and gaining control of four states, including Uttar Pradesh, the most populous state in India. Even these gains, however, meant that support for Hindu extremism does not yet exceed 20 percent of the vote.[19]

An important part of the explanation of India's stability to date has been the coalition nature of the Congress Party: It has succeeded in yoking together widely disparate elements, ensuring that, in principle (although, clearly, not everywhere in practice), no politically significant segment of society was consigned to perpetual minority status. However, the Sikhs, who comprise 2 percent of the population, and some of whom agitate for a purely Sikh nation, Khalistan, see themselves as victims of the tyranny of the majority.

An important lesson for the management of ethnic conflict is that no salient group should be prohibited from a share of effective power. Political institutions should be designed to ensure that minorities are proportionately represented in parliaments and bureaucracies and that their interests—political, cultural, and economic—are heeded. To the extent that minority votes are sought by political parties, minority interests are likely to be respected.

In institutional terms, a crucial conflict-regulating device appears to be, on the basis of the cases examined here, broad-based coalition government. This has been part of the explanation of Switzerland's success, and, in different form, it has been a characteristic of Indian politics. Equally striking as another rare example of democratic stability in a developing state is Mauritius, a small island whose population of 1 million consists of an Indian (Hindu) majority of 52 percent, a Creole minority of 27 percent, and other small minorities. Since gaining independence in 1968, Mauritius has enjoyed a stable democratic system and, in recent years, economic prosperity, which has helped to blunt the cutting edge of potential ethnic conflict. It has also benefited from a vigorous civil society, including a robust free press. Coalition government has been the norm in Mauritian politics; this has been a stabilizing factor, inhibiting ethnic conflict and giving all salient parties a share (or the prospect of a share) of power. Eliphas Mukonoweshuru writes: "Mauritian politicians, over the years, have managed to turn this potentially explosive diversity into a political strength. Out of this polyethnic plethora, they have woven a political spoils system which has ensured that each ethnic group has an established stake in the system. This has resulted in the emergence of rules of the political game whose legitimacy and legality is accepted by all the dominant forces on the island."[20]

It follows from the cases examined in this article that if multiethnic states are to have any hope of sustaining democratic political systems, "winner-take-all" outcomes have to be avoided. The principle of majority rule has to be tempered by a recognition of the destabilizing and alienating consequences that ignoring or riding roughshod over minority interests is bound to have. If a political community does not exist, relationships among the major actors are likely to resemble international relations; this implies that careful and sensitive diplomacy is a primary requirement of political stability.

In the literature on the politics of divided societies, there has often been some (usually latent) tension between those who pin their faith on the efficacy of political institutions to promote accommodation and those who, being skeptical of the value of institutional design, place more emphasis on the skills and prudence of political leaders and the accommodative potential of different political subcultures in a divided society.[21] This is a false dichotomy because both are surely necessary. It is clear that skillful political leadership and the encouragement of accommodative attitudes are of prime importance: Their absence (especially on the Protestant side) has bedeviled Northern Ireland's quest for a solution; a succession of insensitive Sinhalese leaders pushed the Tamils into civil war; and widespread anglophone indifference to, and even contempt for, the legitimate concerns of French-Canadians, goes a long way toward explaining Canada's problems. Conversely, the political skills and prudence of Tunku Abdul Rahman, Malaysia's first prime minister, explains much of Malaysia's success in mediating and moderating its ethnic problems, just as the deliberately cultivated emphasis on "amicable agreement" in Swiss political culture underpins its institutional mechanisms for neutralizing potential ethnic conflict.

It is also apparent that ethnicity cannot be disinvented easily. Forced assimilation—except perhaps in the case of small, dispersed immigrant communities—is unlikely to succeed, to say nothing of the incompatibility of such a strategy with any notion of democracy and justice. Ethnic groups, as a general principle, must be permitted to enjoy and foster their cultures, and, although a proliferation of claims for languages to be given "official" or "national" status creates significant problems, the general principle should be that, as far as possible, language preferences should be respected and provided in schools, courts, elective bodies, and bureaucracies. It follows from these principles that, as far as possible, the principle of cultural autonomy should be respected. Governments should respect religious freedom and other institutional manifestations of ethnic culture.

The potential accommodative uses of federalism have been touched on at various points in this chapter. The conventional argument is that federalism is the most appropriate approach if ethnic groups are territorially based, as in the case of Canada's francophone population. As seen, however, federalism is by no means a guarantee of ethnic accord.

Belgium has substantially "territorialized" its rival ethnic groups, and it has formally embraced federalism, but it does not follow that federalism is likely to result in a durable accommodation. It may be possible to maintain that Belgium has no alternative to federalization and that federalism, although not a sufficient condition, is a necessary condition for any chance of an accommodation to be reached. Even this, however, is not a persuasive argument in view of the apparently unstoppable drive toward dismemberment of the state. Apart from the intractable problem of what would happen to Brussels, would dismemberment actually make much difference to an independent Flanders or Wallonia, given continuing membership in the European Community?

In this latter consideration lies a potential answer to part of the problem posed by the lack of congruence between the (putative) model of the nation-state and the ethnic diversity of most modern states. Wider economic associations, becoming, perhaps, also political associations (initially confederations, possibly later, federations) offer a potential safety-net to the political entities that could result from dismembered states. However, this is a long-term prospect that does not address the immediate problems of ethnically divided states in most parts of the world.

Further advantages claimed for federalism restate traditional arguments that may have little to do with ethnic issues: that federalism reduces the administrative load on the center, that it brings government "closer to the people," and that it establishes barricades against tyrannical government by diluting the power of central government and by securing certain powers (and they vary considerably among federations) for regional governments. There is truth in all of these contentions, and many have been voiced in the vigorous debate in South Africa about whether its highly centralized government should in the new, democratic system be unitary or federal.

Scale seems to be a critically important variable: All democratic states (with the possible exception of France) that are large either in terms of geographical size or population are federations. It is highly unlikely that India, Nigeria, Sudan, or Brazil could be effectively governed other than by federal means. Multiethnic Russia, therefore, should embrace federalism.

CONCLUSION

This article has emphasized the inappropriateness of the nation-state model for political organizations in most cases, but has tried to avoid the simplistic view that the logical and preferable alternative is secession or partition. The Baltic states unilaterally seceded from the Soviet Union, but each faces the problem of accommodating sizable Russian minorities.

Partition, as in Northern Ireland or India, faces the problem of accommodating those remaining on the "wrong" side of the boundary. Cyprus, which was forcibly partitioned by the Turkish army in 1974, may be considered an exception because only tiny numbers of Greeks and Turks remain on the "wrong" side of the border. However, the forced relocation of some 200,000 people and the fact that Turkish-Cypriots, who number 18 percent of the total population of Cyprus, now occupy nearly 40 percent of the island, are hardly compatible with conventional notions of fairness.

For the foreseeable future, individual states with ethnic problems will have no alternative but to grope toward political accommodation. This chapter has discussed some of the constitutional and political techniques of coping with ethnic conflict. Several broad propositions have been advanced: avoidance of "winner-take-all" outcomes, the desirability of coalition government, tolerance of ethnic groups' desire for cultural autonomy, and, in some situations, adoption of federalism. There are no general solutions to ethnic conflict, however. Each case differs from others in terms of its possible amenability to particular techniques of accommodation.

As international organizations strengthen and their scope increases, international concern with human rights abuse and the maintenance of democratic polities will grow. In turn, this will strengthen individual states' sensitivity to international criticism of the mistreatment of minorities. One hopes that these tightening bonds of accountability to internationally accepted norms will have a deterrent effect on the future practitioners of ethnic cleansing or those, like Saddam Hussein, who persecute and tyrannize defenseless minorities. For those seeking to establish and maintain democratic institutions in divided societies, the test of whether a country is really free will increasingly depend on the security enjoyed by the minorities within that country.

Notes

[1] Calculated from the chronology in Patrick Brogan, *World Conflicts: Why and Where They Are Happening,* 2nd ed. (London: Bloomsbury Publications, 1992), pp. 621–625.

[2] Alexis de Tocqueville, *The Old Regime and the French Revolution* (New York: Anchor Books, 1955), p. 77.

[3] E.J. Hobsbawm, *Nations and Nationalism since 1780: Programme, Myth, Reality* (Cambridge: Cambridge University Press, 1990), p. 60.

[4] Rupert Emerson, *From Empire to Nation: The Rise to Self-Assertion of Asian and African Peoples* (Cambridge, Mass.: Harvard University Press, 1960), p. 94.

[5] Ronald Cohen, "Conclusion: Ethnicity, the State, and Moral Order," in Judith D. Toland, ed., *Ethnicity and the State* (New Brunswick, N.J.: Transaction Publishers, 1993), p. 242.

[6] John Stuart Mill, *Representative*

Government (London: J.M. Dent and Sons, 1910), p. 362.

[7] John Acton, *Essays on Freedom and Power* (London: Thames and Hudson, 1956), p. 169.

[8] Donald L. Horowitz, *Ethnic Groups in Conflict* (Berkeley, Calif.: University of California Press, 1985), p. 86.

[9] John Darby, *Conflict in Northern Ireland: The Development of a Polarised Community* (Dublin: Gill and Macmillan, 1976), p. 76.

[10] David K. Shipler, *Arab and Jew: Wounded Spirits in a Promised Land* (New York: Penguin Books, 1987), p. 191.

[11] K.D. McRae, "Consociationalism and the Canadian Political System," in Kenneth McRae, ed., *Consociational Democracy: Political Accommodation in Segmented Societies* (Toronto: McLelland and Stewart, 1974), p. 244.

[12] Barry L. Strayer, "The Canadian Constitution and Diversity," in Robert A. Goldwin, Art Kaufman, and William A. Schambra, eds., *Forging Unity Out of Diversity: The Approaches of Eight Nations* (Washington, D.C.: American Enterprise Institute, 1989), pp. 176–180.

[13] Minister of Supply and Services, *Canada, Our Future Together: An Agreement for Constitutional Renewal,* Cat. no. CP 43–45/1992 (Ottawa: Ministry of Supply and Services, 1992).

[14] Stephanie Lawson, "Constitutional Change in Fiji: The Apparatus of Justification," *Ethnic and Racial Studies*, vol. 15, no. 1, January 1992, p. 75.

[15] Vernon Bogdanor, "Federalism in Switzerland," *Government and Opposition*, vol. 23, no. 1, Winter 1988, pp. 86–87.

[16] Charles V. Hamilton, "On Parity and Political Empowerment," in Janet Dewart, ed., *The State of Black America 1989* (New York: National Urban League, 1989), p. 115.

[17] Bogdanor, "Federalism in Switzerland," pp. 71–73.

[18] Ainslie T. Embree, "Pluralism and National Integration: The Indian Experience," *Journal of International Affairs*, vol. 27, no. 1, 1973, p. 47.

[19] *The Economist*, December 19, 1992, p. 53.

[20] Eliphas G. Mukonoweshuru, "Containing Political Instability in a Polyethnic Society: The Case of Mauritius," *Ethnic and Racial Studies,* vol. 14, no. 2, April 1991, p. 220.

[21] See Horowitz, *Ethnic Groups,* for a splendid overview that judiciously combines both approaches.

Chapter 4

Democratization and Ethnic Conflict

Renée de Nevers

The recent spread of democracy in Eastern Europe and other parts of the world has been accompanied by a rise in the number of bloody ethnic conflicts. This has led some to observe that ethnic conflict may be an inevitable result of the disintegration of authoritarian control. Given the difficulties inherent in mitigating ethnic conflict, one might be tempted to conclude that ethnic hostilities will invariably overwhelm efforts to establish new democratic governments.

Must democratization be accompanied by ethnic unrest, or might the process of democratization actually provide an *opportunity* to prevent ethnic conflicts from defining the political debate in newly democratic states? The aim of this chapter is to identify the conditions in which democratization is likely to temper ethnic tensions, as well as those conditions likely to exacerbate ethnic conflict. Its initial premise is that democratization can prevent or dampen ethnic conflicts if the forces pushing for democratization, first, recognize and acknowledge the ethnic differences that exist within the state and, second, if they can accommodate the interests of different groups in a way that is perceived to be fair and evenhanded. Neither of these is automatic. One precondition for successful democratization is national unity; that is, potential ethnic problems must be at least temporarily submerged in the effort to defeat authoritarian regimes.[1] Yet, this suggests that the democratization process provides a window of opportunity to allay potential ethnic problems.

Several factors help determine whether democratization mitigates or exacerbates ethnic tension. Among these are the speed with which ethnic issues are recognized, the level of ethnic tension when the democratization process begins, the size and power of different ethnic groups within the state, the ethnic composition of the previous regime and its opposition, the political positions of the leaders of the main ethnic groups, the presence or absence of external ethnic allies, and the ethnic composition of the military. It is not yet clear how other factors—for example, the balance between political competition within an ethnic group and inter-ethnic competition or the level of homogeneity of ethnic communities—affect efforts to develop moderate policies.

Presented first is a brief examination of the causes of ethnic conflict and options for attempting to mitigate such conflicts. Second, the process of democratization is discussed, and three models of the democratization process are outlined, as are the ways in which the behavior of preceding authoritarian regimes helps to shape the ethnic issues confronting new democratic governments and the conditions under which democratization might dampen ethnic tensions, along with those that have the potential to exacerbate such tensions. The effect different processes of democratization may have on ethnic tensions are then examined, as is the role that the international community can play in preventing and dampening ethnic disputes.

ETHNIC CONFLICTS: CAUSES AND OPTIONS

What causes ethnic conflict?[2] The prerequisites are fairly simple. First, conflict requires the presence of a mixed ethnic community within a single state. Because ethnic conflict is based on the struggle between different groups for political power and status, it is fundamentally linked to the existence of states.[3] Thus, the potential for ethnic conflict is almost universal because there are very few states in which only one ethnic group resides.[4] Second, ethnic conflict requires a situation in which at least one group feels aggrieved. It could be unhappy about the existing distribution of power among the ethnic groups making up the state, or it could feel that it is being discriminated against. If it is impossible—or perceived to be impossible—to redress these grievances through legal or political channels, then violent conflict may result.[5]

Conflict Prevention and Mitigation

Recent history has shown that ethnic conflict can be resolved through forced expulsion and genocide. Yet, short of these morally repugnant options, as long as different groups continue to cohabit states, the potential for ethnic conflict remains. This raises two questions. How is it possible to prevent latent ethnic tensions from being inflamed? When ethnic tension is acute, how can these conflicts be mitigated? The key to answering both questions lies in creating an environment in which political moderation prevails. Leaders of all the relevant ethnic groups must perceive that it is in their interest to avoid adopting extremist rhetoric or policies in the search for solutions to potential or existing problems. More often than not, however, group leaders feel that either their personal political aims or those of the group they represent will be better served by doing just the reverse—exacerbating tensions or raising the level of violence.[6]

How can moderation be promoted? If possible, it is best to prevent serious tension from developing, thus avoiding the situation in which a potential conflict becomes a real conflict. One way to do this is to structure the electoral system of the state so that most political parties and mainstream politicians cannot perceive a political advantage in adopting extremist positions on ethnic issues. If possible, regional and national leaders should be made dependent on support from other ethnic groups for political success. This can be done by creating an electoral system that takes into account the relative strength of different ethnic groups within the state and requires successful candidates for regional and national offices to receive a larger percentage of the vote than can be met by support from any one group.[7]

In states in which ethnic tensions have already led to violence, little can be done until conflicts have spent themselves. There may, however, be windows of opportunity to encourage the adoption of moderate policies. Such opportunities could emerge if the main parties in a conflict are simultaneously weakened or if they decide that futher fighting could lead to a worse outcome for their side: That is, they would be better off ending the conflict, rather than continuing in the hope of improving their position. If either of these situations occurs, it may be possible to negotiate a political settlement that will accommodate all sides, thus promoting a political climate of moderation.[8]

A variety of options are available to a government seeking to dampen ethnic tensions by reconfiguring the state. The most extreme policies involve denying ethnicity altogther, either by extermination and expulsion or by forced assimilation. Less extreme, but still radical, options would mean the end of the state in its current form. A complete devolution would entail either partitioning the state or allowing some regions to secede; a partial dismantling would be brought about by creating a federal state or a confederation. Of these, only a federal arrangement would have much likelihood, in the long run, of preserving the existing state.

Devolution does not appear to be a viable option, given the prevailing tendency of governments to try to preserve their states regardless of the contradictions between ethnic groups and national borders. Because maintaining states as coherent units remains an important goal for leaders trying to solve ethnic problems, two alternative types of solutions are available for reducing ethnic tension: electoral and territorial.[9]

For an electoral system to avoid or mitigate ethnic tension, it must be designed to ensure power-sharing among different ethnic groups. There is no single model that can address all ethnic concerns; an electoral solution must be customized to the ethnic mix within the given state if it is to be effective. Arend Lijphart suggests that for power-sharing to be effective, it must provide for the following: a joint exercise of power by the relevant groups in a given state, group autonomy, proportionality in representation, and a minority veto.[10] The degree to which the state's ethnic mix is geographically heterogeneous or homogeneous, and the relative differences in size of various ethnic groups, will play a major role in determining the appropriate type of electoral arrangement.[11] There is general agreement, however, that the parliamentary model is more useful than the presidential model in ethnically diverse states; a system of power-sharing through proportional representation can best meet the needs of multiethnic societies.[12]

Territorial solutions can either be part of electoral solutions or alternatives to them. The shaping of electoral districts can play a key role in the relative power of different ethnic groups; the territorial aspects of any electoral system, therefore, must be carefully considered. If opposing ethnic groups live in different parts of a given state, then regional autonomy or self-rule for minority groups may be an option. Although an obvious objection is that regional autonomy could be the forerunner to secession, the historical evidence suggests that this is rarely the case. In any community, homogeneous or heterogeneous, competition for power will develop; if regional autonomy is granted, the local population is more likely to be occupied with internal politics than with secession.[13] Finally, power-sharing will be facilitated if no ethnic group in the state has a clear majority and if the socioeconomic levels of the various ethnic groups are not widely divergent.

In contrast, states with severe ethnic conflicts share certain similarities. First, it is common for the smaller ethnic groups in such states to have ethnic ties across state borders, giving them external allies in their domestic disputes. Second, ethnic groups in these states tend to have strong stereotypical views about other ethnic groups in the state. Indeed, if one of the ethnic groups in the state subjugated other groups in the past, this could be the root of current conflicts. Third, in states with high levels of ethnic tension, extremist ethnic positions can be a very useful tool in intra-ethnic political competition, which can perpetuate ethnic tensions.

THE IMPACT OF ETHNIC CONFLICT
ON DEMOCRATIZATION

In principle, democratization presents a golden opportunity for resolving ethnic conflict. Such solutions generally require negotiated settlements. In the absence of democratization, governments must agree to hold negotiations with opposing ethnic groups to reach a compromise; if the conflict has led to civil war, then the warring groups must be willing to find a solution together. Because in most cases democratization includes a negotiating phase, there is an inherent opportunity in the process to address issues raised by ethnic tensions—especially when constitution-building is part of the democratization process. However, simply because such an opportunity exists, this does not guarantee the successful resolution of tensions, as has been clearly demonstrated in recent years by the breakup of Czechoslovakia and continuing tensions in Cambodia. For democratization to reduce ethnic tension, the inclusion of all relevant groups in the negotiating process is required; in addition, there must be a willingness by all parties to work for, and then accept, a mutually beneficial arrangement.[14]

Processes of Democratization

The process of democratization tends to follow a general pattern.[15] First, in many cases, an external catalyst changes popular perceptions about the options available to nondemocratic regimes and, thus, increases popular support for opposition movements. Second, authoritarian governments reject change, which then leads to an expansion of popular opposition to the regimes. Third, the regimes recognize that they cannot continue to rule without including opposition forces in some way, which leads, fourth, to negotiations on new political structures between regimes and opposition groups. The fifth and final step is elections. In this respect, the goal of democratization and the means to achieve it are the same: the expansion of political participation and the creation of stable democratic governments, established by competitive elections in which the majority of the population has the right to vote.

Expanding on this foundation, Samuel Huntington has recently proposed three more specific models to explain the recent wave of democratization.[16] In transformations, reform is initiated from above by the elite within the authoritarian regimes. For transformations to occur, democratic reformers must come to power within the regime. Transformations generally begin with a period of liberalization by regimes, during which reformers both legitimize and solidify their rule, and of neutralizing opposition within the regime to democratization. To succeed, reformers look outside their regimes for alternative sources of support, thereby expanding the political arena and beginning a process of negotiation that eventually leads to democratization. Transformations require that the governments in question are stronger than the opposition when the process begins (although this could change drastically by the time the process ends) and that moderate opposition groups are stronger than extremist groups. Spain after Francisco Franco's death is one example of such a transition. Brazil's transformation also fits this pattern; indeed, the process was so gradual in Brazil that there was no clear break between the dictatorship and democracy.[17]

Replacement occurs when authoritarian regimes collapse or are overthrown by popular pressure. There are three stages to this process: the struggle against the regime, during which the opposition movements gain strength, while the government loses strength; the fall of the regime; and the struggle for power after the government has fallen. Replacements are more common when authoritarian regimes are one-man dictatorships, as opposed to governments run by larger coalitions. Unlike transformations, any negotiation in this process occurs during or after the collapse of the regime, at a time when the regime is not in a strong position to affect the negotiation's outcome. In addition, although opposition forces tend to be strong and united in rejection of previous governments, they may fragment during the struggle over the replacement of the regime in question. Replacement occurred in the Philippines after Ferdinand Marcos's removal from power and in Romania after Nicolae Ceausescu's death. However, leaders such as these are as likely to be replaced by other dictators or authoritarian regimes as they are by democratic institutions and processes; in the cases of Argentina and Greece, military leaders assumed control for an interim period before democracy eventually prevailed.[18]

Transplacement results from joint actions by governments and opposition movements. Generally, transplacement occurs when both governments and opposition leaders recognize that they are not strong enough to determine the country's political future individually. Both must also recognize their inability to prevail and, thus, be willing to negotiate a settlement. As with transformations, this process often includes a liberalization phase, during which the regime begins to lose power, while the opposition gains broader support. The government responds to these shifts in power by attempting to contain the liberalization process and opposition support, but it may no longer be strong enough to maintain control. In such cases, standoffs result, during which negotiations can begin. In contrast to the other two models, transplacement requires that opposition and government are relatively equal in strength; neither can count on prevailing in a direct confrontation. The transition in Poland began as a transplacement, although the balance of power between regime and opposition shifted quickly in the more open environment created by negotiations.

Authoritarian Regimes and Ethnicity

To determine the effect democratization efforts are likely to have on possible ethnic conflicts, it is necessary to look at the conditions that exist when the democratization process begins. The presence or absence of ethnic tensions in the previous authoritarian regime will affect the likelihood of serious ethnic problems erupting and may highlight issues to avoid or address immediately. Four factors are important in this regard: the ethnic composition of the regime, the ethnic distribution of the population, the ethnic makeup of the military, and the level of ethnic conflict in the state prior to democratization.

The ethnic makeup of the authoritarian regime itself could be a source of ethnic resentment. Members of the regime may have been members of the main ethnic group in the state in a country with a dominant ethnic group. Alternatively, the regime could be associated with a minority group in the country, thereby creating an impression of minority rule, regardless of whether this group supported the authoritarian regime's policies. Finally, the regime may have shown no particular ethnic distinctiveness and instead reflected a cross section of ethnic groups, representing a similar mix to the groups in the population at large. These differences could have important consequences for the level of tension between ethnic groups during the democratization process.

As with other states, there could be either a homogeneous or heterogeneous geographic mix of ethnic groups within a state ruled by an authoritarian regime. What is important to consider in terms of problems that might emerge during democratization is whether the authoritarian regime, or some previous government, took deliberate steps to affect this ethnic distribution. An authoritarian regime might have adopted expulsion or extermination policies to create a homogeneous population; alternatively, it might have forcibly moved ethnic groups to different parts of the country to preclude homogenous regions. Both policies reflect the aim of maintaining control. The Soviet practice of settling Russians in the Baltic and Central Asian republics is an example of deliberate intermixing, while the ethnic cleansing under way in Bosnia-Herzegovina is an example of expulsion designed to create ethnically homogeneous regions.

The ethnic composition of the military under the authoritarian regime could also have important consequences. Because authoritarian regimes frequently depend on the military to aid in suppressing ethnic or other societal tensions, some regimes in multiethnic states have manipulated the ethnic makeup of the armed forces and the deployment of ethnic troops to prevent a situation in which military forces might choose to align themselves with the local population against the regime in power. This may have an effect on the attitude of the military toward democratization and its willingness, or lack of resolve, to become involved in politics—especially if ethnic tensions are already inflamed in the state.

In an ethnically mixed society, the military may be heterogeneous. If there is a dominant ethnic group in the regime, most of the military is likely to be from this group as well; it is unlikely that most of the military would be from a different ethnic group, although this is not impossible. For example, the regime may not have had sufficient time in power to implement changes in the military hierarchy; alternatively, it may have relied on different organizations (such as an internal police force) to maintain control and was therefore willing to tolerate a different ethnic mix in a marginalized military.

The level of ethnic conflict under the previous regime will also have an effect on the role that ethnicity plays in the democratization process because this could determine the degree of attention ethnic concerns receive in negotiations on new political arrangements. There are three possibilities in this respect. First, tension between ethnic groups could be evident, but suppressed. Given the repressive mechanisms of the state, the regime might have taken steps to contain existing tension; these ethnic groups may have played no role in the demise of the regime, but societal cleavages were clearly visible. This may have been the case in Romania, where the regime's repressive powers did much to intimidate the population, but little to mask the existence of continued distrust between Romanians and ethnic Hungarians in Transylvania.[19]

Second, ethnic tensions might be latent. Because of repression or a limited history of ethnic problems, there might be little indication of potential conflicts between ethnic groups in a given state. For example, there was little evidence suggesting that the Tamils and Sinhalese could not live together peacefully in Sri Lanka prior to decolonization.[20]

Third, ethnic conflict might be a factor in the authoritarian regime's downfall. This could be the result either of direct ethnic pressure for change or simply of ethnic conflict causing overwhelming problems in the society—problems that the regime was unable to solve. South Africa would appear to be a case in which ethnic pressure has pushed the regime toward democratization, while it could be argued that the Soviet Union's demise was due in part to its inability to allay growing ethnic conflicts and secessionist tendencies.

Democratization and the Mitigation of Ethnic Conflict

When can democratization reduce the prospects and dangers of ethnic conflict? In the most general sense, it can do so if the negotiating process associated with democratization can establish a workable distribution of power among ethnic groups, so as to preclude the development of severe tension. Under what conditions is this likely to occur? One must distinguish between the ability of the democratization process to mitigate problems and the likelihood that it will not exacerbate tensions.

Democratization is most likely to succeed in mitigating ethnic tensions if ethnic issues are addressed early in the transition process. A comparison of cases in which ethnic tensions were either addressed or ignored in early negotiations underscores the importance of providing for the concerns of various ethnic groups, even in situations in which there is no apparent tension. The lack of such provisions in Sri Lanka had devastating consequences by inadvertently encouraging the use of ethnic extremism in electoral competition, while the early introduction of a system of ethnic power distribution in Malaysia helped establish a moderate political climate. If potential ethnic grievances can be anticipated early and avoided during the writing of a new constitution, before there is an obvious need for such efforts, ethnic conflicts may be prevented or mitigated.

Second, if ethnic tension is low to begin with, democratization is less likely to unleash ethnic conflict. Whether ethnic tensions later emerge would depend on the degree to which ethnic issues were manipulated in subsequent political campaigns. The disintegration of Czechoslovakia is a warning, however, that even in countries with few ethnic problems, ethnic issues can severely hinder the search for new constitutional arrangements; democratization is less likely to lead to ethnic conflicts, but only if ethnic issues are addressed carefully.

Third, democratization should have a greater chance of preventing or lessening tension if ethnic groups are relatively equal in size and power. Thus, it would be unlikely that one group would dominate another or exclude it from the political process. In cases such as these, avoiding ethnic tension would be dependent on the development of an electoral system that promotes intra-ethnic voting. Relative parity in strength means that ethnic groups are less likely to see much gain in adopting extremist positions; similarly, they are less likely to feel threatened by the possibility of being dominated or exploited by other groups.[21] Given that avoiding ethnic conflict is easier when group leaders perceive their interests to lie with cooperation, the perception that extremism is unnecessary or may be politically harmful is important to cultivate. The case of Switzerland suggests that it is indeed possible to prevent ethnic tension from developing. Similarly, Lebanon's constitutional distribution of power among ethnic groups allayed ethnic problems from 1943 to 1975. The Lebanese case, however, illustrates how problematic it is to base solutions to ethnic conflicts on fixed quotas in representation.[22]

Fourth, democratization has a better chance of avoiding ethnic conflict if the previous authoritarian regime was not dominated by an ethnic minority. If the regime either contained a representative ethnic mix or was dominated by the majority ethnic group in the population, there is less likelihood that ethnic resentment will develop because of antipathy for the previous regime. It is also less likely that ethnic conflict would have been the cause of the regime's downfall. Under such circumstances, ethnic tension is unlikely to be severe when the democratization process begins. Similarly, demands for retribution against the regime's ethnic group are less likely to materialize. Ethnic resentment of this sort could be a political factor in some republics of the former Soviet Union, in which the ethnic Russian population in the state may bear the onus of affiliation with previous Communist Party leadership.

Fifth, if all the main ethnic groups in the state were united in opposition to the previous regime, either in one movement or a coalition, democratization has a better chance of avoiding or mitigating ethnic tension. This would particularly be the case if the leadership of the opposition included members of different ethnic groups. This would give groups a cooperative foundation on which to build when working to create a new system of government, as well as ensuring that members of different groups would participate in the negotiating process for a new political structure. Czechoslovakia provides an example of the harmonizing effect this can have; the two heroes of the Velvet Revolution were Vaclav Havel, a Czech, and Alexander Dubcek, a Slovak, while the main opposition to the communist regime was a coalition between Civic Forum in the Czech lands and the Public Against Violence in Slovakia.[23]

Sixth, the likelihood that democratization will mitigate ethnic problems is greater if the leaders of large ethnic groups are moderates, rather than extremists. Moderation has two definitions in this context. In the context of democratization, moderation means support for negotiated settlements to change power balances, rather than revolutions.[24] In ethnic disputes, moderation means avoidance of extremism and hostility in developing positions vis à vis other ethnic groups. The democratization process has the greatest chance of avoiding ethnic conflict if both of these definitions apply to the major opposition leaders.

Seventh, if external ethnic allies are not present, democratization is less likely to exacerbate ethnic tension. The absence of an ethnic link outside the state does not remove the possibility of external allies entirely because there are always states or leaders who will see an advantage in destabilizing neighboring countries. Yet, the immediate affinity of a shared ethnic background is a powerful force, the absence of which improves democratization's odds of avoiding ethnic tension.

Eighth, if the army is loyal to the state, rather than to a particular ethnic group, democratization is less likely to lead to ethnic conflict. The Yugoslav army's dominance by Serbian officers loyal to Serbian leaders greatly complicated efforts either to maintain the Yugoslav state or to defend moves by Slovenia and Croatia toward independence.[25]

The presence of these eight factors does not guarantee that democratization will be able to resolve ethnic issues. The key to preventing or quelling ethnic grievances remains the negotiation of a farsighted and equitable balance among ethnic groups in a state. Favorable conditions alone do not guarantee that potential pitfalls will be avoided, but they do help to improve the odds that democratization can meet potential problems successfully.

Democratization and the Exacerbation of Ethnic Conflict

Just as certain factors enhance the odds that democratization can mitigate ethnic tension, others increase the likelihood that ethnic conflict will emerge either as a result of, or in spite of, democratization. This does not mean that efforts to mitigate ethnic tension should be abandoned—just the reverse. Democratization by definition provides an opportunity to expand political participation, and the transition period to democracy provides a window of opportunity that should be utilized, even if obvious obstacles exist.

First, the existence of historical grievances and the presence of strong ethnic stereotypes may not exacerbate ethnic conflict, but they will certainly make bargaining among different groups more difficult. This is the sort of situation in which addressing potential ethnic grievances immediately is especially important.

Second, the previous regime's identification with a specific ethnic group—in particular, one that was a minority in the state—is likely to hamper efforts to avoid ethnic conflict. This increases the odds that demands for retribution against or punishment of the old regime will take on ethnic overtones.

Third, if the previous regime manipulated the ethnic mix in parts of the country, there is a greater likelihood that ethnic tensions will emerge. Again, this could cause resentment toward the old regime's ethnic group, as well as demands for repatriation or resettlement. Given the upheaval such adjustments would invariably create, this could greatly complicate the process of reaching an equitable distribution of power among national and regional groups.

All three of these factors can be seen in the current political situation in the Baltic republics—Lithuania, Latvia, and Estonia. Due to Russia's former domination of the Baltic republics, there is long-standing hostility toward Moscow and toward Russians in these newly independent states. This combination of hostility and fear about potential domination by the large ethnic Russian population that was settled in these republics explains why the republics—Estonia, in particular—have tried to adopt harsh, restrictive citizenship requirements, which would effectively exclude ethnic Russians from citizenship and the right to vote. In part, this is simply ethnic discrimination. It also reflects concern about losing political control to what is perceived to be an alien ethnic group. Similar policies have been adopted by the indigenous population in Fiji to prevent political domination by ethnic Indian immigrants.[26]

Fourth, if opposition to the authoritarian regime were dominated by a single ethnic group or fragmented along ethnic lines, the process of negotiating new political structures would be complicated. If only one ethnic group is involved in the negotiations in a multiethnic state to create a new political structure, it is unlikely that the end result will satisfy all the major ethnic groups. Negotiations dominated by one ethnic group will be less likely to address the issue of equal rights or strive for adequate representation for all groups when creating a new constitution. Although this may be inevitable if an ethnic balance is severely skewed toward the dominant ethnic group, the case of Sri Lanka shows that the existence of a strong majority does not mean that ethnic conflicts can be avoided in the long run. Instead, other groups may be driven to violent protest against majority domination.

Fifth, if some ethnic leaders embrace extreme positions with regard to ethnic rights, the ability of the democratization process to lessen ethnic tension will be weakened. All ethnic groups must be willing to work together to find solutions to ethnic conflicts; if one side—or one side's leadership—sees an advantage in continuing the conflict, it will continue. For years, this situation prevented solutions to the civil war in Sudan from taking root. As long as leaders of different factions think that continued fighting favors their ends, they will be unwilling to consider negotiated settlements.[27]

Sixth, the mitigation of ethnic conflicts will be more complicated if ethnic groups are of greatly uneven sizes. In this situation, it is more likely that a majority group will be able to dominate others and that minority fears that their interests will be overlooked will be heightened. Furthermore, if homogeneous communities exist, regional voting may work, but in heterogeneous communities, it may be difficult to ensure minority representation. A successful example is Malaysia, in which voting districts were designed in many cases to require candidates to gain multiethnic support to ensure victory, thus mitigating minority fears about being excluded from political power. The Malaysian example illustrates the possibility of finding solutions even to complex problems. The continuing struggle in Canada to find an acceptable solution to Quebec's insistence on greater protection for French-speaking Canadians, however, illustrates the difficulty of assuaging every group's concerns, even in societies with a low level of ethnic tension.[28]

Seventh, if one or more groups in a given state are members of an ethnic group that governs a neighboring state, democratization could face additional challenges.[29] This could lead to the existence of, or accusations about, alternative loyalties. Indeed, some groups may choose to exploit potential external allies to gain leverage in their internal bargaining process. Ensuring that negotiations on new political arrangements remain domestic in character is preferable because it keeps any conflicts comparatively simple and reduces the number of actors involved.[30] There are many examples of the problems that can be created when ethnic groups claim external allies, including Northern Ireland, Armenia, and Romania.

Eighth, if the military is loyal to one ethnic group, it can cause severe problems for the democratization process and the search for solutions to ethnic conflicts. If the military is part of the majority group, the consequences might not be as severe, unless ethnic tensions already exist. If both the military and the previous regime are run by members of the same minority group and feel threatened by retribution during the democratization process, the military may attempt to stop the democratization process or to defend its ethnic views with force. The efforts of Red Army units stationed in Moldova to defend ethnic Russians there in 1992 illustrates the problems that can arise in such a situation.

Finally, if ethnic issues are ignored in the early stages of constitution-building, democratization may do more to exacerbate than mitigate ethnic tension. The evidence from cases such as Sri Lanka and Nigeria, in which constitutional safeguards for minority rights were not established at the time of independence, points to the importance of addressing ethnic issues early. It is also important to avoid creating opportunities for extremist ethnic views to dominate. Even in countries with no obvious ethnic problems, safeguards against ethnic tensions should be built into the system.

Indeterminate Issues

It is also important to note some factors that complicate attempts to resolve ethnic disputes that are likely to require special attention during the democratization process. First, previous attempts to manage ethnic conflicts do not provide a clear assessment of the effect that competition among parties within an ethnic group will have on inter-ethnic disputes.

In some cases, intra-ethnic competition appears to lessen the degree of conflict between ethnic parties by denying any party a clear victory on the basis of support from its ethnic group membership alone. The need to garner votes from other ethnic groups favors political candidates who endorse policies acceptable to many groups, rather than just one, and these politicians will generally hold more moderate ethnic policies.

In other situations, however, intra-ethnic competition can lead to a battle to determine which party can win the support of a single ethnic constituency. In states in which ethnic grievances are close to the surface, this can exacerbate tensions as parties compete to defend ethnic interests more fiercely than their political opponents—with negative consequences for inter-ethnic relations. It is not clear whether ethnic homogeneity or heterogeneity within the state creates a greater likelihood of ethnic conflict. In either case, if the ethnic balance has been manipulated by previous regimes, there is a greater chance that ethnic grievances will exist.

What both of these issues highlight is the importance of finding a solution that fits the unique circumstances that exist in each state; there is no standard formula that will ensure the prevention of ethnic conflicts. Given that many of the groups and parties in newly democratizing states have little experience with political participation, it is particularly crucial that those negotiating democratic transitions use great care while constructing either electoral or territorial solutions to potential ethnic conflicts.

Assessing Democratic Models and Ethnic Tensions

Given this assessment of factors influencing the likelihood and intensity of ethnic conflict, which democratization processes have the greatest chances of dampening ethnic conflict?

Because of the importance of negotiating adequate power-sharing arrangements, transformations and transplacements may provide a greater opportunity than regime replacement to address ethnic problems early. Both of these processes rely on negotiation in the creation of new political structures, which means that mechanisms for addressing possible ethnic conflicts are in place prior to the collapse of the previous regime.

Because transformations are more gradual approaches to democracy, they may provide more time to quell ethnic tension. Furthermore, because transformations are only likely to occur when moderates are stronger than radicals in both regimes and opposition movements, it is more likely that moderate ethnic policies can be forged early in the negotiation process.[31]

Transplacements, on the other hand, may have an advantage in that opposition movements are generally better established. It also means that diverse ethnic groups are likely to have had more experience cooperating to evict the previous regime than those opposition forces in transition or replacement situations. This could enhance their ability to sustain moderate policies during the formation of democratic governments.

Replacement processes do not provide great opportunities to take account of ethnic concerns in the creation of new governments. Because replacements generally result from the collapse of the previous regime, negotiations in replacement situations are more likely to encourage power struggles among the opposition groups involved because of the power vacuum left by the previous regime. Negotiated solutions will be hurriedly thrashed out among indigenous opposition groups, while a caretaker regime, if in place, will have little influence on decision-making. This means that there is a greater likelihood that some political leaders will see an advantage in exploiting or exacerbating ethnic tensions for their own gain.

On the other hand, the euphoria that can accompany the rapid and peaceful collapse of an authoritarian regime that occurs in some replacement and transplacement processes does provide a moment of national unity that might discourage opposition leaders from exploiting ethnic tension. Because the pace of change is more gradual in transformation processes, countries undergoing transformations may not experience this cathartic moment of national solidarity and the cohesive benefits it may have on the population.

Whether ethnic conflicts are mitigated or exacerbated will depend on the particular mix of problems in each case and the weight political leaders and ethnic groups attach to reaching accommodation for all, as opposed to promoting their own aims. In addition, ethnic issues are only one of many complications likely to be present during democratization. The myriad issues involved in a democratic transition may make it harder to focus sufficient attention on ethnic problems in a timely fashion, but the evidence from previous transitions underscores the urgency of addressing ethnic concerns as soon as possible.

CONCLUSION

This examination of the relationship between democratization and ethnic conflict suggests that democratization has the potential to help mitigate ethnic tension by allowing for the establishment of an inclusive means of governance to address the needs of all ethnic groups in the state. This will not happen automatically, however; moving from an authoritarian environment to one that is more open creates a fertile climate for hatred and prejudice.

What can outside powers or the international community do to promote democracy without exacerbating ethnic conflict? First, to the degree that democratizing states look to other democracies for blueprints of ways to shape their own systems, established democratic states have both an opportunity and an obligation to provide useful examples of ways to avoid ethnic conflict. The best means of doing so is to pursue fair policies at home, making provision for group rights where necessary, as well as individual human rights.[32] Given the importance many newly democratizing states place on inclusion in Western institutions and the international economic system, it may be worthwhile for the United Nations and relevant regional organizations to develop a set of guidelines for the protection of group rights, short of changing borders.[33]

Second, the international community should make clear that it will not reward or support extremist ethnic politics, and to the degree that it can, it should impose sanctions on groups that promote extremism. The utility of such a stand will vary, depending on the importance indigenous groups attach to international approbation.

For sanctions to have teeth, they must be honored by virtually all international and regional powers in the system. This leads to a third suggestion: The major powers should make clear to regional actors that share ethnicity with neighboring groups in a democratizing state that they must act responsibly. Regional actors wishing to expand their influence must recognize that taking advantage of the instability inherent in government changes will have negative consequences in the broader international community. External actors should be discouraged from trying to goad ethnic conflict.

Paradoxically, unless ethnic conflict spills across borders or begins to impinge directly on the interests of other states, outside powers have difficulty justifying interference in what appear to be domestic disputes. The dire predicament in which the Kurds find themselves shows this only too well, to say nothing of the Bosnian Muslims. This means that there may be little outside powers can or will do to prevent the worsening of conflicts.

In the end, whether democratization is likely to allay ethnic tension or not depends on the circumstances that exist when the process of democratization takes place, as well as the early and careful attention given to ethnic issues by political leaders. Outside powers may be able to encourage moderation by providing economic incentives or political advice. However, so long as the international community vacillates in the face of ethnic catastrophes, such as the one in Bosnia-Herzegovina, it is unlikely to succeed in deterring ethnic extremism.

Notes

[1] Dankwart Rustow, "Transitions to Democracy: Towards a Dynamic Model," *Comparative Politics*, vol. 2, no. 3, April 1970, p. 15.

[2] This article will outline some of the main points of agreement in the literature on this subject. See Walker Connor, "The Politics of Ethnonationalism," *Journal of International Affairs*, vol. 27, no. 1, 1973, pp. 1–21; Donald L. Horowitz, *Ethnic Groups in Conflict* (Berkeley, Calif.: University of California Press, 1985); Arend Lijphart, *Democracies: Democracy in Plural Societies* (New Haven, Conn.: Yale University Press, 1977); Joseph V. Montville, ed., *Conflict and Peacekeeping in Multiethnic Societies* (Lexington, Mass.: Lexington Books, 1990). On the relationship between ethnicity and nationalism, see also Anthony Smith, *The Ethnic Origins of Nations* (New York: Basil Blackwell Ltd., 1986); Benedict Anderson, *Imagined Communities* (London: Verso, 1983).

[3] When conflicts cross borders, they become international disputes and take on different significance. See Donald L. Horowitz, "Making Moderation Pay: The Comparative Politics of Ethnic Conflict Management," in Montville, *Conflict and Peacekeeping*, p. 453.

[4] Uri Ra'anan, "The Nation–State Fallacy," in Montville, *Conflict and Peacekeeping*, p. 7.

[5] See Horowitz, *Ethnic Groups*, pp. 455–456; Jack Snyder, "Nationalism and the Crisis of the Post-Soviet State," chapter 5 in this volume.

[6] Donald L. Horowitz, "Ethnic Conflict Management for Policymakers," in Montville, *Conflict and Peacekeeping*, pp. 116–118.

[7] Horowitz, *Ethnic Groups*, p. 471.

[8] All of the main antagonists in these cases must reach the same conclusion at the same time. If only one side is weakened or perceives continued conflict to be counterproductive, then the other party has an even greater incentive to continue the conflict, rather than moderating its behavior. See Horowitz, *Ethnic Groups*, pp. 116–120; I. William Zartman, "Negotiations and Prenegotiations in Ethnic Conflict: The Beginning, the Middle, and the Ends," in Montville, *Conflict and Peacekeeping*, pp. 511–534.

[9] The obvious exception to this, of course, is the dissolution of Czechoslovakia into its two constituent republics at the end of 1992; this option does not appear to be open to many other countries today. On the importance of state preservation, see Connor, "Politics of Ethnonationalism," p. 12.

[10] Lijphart stresses the importance of creating a system that allows for fluidity over time by allowing individuals to determine whether they wish to be identified as members of particular ethnic groups. See Arend Lijphart, "The Power-Sharing Approach," in Montville, *Conflict and Peacekeeping*, pp. 491–509; Arend Lijphart, "Consociational Democracy," *World Politics*, vol. 21, no. 2, January 1969, pp. 205–223.

[11] For discussions of a variety of cases, see Montville, *Conflict and Peacekeeping*.

[12] Ibid.

[13] Zartman, "Negotiations and Prenegotiations," p. 527.

[14] I do not intend to discuss the negotiating process involved in democratization in any detail here. The important point about negotiations in ethnic conflicts or in democratization is that, even in cases in which a demonstration effect from one state to the next plays an important role in catalyzing democratization, negotiations must address the specific issues facing the state. Given the diverse nature of ethnic conflicts, a formulaic approach could be counterproductive.

[15] "On Negotiating Democratic Transitions," *Third World Quarterly*, vol. 7,

no. 2, April 1985, pp. vii–xvi.
[16] See Samuel Huntington, *The Third Wave: Democratization in the Late Twentieth Century* (Norman, Okla.: University of Oklahoma Press, 1991), pp. 109–163. On transitions to democracy see, for example, Guillermo O'Donnell, Phillippe Schmitter, and Laurence Whitehead, eds., *Transitions from Authoritarian Rule* (Baltimore, Md.: Johns Hopkins University Press, 1986), especially Vol. 4; Adam Przeworski, *Democracy and the Market: Political and Economic Reforms in Eastern Europe and Latin America* (Cambridge: Cambridge University Press, 1991).
[17] Huntington, *The Third Wave*, pp. 125–126.
[18] Ibid., p. 143.
[19] During the revolution, Romanians and ethnic Hungarians worked together in opposition to Ceausescu's rule. Ethnic conflicts quickly resurfaced in the postrevolutionary period, however.
[20] See Montville, *Conflict and Peacekeeping*, part 3; Horowitz, *Ethnic Groups*.
[21] Horowitz points out that one of the dangers in situations with two relatively equal ethnic groups is that if ethnicity is a major political factor, elections can become merely censuses favoring the larger group, rather than true political competition. See Horowitz, *Ethnic Groups*, p. 116.
[22] See David Welsh, "Domestic Politics and Ethnic Conflict," chapter 3 in this volume. This also supports Lijphart's conclusion that proportionality must be fluid, rather than fixed, in constitutions, which cannot take into account future birthrates.
[23] The tragedy of Czechoslovakia is that an agreement could not be reached on an ethnic balance in the formation of the new government's structure, but this was due primarily to the obstinacy of some key figures and the exploitation of extremist ethnic positions in Slovakia.

See Jiri Pehe, "Czechoslovak Parliament Votes to Dissolve Federation," *Radio Free Europe/Radio Liberty Research Report* (hereafter *RFE/RL Research Report*), vol. 1, no. 48, December 4, 1992, pp. 1–5; Paul Wilson, "Czechoslovakia: The Pain of Divorce," *The New York Review of Books*, vol. 39, no. 21, December 19, 1992, pp. 69–75.
[24] Huntington, *Third Wave*, p. 121.
[25] On Yugoslavia's demise, see John Zametica, *The Yugoslav Conflict*, Adelphi Paper 270 (London: Brassey's for the IISS, 1992); James Gow, "Deconstructing Yugoslavia," *Survival*, vol. 32, no. 4, July–August 1991, pp. 291–311.
[26] Welsh, "Domestic Politics."
[27] Horowitz, *Ethnic Groups*, pp. 117–119.
[28] Welsh, "Domestic Politics."
[29] Kurds are scattered across several states, but because they are not in power in any state, they have little leverage.
[30] Zartman, "Negotiations and Prenegotiations," pp. 520–524.
[31] Huntington, *Third Wave*, pp. 123–124.
[32] The different ways that states and cultures define nationality, based on different views of group and human rights, must be kept in mind. See Ra'anan, "Nation–State Fallacy," pp. 12–19; Snyder, "Nationalism and the Crisis of the Post-Soviet State."
[33] The experience of Czechoslovakia is hopeful in this respect. The Czech and Slovak governments' desire to be included in European institutions, particularly the European Community (EC), and the EC's insistence that continued association depended on cooperation between the two new states, appears to have played an important role in promoting the careful legalistic devolution of Czechoslovakia into two new republics. See Jiri Pehe, "Czechs and Slovaks Define Post-Divorce Relations," *RFE/RL Research Report*, vol. 1, no. 45, November 13, 1992, pp. 7–11.

Chapter 5

Nationalism and the Crisis of the Post-Soviet State

Jack Snyder

Nationalism is one of the gravest but least understood issues facing the international community today. Twice in this century, nationalism provided the impetus for world war. Now, the collapse of the Soviet and East European communist states is unleashing a new round of nationalism. The result is ethnic warfare in the post-Soviet periphery and mounting nationalist opinion in Russia itself.

So far, public discussion of this outbreak of nationalism has been dominated by two views: the "ancient hatred" schema, applied especially to the Balkans and the Caucasus, and the Weimar analogy, applied mainly to Russia. Each is misleading.

It has become standard journalistic fare to portray ethnic and tribal enmities among the peoples of the former communist states as seething since time immemorial. Moscow's collapse, it is said, simply took the lid off and allowed the pot to boil over. US President George Bush, like many political leaders in the West, contended that Balkan strife grew out of "age-old animosities." Therefore, he said, "let no one think there is an easy or a simple solution to this tragedy . . . whatever pressure and means the international community brings to bear."[1] The implication is that flare-ups of irrational nationalist hatred are hard to prevent and impossible to stop, so the prudent policy is to limit the West's involvement in such quagmires.

Most scholars of nationalism condemn the ancient hatred view. They argue that nationalism is primarily a modern phenomenon and that the intensity of ethnic conflict varies greatly with changing social and political conditions.[2] Contrary to what some would suggest, Serbs and Croats fought each other very little before this century: 29 percent of Serbs living in Croatia who married in the 1980s took Croatian spouses. Likewise, conflicts in this century between Azeris and Armenians were triggered not by festering feuds, but by the impact of outside forces—in particular, economic change and revolution. Even national identity is changeable. Many post-Soviet national identities, such as Uzbek or Moldovan, scarcely existed in people's consciousness until Soviet policy arbitrarily made them titular nationalities of republics. More broadly, a recent report by Human Rights Watch on 53 countries contends that contemporary ethnic violence stems as much from deliberate government policies as from traditional communal antagonisms.[3] In short, the widely invoked schema of ancient unchangeable, irrational hatred is an inadequate basis for public discourse on nationalism.

The other popular schema for thinking about post-Soviet nationalism, the analogy between Weimar Germany and contemporary Russia, emphasizes the effect of transitory circumstances on nationalist feeling. The analogy has as its centerpiece the fear that nationalists could exploit economic difficulties by promising to protect people from the cruelties of the market. Galina Starovoitova, Russian President Boris Yeltsin's former adviser on nationalities, recently warned: "One cannot exclude the possibility of [a fascist period] in Russia. We can see too many parallels between Russia's current situation and that of Germany after the Versailles Treaty. A great nation is humiliated, [and] many of its nationals live outside the country's borders. The disintegration of an empire [has taken place] at a time when many people still have an imperialist mentality. . . . All this [is happening] at a time of economic crisis."[4]

Unfortunately, some of the Western policies designed to prevent a Weimar scenario from unfolding in Russia might actually cause it. At the height of the Russian policy of economic "shock therapy" in spring 1992, former US President Richard Nixon captured headlines with his warning that a failure to back Russian reform with substantial economic assistance could lead to a dramatic failure and the emergence of a nationalist, fascist, militarist regime.[5] However, along with Western assistance would come Western conditions, which include requirements to balance budgets and to end subsidies to uncompetitive industries. This will consequently increase unemployment, which could trigger a nationalist backlash. Thus, if Nixon's political analysis is correct, his prescription should have been to stop economic shock therapy, not encourage it.

In short, much public commentary misunderstands the nature of contemporary nationalism or advances prescriptions that do not follow from its diagnoses. By overrating the immutability of ethnic hatred, the West may be overlooking opportunities to prevent nationalist conflicts from developing. At the same time, by promoting economic shock therapy in post-Soviet states, the West may be laying the groundwork for a nationalist reaction.

Recent scholarship suggests that nationalism reflects a need to establish an effective state to achieve a group's economic and security goals. The most aggressive nationalist movements arise when states fail to carry out those tasks, spurring people to create more effective states. Today, nationalism is flaring up where old states have collapsed and where mobilized populations are consequently demanding the creation of effective new states. The problem is that many of these new states lack the institutional capacity to fulfill popular demands. Their borders and sovereignty are in doubt; their armies are in disarray; their economies are out of control. These shortcomings redouble the intensity of nationalistic sentiments, as militants demand the creation of effective national states to manage social problems. Managing post-Soviet nationalism, therefore, hinges on improving the effectiveness of post-Soviet states.

In developing this argument, some key terms are defined, a theory of nationalism and state effectiveness is outlined, and, from that theory, some hypotheses are derived that help illuminate the problems of post-Soviet nationalism. Discussed within the concluding section is the impact on post-Soviet nationalism of possible policy choices by some of the successor states and by the Western powers.

WHAT IS NATIONALISM?

People form groups to advance their interests through collective action, including defense against other groups. Some scholars call these "conflict groups."[6] Here, nationalism is defined as the doctrine in which the most important line of cleavage for establishing membership in a conflict group is nationality. That is, nationalists contend that nationality overrides or subsumes alternative criteria for alignment and enmity, such as social class, economic class, or patronage networks.[7]

Nationality, in turn, may be defined in one of two ways: by ethnic or civic criteria. Ethnic nationality is based on the consciousness of a shared identity within a group, rooted in a shared culture and a belief in common ancestry. Civic nationality, by contrast, is inclusive within a territory. Membership in the national group is generally open to everyone who is born or permanently resident within the national territory, irrespective of language, culture, or ancestry.[8] Today, Serbian, Armenian, and Azeri nationalists advance ethnic criteria for group membership. Russian President Boris Yeltsin and Ukrainian President Leonid Kravchuk generally argue for civic criteria.

A THEORY OF NATIONALISM AND
STATE EFFECTIVENESS

A useful theory of nationalism ought to be able to answer the following questions: When do people accept nationality as the overriding criterion for inclusion in their principal conflict group? When does nationalist identification intensify? When do groups adopt civic rather than ethnic national identities? When does the intensification of nationalism cause conflict with other groups?

In working toward hypotheses on these questions, it is useful to begin with individuals' basic needs and the advantages of forming groups to achieve them. Some commentators posit a basic need for meaning and identity, which can only be satisfied in culturally distinctive communities.[9] If this is true, it would "explain" why nationalism occurs, but not why it is sometimes absent; moreover, it explains little about large variations in the intensity and forms nationalism takes. Instead of prejudging the question by assuming an innate need for social and cultural distinctiveness, here less controversial needs will be assumed—namely, the need for physical and economic security.

In virtually all societies, individual households are seen as insufficient to achieve these goals. Larger groups are more effective for military defense. Likewise, a larger group enhances economic productivity by allowing a more efficient division of labor. Even in very primitive economies in which the division of labor is minimal, group membership permits the pooling of economic output, so that risk can be distributed across several households.

However, collective action will not necessarily happen just because it is advantageous to the group. Individuals have an incentive to shirk collective efforts. Rational choice theory suggests that cooperation is very difficult in large groups, unless a smaller "privileged" group can find a way to keep for themselves a portion of the gains obtained from organizing and enforcing the collective action of others. Sociologists note that social ties, norms, habits, and institutions allow a group to overcome shortsighted, selfish behavior that would hinder collective action. Barry Posen notes that groups' capacity for collective action (what he calls their "groupness") may vary and that a group's capacity for effective social and military organization is inherently threatening to groups that lag behind.[10] In short, because of the interrelated needs of common defense and economic security, groups have strong incentives to use social networks, social norms, and political institutions to enhance their ability for collective action.

In traditional societies, collective action rarely takes the form of nationalism. In such cases, the capacity for collective action begins with kinship, but extends to include other face-to-face relationships involving reciprocity among neighbors and between patrons and clients. The solidarity of these networks is reinforced by social norms that morally prescribe individuals' obligations toward each other. In traditional societies, economic production and distribution are typically regulated by such norms more than they are shaped by bargaining and calculations of interest. Cooperation within the group is further reinforced by group myths and rituals that instill in the individual a sense of the group as a sacred corporate body in which social roles and behavior are defined by custom.[11]

Most groups have some political organization that promotes and organizes collective action. In more complex traditional societies, this includes the extraction of taxes or services to support specialists, such as political leaders, soldiers, and religious elites, who provide "collective" goods. Of course, the distribution of the benefits from providing security and economic stability was often skewed toward these privileged elites. This was accomplished both by coercion and by ideological justifications, such as the divinity of kings and religious obligations to accept the existing social order.

Under such premodern conditions, which prevailed before the sixteenth or seventeenth centuries in Western Europe and even later elsewhere, national identification was weak. Among less advanced societies, some groups occasionally developed a sense of belonging to a broader linguistic or ethnic unit, but local, clan, and patronage ties had more significance as units for collective action toward economic and military ends. Even in more complex and geographically extended traditional societies, the bases for ethnic or civic nationalism were absent. Elites of one ethnic and linguistic group often ruled over peasants of varied cultures and dialects. Moreover, elites typically made little pretense of contributing to the collective good and, thus, relied on ideological justifications other than national solidarity. As a result, people thought of themselves as Christians or as peasants from a certain locality, not as members of a nationality.[12]

The modernization process changed this in ways that intensified national identification. The modern nation-state emerged as the most effective instrument promoting collective action in more complex, more highly mobilized societies. Where such states were effective in promoting economic and military security, they attracted loyalty because of their effectiveness; where they lagged in effectiveness, they stimulated an even more urgent form of nationalism, spurred by the demand to create a more effective state.

Underpinning these developments were the more complex division of labor, the increasing scale and complexity of warfare, the wider diffusion of political power in society, and the technology of mass communications. Each of these four phenomena is the focal point of a major theory of nationalism. Each partially explains the means by which the modern state, in managing these processes of social change, created modern nationalism.

The Division of Labor

The increasingly complex economy of commercial and, later, industrial capitalism posed qualitatively new challenges for collective action. It also promised dramatic payoffs for those who could overcome those challenges. Successful sovereigns were those who created incentives that made it possible for individuals to work simultaneously for their own benefit and for the national commonwealth. Sovereigns did this by creating efficient property rights, promoting a unified national market, reducing internal barriers to trade, establishing uniform laws and standards, and meting out predictable justice.[13] Moreover, argues Ernest Gellner, the emergence of common cultures and languages was indispensable to meeting the communication requirements of vastly more complex economic relationships.[14] Nation-states that fulfilled these requirements prospered and set the trend.

Military Mobilization

The increasing scale and technological complexity of warfare placed heavy financial and manpower burdens on sovereigns who wished to survive in Europe's intensely competitive international environment. Winners in the competition were those who created effective state bureaucracies to collect taxes and to organize regular armies. States also had strong incentives to foster nationalism, which became a potent weapon facilitating the mobilization of military power.[15]

Political Participation

Given a more complex division of labor, consent became a more effective means for promoting collective action than compulsion. Moreover, many states found that they could enhance their effectiveness in military competitions by giving social groups a stake in the state, allowing their political participation in exchange for contributions to military efforts, and, consequently, fostering a patriotic attachment to the state.[16]

Mass Communications

Whereas in traditional societies the symbols of community solidarity were transmitted in small groups through face-to-face rituals, in modern society, mass media created what Benedict Anderson calls an "imagined community" throughout the literate population of national states. In part, this community was the unintended by-product of the common concepts marketed in the mass media—first, in books for the middle class and, ultimately, in newspapers and electronic media for everyone. At the same time, this sense of community was consciously promoted by the state and other elite groups through propaganda, the dissemination of nationalistic versions of history, and public education.[17]

Nationalism and the Modern State

In sum, the process of organizing collective action in modern times gave a strong impetus to the development of the modern state and its offspring, nationalism. In contrast to traditional society, spontaneous social networks were unable to carry the burden of organizing efficient collective action without political intervention. To free markets from stifling exploitation by predators, states had to intervene to create the legal framework needed to foster economic efficiency. At first, state activities focused on regularizing laws and bureaucracies. Later, the state's equally important task was to create a constitutional framework through which social interests could be represented and reconciled to state policy. Ideologically, the success of the nation-state as a framework for collective action made plausible the nationalist doctrine that nationality should be the main cleavage in politics. Thus, nationalism was a natural concomitant of, and prop to, successful states. Moreover, groups that lacked a successful state had a strong incentive to mobilize a nationalist movement in order to keep pace with the competition.

HYPOTHESES ON NATIONAL IDENTITY

The foregoing theory of nationalism suggests a number of hypotheses about national identity and conflict. First, national identity will be the primary line of political cleavage whenever states are seen as indispensable forms of group organization for providing economic and physical security. Some people argue that, because of such contemporary developments as global economic interdependence and the obsolescence of great-power wars, the nation-state is becoming obsolete as an efficient unit for organizing collective action. They offer as evidence the pincer-like attack on existing European nation-states from a supranational competitor in the West and subnational ones in the East.[18] In fact, recent European developments confirm the centrality of the state and its links with nationalism. In the East, people are abandoning failed communist states and attaching nationalist sentiments to whatever unit might serve as a basis for forming a new state, be it an ethnic group or an arbitrarily constructed republican administrative apparatus. States are seen as indispensable, and many groups in the East want one. In the West, the real question is not whether states will be overtaken by some other form of organization, but whether the technocrats who favor European unification will devise a convincing formula for the democratic and national legitimization of a new state on a larger scale.

Second, national identity takes different forms in different social circumstances. Civic nationalism normally appears in well institutionalized democracies. Ethnic nationalism, in contrast, appears spontaneously when an institutional vacuum occurs. By its nature, nationalism based on equal and universal citizenship rights within a territory depends on a supporting framework of laws to guarantee those rights, as well as effective institutions to allow citizens to give voice to their views. Ethnic nationalism, in contrast, depends not on institutions, but on culture. Therefore, ethnic nationalism is the default option: It predominates when institutions collapse, when existing institutions are not fulfilling people's basic needs, and when satisfactory alternative structures are not readily available. This is the reason, according to Gellner, that ethnic nationalism has been so prominent in the wake of the collapse of the Soviet state.[19]

This assessment may be too pessimistic. Post-Soviet society is not operating in an institutional vacuum in which ethnicity is the only basis for forming conflict groups. Republican institutions are serving as the nuclei for new states, which may be infused with either ethnic or civic content, depending in part on the state-building strategies of republican elites. Civic nationalism suits Yeltsin's strategy for evolving toward a free-market, Western-style state that recognizes basic individual rights. Civic nationalism also fits the strategic needs of the leaders of Ukraine and Kazakhstan because a highly ethnic definition of nationalism would gratuitously provoke dangerous Russian opposition inside and outside their borders. In Estonia and Latvia, however, the fact that Russian-speakers are so near a voting majority makes granting them full citizenship a risky proposition. A strategy based on ethnic nationalism is, consequently, tempting in these republics.

HYPOTHESES ON THE INTENSITY OF NATIONALISM

Particularly intense nationalism results from a gap between a group's inadequate capacity for collective action and acute threats to the group's military or economic security. This effect is compounded by the secondary consequences of the nationalist ideology used to mobilize support for national collective action. It may be intensified still further by attempts of parochial interest groups to exploit nationalist mobilization for their own purpose.

Historically, gaps between threats and group capacity have appeared as crises of military survival, economic disorder, expanding political participation, and ideological legitimacy—that is, the same problems that led to the emergence of the modern nation-state. The following sections explore the effects of each of these four types of crisis on the intensification of nationalism.

Hypotheses about Nationalism and Military Threats

In the medieval period, military threats rarely led to an increase in national identification because wars were the affairs of elites and mercenaries, the outcome of which was of marginal interest to the broader community. Once states began to reach out for popular support, however, military threats gave a powerful boost to nationalism. As Charles Tilly put it, "war made the state, and the state made war," and together they made nationalism.[20] The decisive turning point came with the wars of the French Revolution in which foreign military threats led to the *levée en masse* to defend the people's revolutionary state. In turn, French military conquests triggered a leap in national consciousness throughout Europe, as people perceived a dangerous gap in the mobilization capacities of their absolutist states and France's popular national one.

From that point on, the connection among military threats, national consciousness, and the enhancement of state capacity has been a constant theme. It was especially prevalent during the heyday of aggressive nationalism in the late nineteenth and early twentieth centuries. In Germany and France, threat perceptions spurred nationalist revivals and social mobilization to strengthen fighting capacity. In Russia, an archaic state that was unable to tap the capacities of the nation was smashed in war and replaced by one that could.[21]

The post-Soviet period offers some evidence that the links among military threats, nationalist mobilization, and state-building still hold. The creation of 15 new political entities from the rubble of the former Soviet Union could lead to an accelerated process of state formation. In Baku, at least, the process is well under way. The speeches in the Azeri parliament during the March 1992 ouster of moderate, former communist President Ayaz Mutalibov read as if Tilly had ghostwritten them. Critics charged that Armenia was winning the war in Nagorno-Karabakh because Mutalibov's regime had been too weak to create a standing army or the strong fiscal structures needed to pay for it. Mutalibov and his ex-communist cronies should stand aside, they said, and let new elites, more closely tied to popular national groups, forge a social consensus behind a new, war-making state. The political platform of Abulfez Elchibey, elected Azerbaijan's president in June 1992, featured the reconquest of Nagorno-Karabakh and the creation of a standing army and a national currency to achieve that end.[22]

In much more muted form, the Russian–Ukrainian face-off about Crimea and the Black Sea Fleet contains some of the same elements: the hypersensitivity of new states, the rallying of supporters through the specter of foreign competition, and the agglomeration of military power as the constitutive act of statehood. Still, there are many forces working to prevent a general replay of the Tilly dynamic, including caution induced by the existence of nuclear arsenals on both sides, the economic cost of Western disapproval, and the dim view of big-stick diplomacy taken by "new thinkers" such as Russia's embattled foreign minister, Andrei Kozyrev.

Hypotheses on Nationalism and Economic Threats

Outbursts of aggressive nationalism correlate strongly with historical instances of rapid industrialization, the introduction of market forces into nonmarket or regulated market economies, and the disruption of local markets due to integration into world markets with radically different relative prices. Under such conditions, nationalism may play a number of political roles. Entrepreneurs may use nationalism to knock down barriers to the creation of national markets, as in Bismarck's Germany or revolutionary France, or to promote the expansion of international markets, as in Palmerston's Britain. Market forces may also trigger nationalist reactions if, as in contemporary Bohemia and Slovakia, some ethnic groups benefit, while others are hurt.

The most virulent form of economic nationalism has come in response to popular demands for state protection from the pain of adjusting to unregulated markets. Wilhelmine nationalism, for example, was stoked by the backlash from farmers, artisans, and shopkeepers who demanded protection from the disruptive impact of international economic interdependence on their traditional market niches. As Karl Polanyi argued in *The Great Transformation*, the turn toward hypernationalism and fascism in the first half of the twentieth century stemmed from the incompatibility of mass-suffrage democracy with the adjustment shocks of laissez-faire economics. Under the gold standard, for example, countries facing an imbalance of payments had no choice but to deflate their domestic economies, which created severe unemployment. Once the working class obtained the vote, this sort of economic shock therapy was hard to sustain politically. In particular, the Great Depression sparked a revolt against laissez-faire economics, giving rise to the political management of markets by either Keynesian or fascist methods.[23]

Similarly, in Russia today, the people who are most likely to suffer from Yeltsin's economic shock therapy have organized themselves to create a nationalist–protectionist coalition. Arkady Volsky, who as head of the Russian Union of Industrialists and Employers claims to represent firms accounting for 65 percent of 1991 industrial output, has sought to replace Yeltsin's free-market policies with a more "managed transition to the market." Backed by military-related heavy industry, Volsky's organization advocates a continuation of budget-busting soft government credits for industry, gradual increases in energy prices, little foreign borrowing, no cut-rate foreign buy-outs of Russian assets, and a reassertion of economic ties with non-Russian republics. The government installed by Prime Minister Viktor Chernomyrdin in December 1992 represents a compromise between Yeltsin and Volsky supporters.

Volsky claims that industrial workers will back his policies. In the spring of 1992, he threatened a joint labor–management strike if cutbacks in industrial subsidies forced massive layoffs. In fact, there was little labor unrest during 1992, mostly because the independent central bank refused to go along with Yeltsin's shock therapy; it extended huge credits to maintain full employment in unproductive enterprises.[24]

Many moderate Russian nationalists, such as Vice President Alexander Rutskoi, have joined Volsky's political faction, the Civic Union. Some erstwhile new thinkers from liberal foreign policy think tanks have also joined with Volsky, military figures, and other critics of the Yeltsin–Kozyrev foreign policy. One recent manifesto penned by a high-level group of this kind called for less economic reliance on the West, more emphasis on Russia's special rights and interests, and the maintenance of adequate military might to deal with the latent threat from the West. Curiously, it also called for an alliance with the West to counterbalance threats from Japan and Asia.[25]

More extreme nationalists have joined organizations, such as the proto-fascist National Salvation Front, whose platform calls for imposing price controls, stopping inter-ethnic conflicts by force, "restoring the state's defense capability," "supporting the military–industrial complex," strengthening executive powers, and, above all, "preventing the approaching collapse of the state." Echoing the appeals made by nationalists in past economic depressions, today's Russian nationalists are calling for strengthening the national state to protect the Russian people from foreign manipulators of the market and from predations by non-Russian successor states.[26]

Although painful adaptations to market forces have often triggered nationalist backlashes, there is no connection between mature, successful market economies and nationalism. Advanced market societies deeply integrated in the international division of labor are among the most benign, moderately nationalistic states. Since the ugly days of the unregulated gold standard, advanced capitalist states have developed Keynesian economic methods, corporatist bargaining practices, and international mechanisms, such as International Monetary Fund (IMF) loans, that ease the pressures of market adjustment.[27] The lesson of history and theory would seem to be that marketization intensifies nationalism in inverse proportion to the effectiveness of the political institutions, both domestic and international, that are available to manage the process. Such institutions are now very weak in the Soviet successor states, and adequate international substitutes for them have not been deployed.

Hypotheses on Political Participation

Nationalism typically intensifies when there is an increase in the proportion of people who have a voice in politics. Since its earliest appearance in Britain and France, nationalism has been connected with the notion of popular rule.[28] Often, nationalists claim that old elites are ineffective in meeting foreign threats and that a new, popular government is needed to pursue national interests more forcefully.

The first modern British nationalists in the 1750s argued, for example, "that England's vital affairs were in the hands of hardened [aristocratic] Francophiles, addicted by both taste and fashion to the superiority of the national enemy," says historian Gerald Newman. Even after the Crimean War, middle-class nationalists who sought to expand their participation in government claimed that the aristocratic elite was lax and inept in creating effective national power, whether military, economic, or ideological. The French Revolution, however, encouraged the old elites to try to turn the tables on middle-class radicals: They, not the aristocracy, were now said to be the stalking horse for the French, as Edmund Burke argued.[29]

This pattern was repeated in a more intense form in other states, where pressure for popular political participation mounted more abruptly. In Wilhelmine Germany, for example, old elites tried to use nationalism to split apart working-class and middle-class proponents of political change, while counting on imperial successes to demonstrate the aristocracy's continued ability to govern. However, middle-class groups turned these arguments against the Junker ruling class, contending that the aristocratic army was too small and national diplomacy too conciliatory to meet the international threats that the old elites themselves had conjured up.[30]

Today, similar developments are unfolding in some of the Soviet successor states. Former communist elites, where they have clung to power, have tried to outdo the nationalists to establish new bases for their popular legitimacy. For example, Kravchuk has successfully preempted the Rukh movement's monopolization of the nationalism issue by standing firmly for Ukrainian independence and sovereign rights. As a result, Rukh has been split in two, with the more moderate half backing Kravchuk. Similarly, Serbian President Slobodan Milosevic and the Yugoslav army maintained their political positions by exploiting the nationalism issue. In Azerbaijan, Mutalibov was ousted because he failed to coopt the nationalist agenda of the Popular Front.[31]

Although democratization often goes hand in hand with the rise of nationalism, it does not follow that well institutionalized mass democracies are extremely nationalistic. On the contrary, they have been among the least nationalistic states. The United States and Britain have had jingoistic moments, but US and British nationalism never reached the self-destructive intensity seen in Germany or Japan, for example.

The problem, in other words, is not democracy per se, but the turbulent transition to democracy. In fully fledged democracies, voters usually have the information and the power to punish leaders whose reckless foreign policies impose excessive costs on them.[32] The archetype is William Gladstone's successful Midlothian campaign against Benjamin Disraeli's imperial policy. In Wilhelmine Germany's proto-democracy, however, mass political participation had a different effect. All men could vote for representatives to the Reichstag, but their votes did not determine who led the government, the army, or the foreign ministry. To have real political impact, people had to join extraparliamentary pressure groups, such as the Agrarian League or the Navy League, which were organized by various factions of the elite. These organizations then used nationalism to justify their parochial concerns in terms of the national interest. In short, mature representative, party, and press institutions have tended to act as a check on the more extreme forms of nationalism. Conversely, expanded political participation without these institutions can yield a clamorous contention of elite and mass interest groups that use nationalism to create a smoke screen of illusory public-spiritedness.[33]

Politics in the Soviet successor states has involved sporadic voting and continual appeals by politicians for popular support. However, these democratic activities have been carried out in a context of weak political parties, manipulative political machines, and unstable constitutional rules. Russia's legislature remains dominated by former communists because neither Yeltsin nor his opponents want to risk an unpredictable electoral showdown. All of this makes it doubtful that the moderating influence of the median voter will prevail. As Timothy Colton puts it, the successor states will remain "pre-democracies" or at best "proto-democracies," exhibiting the pattern of high participation but low institutionalization that has intensified nationalist politics in the past.[34]

Hypotheses on Nationalist Propaganda

Nationalism intensifies and becomes more deeply entrenched in a population when nationalism's proponents enjoy substantial propaganda advantages over their opponents. This is often the case. States have an interest in using schools, the military service, and their public relations apparatus to promote nationalistic versions of history and nationalistic images of opposing groups because this facilitates mobilization of the, population for collective action. Intellectuals have usually been in the nationalistic vanguard, lending their public relations skills to popular movements whose goal is to establish a state whose bureaucracies these intellectuals seek to run.[35]

When nationalists have a near monopoly on public discourse, there exists no counterbalance to this mythmaking. Over time, new generations brought up on a diet of unleavened propaganda lose the ability to distinguish between reality and nationalist myths used for their mobilizing effect. Adolf Hitler imbibed cynical Wilhelmine nationalist mythology in the coffeehouses of Vienna before 1914 and acted on it when he came to power. Even in political systems in which a plurality of opinions is heard, the long-term effects of small propaganda advantages can have significant effects. In the two decades before the Crimean War, a campaign of Russophobic propaganda led by the British foreign ministry left public opinion primed for confrontation at the slightest provocation. In cases in which threats seem great and propaganda advantages are significant, similar effects can be achieved in much shorter periods of time. Under the stimulus of the Great Depression, the Japanese army's propaganda campaign supporting the invasion of Manchuria elicited a dramatic popular response.[36]

Today, despite the temptations to exploit nationalist propaganda for state-building, Yeltsin and Kravchuk have, for the most part, used their pulpits to warn against it. Yeltsin understands that his strategies for Western-oriented market reform and for unifying a multiethnic society would be undermined by an uncompromising ethnic definition of Russian nationality. Arguing that Russia must remain "within the framework of international law" in supporting the civil rights of Russian-speakers in Estonia and Latvia, Yeltsin argues that "you can judge how democratic a state is by the way it treats national minorities."[37] Kravchuk, although urging the "protection of the national revival and national security of Ukraine" by shoring up "all forms of power and state institutions," nonetheless insists that "we cannot allow . . . ethnic enmity to be stirred up in our country."[38] With a large Russian minority potentially backed by the military power of the Russian state, Kravchuk realizes that a civic definition of Ukrainian nationality is the only prudent course to follow.

Thus, one historically potent source of intense nationalism—the power of state propaganda— is working in favor of moderation in Russian–Ukrainian relations today by emphasizing civic, rather than ethnic, forms of national identification.

HYPOTHESES ON NATIONALISM AND CONFLICT

Nationalist criteria for political identity and alignment are, to some degree, inherently conflictual: Any intensification of nationalist sentiment is likely to contribute to an intensification of conflict with other national groups. As Posen shows, under anarchical conditions, the "groupness" of one set of individuals is inherently threatening to others, and an intensification of this "groupness" is more threatening still. Elementary prudence forces groups to maintain a high degree of vigilance, mobilize nationalism in response to the nationalism of others, and weigh the advantages of preventive attacks against potential opponents whenever an opportunity arises. As Posen points out, this is especially true when demography, geography, or technology favor the attacker over the defender. For example, an offensive advantage exists, according to Posen, when hard-to-defend pockets of conationals reside in territories dominated by another national group.

In addition to these strategic sources of conflict, national definitions of identity promote conflict as a result of the psychological consequences of nationalistic in-group/out-group distinctions. Indeed, one of the functions of nationalist doctrine is to sharpen this distinction, so that friends and foes can be more readily identified. As a general rule, there is an inverse correlation between conflict within a group and conflict with other groups. Moreover, the inflation of threats from others and the dehumanization of other groups enhances group solidarity.[39] John Mearsheimer defines hypernationalism as "the belief that other nations or nation-states are both inferior and threatening and must therefore be dealt with harshly."[40] However, if social psychologists are right, this belief is likely to be present to some degree in any nationalism. Thus, any intensification of nationalism is likely to cause an increase in conflict with other groups.

However, this effect is much more virulent in some cases than others. It will be more intense during and immediately after a nationalist campaign to mobilize popular support to counteract a looming military or economic threat. At such times, the state, intellectuals, protectionists, and the military may use the tools of inflating threats and stereotyping to promote national mobilization, so citizens will be especially prone to see the world in Hobbesian terms. Conversely, in open societies with pluralistic, self-critical public debates, there are institutions and processes that limit the

degree and duration of nationalistic propaganda. Cases of civic nationalism are generally of this latter type because they tend to coincide with
democracy, free speech, and a free press.

The degree to which nationalism causes conflict is also affected by the
degree to which parochial interests favoring international conflict attach
themselves to nationalist movements. Nationalism has natural allies in
the military, military-related industries, and protectionist economic sectors. These actors often have self-interested reasons for portraying foreign
competitors as unfair, predatory, and conspiratorial. Nationalism will
often lead to foreign conflict when such groups play a major role in a
regime's ruling coalition, when their position in society gives them an
information monopoly or propaganda advantage, and when the
countervailing power of those who bear the burdens of aggressive policies is weak.

Finally, nationalism produces very intense conflict when an opposing
group presents a barrier to the achievement of full statehood, as defined
by the group's concept of its national identity. For example, if a group
adopts an ethnic definition of its nationality, yet lives intermingled with
other ethnic groups, conflict is unavoidable because the group's achievement of full statehood presupposes the denial of citizenship and protection to members of other ethnic groups. Civic nationalism may provoke
tension with coresident groups who prefer their own ethnic identity. In
many cases, however, conflict will be more manageable because true
civic nationalism offers ethnic minorities easier assimilation, political
equality, and cultural autonomy, whereas ethnic nationalism creates inequalities and greater barriers to assimilation.

CONCLUSIONS AND IMPLICATIONS

What provisional conclusions and policy implications can be drawn
from the foregoing? First, nationalism and ethnic conflict are not primarily rooted in ancient, culturally ingrained animosities. Latent hatred
sometimes exists, but it only becomes decisive in politics when changing
circumstances increase the need for, or feasibility of, nationalist mobilization. Because the intensity of nationalism is responsive to changes in
circumstances and incentives, state policies, including the policies of the
advanced Western democracies can, in principle, influence these incentives. Often, it may not be worthwhile for the international community to
bear the costs of trying to modify these incentives, but sometimes it might
be.

To know where to invest Western resources to prevent aggressive
nationalism, a theory of what causes it is needed. Intense nationalism and
a heightened risk of national conflict are caused when states fail to meet

military and economic threats to their peoples and when they fail to develop effective institutions for managing increased levels of political participation. Thus, intense nationalism is typically a popular movement aimed at creating a state to organize collective action to deal with a group's economic and security problems or to strengthen the capacities of an already existing state. Aggressive nationalism is particularly likely in cases in which propaganda monopolies prevent effective challenges to the nationalists' mobilizing myths and in cases in which groups with a parochial interest in an aggressive foreign policy play a major role in the nationalist coalition.

Many of these conditions exist or are on the horizon in a number of former communist states. What can be done about it? Where security fears fueled by post-Soviet anarchy are fostering nationalist reactions on the part of vulnerable groups, the logical prescription would be to use the power of the international community to reduce these vulnerabilities. Which instruments should be chosen to do this depends on the specific circumstances of the case and on the willingness of the international community to bear the costs of providing security.

Where the security fears of intermingled ethnic groups are the main danger, preventive peacekeeping might be cheap and effective. This is now being attempted in Macedonia. In principle, arms control designed to hinder offensive operations or transfers of defensive types of weaponry to vulnerable groups might also mitigate security fears that promote nationalist agitation. In practice, Posen shows the difficulties of acting on this principle. Diplomacy can attempt to accomplish the same thing by offering strictly defensive alliances, security guarantees, or security regimes to victims of nationalist aggression. At a lesser cost and risk, diplomacy can also offer economic incentives and disincentives according to the same criterion. These efforts could be directed at both sides of a dispute. For example, Latvia and Estonia could be threatened with sanctions if they adopt ethnically biased citizenship criteria, while Russia could be warned that any attempt to settle the dispute by military force would undermine economic relations with the West.

However, the theory advanced in this chapter suggests a drawback to the employment of coercive strategies against fragile nationalist states; humiliating demands from the international community would throw the state's weakness into high relief and thus provide an even stronger impetus for nationalist mobilization. The attachment of coercive political conditions to economic assistance should therefore be done subtly, so as to minimize the affront to the new states' self-esteem.[41]

The failure of some post-Soviet states to provide economic security may also galvanize nationalist reactions. This would be especially dangerous in Russia, where economic nationalists are politically allied with nationalists calling for the forceful protection of co-ethnics whose security is seen to be at risk in neighboring states. An economic depression sweeping nationalists into office might, therefore, change not only Russian economic policy, but also foreign and military policy. What can be done to avert such an outcome?

The initial instinct of internationalists in the West was to urge far-reaching market reforms on the Yeltsin regime and then to propose a "grand bargain" or "Marshall Plan" to make sure it would work. In the first half of 1992, Yeltsin ordered Yegor Gaidar to carry out just such a program, but very little Western support followed. In part, this was because Gaidar's shock therapy was not austere enough for Western economic experts; it also reflected US self-absorption, Japan's obsession with the Northern Territories, and Germany's capital shortage. Yet, even if the West had offered more financial and technical support, it is far from clear that such a high-risk strategy was prudent because a sustained dose of shock therapy might trigger a Weimar-type nationalist backlash.

So far, Russian nationalism has been confined to a rather cautious elite—industrialists, the military, and some mainstream politicians. Extreme forms of nationalism have generated only a small mass following. In the Russian presidential election, the fascist Vladimir Zhirinovsky received only 7 percent of the vote. However, if the theory advanced here is correct, there is a grave risk that a failed experiment with shock therapy, producing 25 percent unemployment under the aegis of the IMF, could generate a mass nationalist movement. As in Weimar Germany, formerly prudent nationalist elites might then scramble to align themselves with the likes of the National Salvation Front. The West needs to remember that its main stake in Russian economic reform is its political outcome, not its consequences for economic growth. Thus, shock therapy is too reckless an approach.

Instead of being disappointed by Russia's retreat from breakneck economic liberalization in the latter part of 1992, the West ought to look for ways to turn it to advantage. Politically, the West now ought to have two goals. First, it should try to ensure that the liberal foreign policy of Yeltsin and Kozyrev is not scuttled along with the liberal economic policy of Gaidar. Now more than ever, the West needs to give Russia an economic stake in maintaining good diplomatic relations. If the Russians conclude that they have nothing to gain from the West's approval and little to lose from its disapprobation, military solutions to the problems of Russians abroad will appear more attractive. Likewise, the West needs to give tangible support to Yeltsin so that he can keep preaching about civic nationalism and keep the state's propaganda tools out of the hands of Rutskoi's ilk.

Second, and related to this, the West needs to exert its economic influence in an attempt to shift the center of gravity of Russia's coalition politics. Volsky's Civic Union is rife with internal divisions: Its alliance with demagogic nationalists is not set in concrete.[42] The nationalist center is united in opposition to the policy of radical economic liberalization, but it is divided about what it wants to put in its place. One line of cleavage seems to pit industrialists in more competitive economic sectors, who might have a future in a regulated market economy, against those in archaic, unadaptable heavy industry, including a substantial part of the military–industrial complex. The former might be lured into a progressive alliance with Yeltsin, the remnants of the Gaidar–Kozyrev team, and other Western-oriented democrats. The latter might be inclined to join a neo-Brezhnevite coalition with former communists, the military, and nationalists. The West needs to offer incentives that make the progressive alliance seem a more attractive option to fence sitters, even if Russian economic discipline fails to meet IMF standards. For this reason, Western aid should not be subject to approval by the IMF, which bases its decisions only on economic criteria. Rather, aid should be determined by the Group of Seven (G-7), which should base its decisions primarily on political considerations.

Of course, a good political strategy will fail if it has unstable economic foundations. Is gradual reform based on state-managed industrial policy economically feasible, given current conditions in Russia?[43] The Chinese example shows that high growth rates can be sustained in an economy that combines centralized state controls with a free-market sector. In the capitalist states of East Asia, the success of state-directed industrial policy has been attributed to various factors: egalitarian starting points, which minimized the role of vested interests; the political weakness of labor; the absence of concentrated industries that lobby for state protection; privileged niches in the international economy; significant foreign threats, which justified state autonomy in economic decision-making; and the values and esprit de corps of the bureaucrats themselves. In Russia, a number of these favorable conditions for successful, state-led industrial policy are absent. Even so, Russia might find a state-directed industrial policy more suitable, given its managerial skills, than a laissez-faire policy. Lacking effective commercial laws, courts, property rights, and accounting capabilities to collect a complicated value-added tax, Russia can hardly expect to copy the policies of advanced capitalist states. Backward countries, in their effort to catch up with more advanced powers, have always found it more effective to rely on an interventionist state to act as a substitute for embryonic social institutions. Attempting to copy competitors' institutions directly rarely works.[44]

The danger of extreme nationalism in the postcommunist states stems from their incapacity to meet social needs in the areas of security, the economy, and the institutionalization of democratization. Nationalism reflects the popular demand that new or revitalized states be created to address these problems. Western policy should try to dampen the force of this nationalist impulse by working with fledgling states to supplement their lagging institutional capacities. In most cases, this will not mean convincing post-Soviet societies to attempt to emulate the practices of the West. Whether the issue is economics, security, democratization, or human rights, it will mean helping successor states pursue a variety of second-best strategies that are suited to their own institutional capacities.

Acknowledgments

I am grateful to Richard Betts, Robert Jervis, Joel Hellman, Jack Levy, Stephen Van Evera, and Stephen Walt for criticizing earlier drafts, and to the MacArthur Foundation and the National Council for Soviet and East European Research for financial support.

Notes

[1] Andrew Rosenthal, "Bush Urges UN to Back Force to Get Aid to Bosnia," *New York Times,* August 7, 1992, pp. 1, 8. Similarly, Serge Schmemann, "Ethnic Battles Flaring in Former Soviet Fringe," *New York Times,* May 24, 1992, p. 10, writes that "the roll call of warring nationalities invokes some forgotten primer on the Dark Ages," fighting "for causes lost in the fog of history."

[2] Ernest Gellner, *Nations and Nationalism* (Ithaca, N.Y.: Cornell University Press, 1983); Eric J. Hobsbawm, *Nations and Nationalism since 1980* (Cambridge: Cambridge University Press, 1990), especially p. 14; Eric Hobsbawm and Terence Ranger, *The Invention of Tradition* (Cambridge: Cambridge University Press, 1983).

[3] Valere P. Gagnon, "Ethnicity, Nationalism, and International Conflict: The Case of Serbia," *forthcoming*; Philip Roeder, "Soviet Federalism and Ethnic Mobilization," *World Politics,* vol. 43, no. 2, January 1991, pp. 196–232; David Laitin, "The National Uprisings in the Soviet Union," *World Politics,* vol. 44, no. 1, October 1991, pp. 139–177; Steven Holmes, "Report Faults Governments in Civil Strife," *New York Times,* December 13, 1992, p. 12.

[4] *Ekho Moskvy,* October 14, 1992, as quoted by Vera Tolz, "Russia: Westernizers Continue to Challenge National Patriots," *Radio Free Europe/ Radio Liberty Research Report* (hereafter, *RFE/RL Research Report*), vol. 11, no. 49, December 11, 1992, p. 3.

[5] *Wall Street Journal,* March 11, 1992.

[6] Donald Horowitz, *Ethnic Groups in Conflict* (Berkeley, Calif.: University of California Press, 1985), p. 76, using the term of Ralf Dahrendorf and Georg Simmel.

[7] Roman Szporluk, *Communism and Nationalism: Karl Marx Versus Friedrich List* (New York: Oxford University Press, 1988). On definitional issues, see also Hobsbawm, *Nations and Nationalism,* pp. 1–13.

[8] Liah Greenfeld, *Nationalism: Five Roads to Modernity* (Cambridge, Mass.:

Harvard University Press, 1992); Anthony Smith, *The Ethnic Origins of Nations* (London: Basil Blackwell, 1986), pp. 21–46.

[9] Horowitz, *Ethnic Groups,* p. 81, citing Ronald Cohen, "Ethnicity: Problem and Focus in Anthropology," *Annual Review of Anthropology,* vol. 7, 1978, pp. 379–405.

[10] Charles Furtado and Michael Hechter, "The Emergence of Nationalist Politics in the USSR: A Comparison of Estonia and the Ukraine," in Alexander Motyl, ed., *Thinking Theoretically about Soviet Nationalities* (New York: Columbia University Press, 1992), pp. 169–204; James Coleman, *Foundations of Social Theory* (Cambridge, Mass.: Belknap, 1990), chapter 12; Barry Posen, "The Security Dilemma and Ethnic Conflict," chapter 6 in this volume.

[11] Karl Polanyi, *The Great Transformation* (New York: Octagon, 1975, orig. ed. 1944); Raymond Firth, *Primitive Polynesian Economy* (London: Routledge & Kegan Paul, 1965, orig. ed. 1939); Emile Durkheim, *The Elementary Forms of Religious Life* (New York: Free Press, 1965, orig. ed. 1912).

[12] Gellner, *Nations and Nationalism,* pp. 8–18.

[13] Douglass North and Robert Thomas, *The Rise of the Western World* (Cambridge: Cambridge University Press, 1973); John Ruggie, "Territoriality and Beyond: Problematizing Modernity in International Relations," *International Organization,* vol. 47, no. 1, Winter 1993, pp. 141–176.

[14] Gellner, *Nations and Nationalism,* pp. 19–38.

[15] Charles Tilly, ed., *The Formation of National States in Western Europe* (Princeton, N.J.: Princeton University Press, 1975), p. 42; Charles Tilly, *Coercion, Capital, and European States, AD 990–1990* (Cambridge: Basil Blackwell, 1990); Barry Posen, "Nationalism, the Mass Army, and Military Power," *forthcoming.*

[16] Tilly, *Formation of National States,* pp. 96–126; David Lake, "Powerful Pacifists: Democratic States and War," *American Political Science Review,* vol. 86, no. 1, Spring 1992, pp. 24–37.

[17] Benedict Anderson, *Imagined Communities: Reflections on the Origins and Spread of Nationalism* (London: Verso, 1983); Paul Kennedy, "The Decline of Nationalistic History in the West, 1900–1970," *Journal of Contemporary History,* vol. 8, no. 1, January 1973, pp. 77–100.

[18] David Lawday, "My Country Right . . . or What?" *The Atlantic,* vol. 268, no. 1, July 1991, pp. 22–26; Hobsbawm, *Nations and Nationalism,* pp. 163–183.

[19] Ernest Gellner, "Nationalism in the Vacuum," in Motyl, *Thinking Theoretically,* pp. 243–254; Greenfeld, *Nationalism,* introduction.

[20] Tilly, *Formation of National States,* p. 42; Tilly, *Coercion, Capital, and European States,* pp. 114–117.

[21] Eugen Weber, *The Nationalist Revival in France, 1905–1914* (Berkeley, Calif.: University of California Press, 1959); Geoff Eley, *Reshaping the German Right* (New Haven, Conn.: Yale University Press, 1980); Theda Skocpol, *States and Social Revolutions* (Cambridge: Cambridge University Press, 1979), pp. 206–235.

[22] Foreign Broadcast Information Service (hereafter FBIS), *Daily Report, Central Eurasia,* March 9, 1992, pp. 50–55; FBIS, *Daily Report, Central Eurasia,* March 10, 1992, p. 52; *New York Times,* June 9, 1992, p. A7.

[23] Polyani, *The Great Transformation*; Peter Gourevitch, *Politics in Hard Times* (Ithaca, N.Y.: Cornell University Press, 1986), pp. 71–180.

[24] Philip Hanson and Elizabeth Teague, "The Industrialists and Russian Economic Reform," *RFE/RL Research Report,* vol. 1, no. 19, May 18, 1992, pp. 1–7.

[25] Sergei Karaganov, et al., "Strategiia dlia Rossii," *Nezavisimaia gazeta*, August 19, 1992. Thanks to Robert Legvold for this citation. More generally, see Hanson and Teague, "Industrialists," pp. 2–4; Tolz, "Russia," p. 8.

[26] "Appeal to the Citizens of Russia by the National Salvation Front Organizing Committee," *Sovetskaya Rossiya*, October 1, 1992, in FBIS, October 6, 1992, p. 27, signed by V.I. Alksnis, S.N. Baburin, and other military, literary, industrialist, and nationalist figures. See also Igor Torbakov, "The 'Statists' and the Ideology of Russian Imperial Nationalism," *RFE/RL Research Report*, vol. 1, no. 49, December 11, 1992, pp. 10–16.

[27] John Ruggie, "International Regimes, Transactions, and Change: Embedded Liberalism in the Postwar Economic Order," *International Organization*, vol. 36, no. 2, Spring 1982, pp. 379–416.

[28] Hans Kohn, *The Idea of Nationalism* (New York: Macmillan, 1961, orig. ed. 1944), chapter 5; Greenfeld, *Nationalism*, chapter 1–2.

[29] Gerald Newman, *The Rise of English Nationalism: A Cultural History, 1740–1830* (New York: St Martin's Press, 1987), pp. 169–170, 229–230; Linda Colley, "Whose Nation? Class and National Consciousness in Britain, 1750–1830," *Past and Present*, no. 113, November 1986, pp. 97–117, especially pp. 100–105; Olive Anderson, *A Liberal State at War* (New York: St Martin's Press, 1976).

[30] Hans Ulrich Wehler, *The German Empire* (Leamington Spa, England: Berg, 1985); Eley, *Reshaping the German Right*.

[31] Roman Solchanyk, "Ukraine: Political Reform and Political Change," *RFE/RL Research Report*, vol. 1, no. 21, May 22, 1992, p. 4; Gagnon, "Ethnicity, Nationalism, and International Conflict"; FBIS, *Daily Report, Central Eurasia*, March 9, 1992, pp. 50–55.

[32] Michael Doyle, "Liberalism and World Politics," *American Political Science Review*, vol. 80, no. 4, December 1986, pp. 1,151–1,169; Anthony Downs, *An Economic Theory of Democracy* (New York: Harper, 1957).

[33] For qualifications and further evidence, see Jack Snyder, *Myths of Empire* (Ithaca, N.Y.: Cornell University Press, 1991), pp. 49–52, 99–105, 154, 158, 209–210, 303.

[34] Timothy Colton, "Politics," in Timothy Colton and Robert Legvold, eds., *After the Soviet Union* (New York: Norton, 1992), pp. 17–48.

[35] Miroslav Hroch, *Social Preconditions of National Revival in Europe* (Cambridge: Cambridge University Press, 1985).

[36] Louise Young, "Mobilizing for Empire: Japan and Manchukuo, 1931–1945," Columbia University Ph.D. dissertation in history, 1992.

[37] *Trud*, October 6, 1992, in FBIS, October 6, 1992, p. 20.

[38] Speech to Ukrainian Supreme Soviet, September 30, 1992, in FBIS, October 1, 1992, p. 28.

[39] Lewis Coser, *The Functions of Social Conflict* (New York: Free Press, 1956).

[40] John Mearsheimer, "Back to the Future: Instability in Europe after the Cold War," *International Security*, vol. 15, no. 1, Summer 1990, reprinted in Sean Lynn-Jones, ed., *Cold War and After* (Cambridge, Mass.: MIT Press, 1991), p. 157.

[41] For analyses that draw different conclusions, see Ted Hopf, "Managing Soviet Disintegration: A Demand for Behavioral Regimes," *International Security*, vol. 17, no. 1, Summer 1992, pp. 44–75; Stephen Van Evera, "Managing the Eastern Crisis: Preventing War in the Former Soviet Empire," *Security Studies*, vol. 1, no. 3, Spring 1992, pp. 361–382.

[42] Elizabeth Teague, "Splits in the Ranks of Russia's 'Red Directors'," *RFE/RL*

Research Report, vol. 1, no. 35, September 4, 1992, pp. 6–10; Alexander Rahr, "A Russian Paradox: Democrats Support Emergency Powers," *RFE/RL Research Report,* vol. 1, no. 48, December 4, 1992, p. 18.

[43] For a well-argued, affirmative answer, see Alec Nove, "Economics of the Transition Period," *Harriman Institute Forum,* vol. 5, nos. 11–12, July–August 1992.

[44] Ziya Onis, "The Logic of the Developmental State," *Comparative Politics,* vol. 24, no. 1, October 1991, p. 117; Stephan Haggard, *Pathways from the Periphery* (Ithaca, N.Y.: Cornell University Press, 1990), pp. 25, 33, 41–42, 48; James Clay Moltz, "Commonwealth Economics in Perspective: Lessons from the East Asian Model," *Soviet Economy,* vol. 7, no. 4, October–December 1991, pp. 342–363; Alexander Gerschenkron, *Economic Backwardness in Historical Perspective* (Cambridge, Mass.: Belknap, 1962).

Chapter 6

The Security Dilemma and Ethnic Conflict

Barry R. Posen

The end of the Cold War has been accompanied by the emergence of nationalist, ethnic, and religious conflict in Eurasia. However, the risks and intensity of these conflicts have varied from region to region: Ukrainians and Russians are still getting along relatively well; Serbs and Slovenians had a short, sharp clash; Serbs, Croats, and Bosnian Muslims have waged open warfare; and Armenians and Azeris seem destined to fight a slow-motion attrition war. The claim that newly released, age-old antipathies account for this violence fails to explain the considerable variance in observable intergroup relations.

The purpose of this chapter is to apply a basic concept from the realist tradition of international relations theory, "the security dilemma," to the special conditions that arise when proximate groups of people suddenly find themselves newly responsible for their own security. A group suddenly compelled to provide its own protection must ask the following questions about any neighboring group: Is it a threat? How much of a threat? Will the threat grow or diminish over time? Is there anything that must be done immediately? The answers to these questions strongly influence the chances for war.

This chapter assesses the factors that could produce an intense security dilemma when imperial order breaks down, thus producing an early resort to violence. The security dilemma is then employed to analyze two cases—the breakup of Yugoslavia and relations between Russia and Ukraine—to illustrate its utility. Finally, some actions are suggested to ameliorate the tendency toward violence.

THE SECURITY DILEMMA

The collapse of imperial regimes can be profitably viewed as a problem of "emerging anarchy." The longest standing and most useful school of international relations theory—realism—explicitly addresses the consequences of anarchy—the absence of a sovereign—for political relations among states.[1] In areas such as the former Soviet Union and Yugoslavia, "sovereigns" have disappeared. They leave in their wake a host of groups—ethnic, religious, cultural—of greater or lesser cohesion. These groups must pay attention to the first thing that states have historically addressed—the problem of security—even though many of these groups still lack many of the attributes of statehood.

Realist theory contends that the condition of anarchy makes security the first concern of states. It can be otherwise only if these political organizations do not care about their survival as independent entities. As long as some do care, there will be competition for the key to security—power. The competition will often continue to a point at which the competing entities have amassed more power than needed for security and, thus, consequently begin to threaten others. Those threatened will respond in turn.

Relative power is difficult to measure and is often subjectively appraised; what seems sufficient to one state's defense will seem, and will often be, offensive to its neighbors. Because neighbors wish to remain autonomous and secure, they will react by trying to strengthen their own positions. States can trigger these reactions even if they have no expansionist inclinations. This is the security dilemma: What one does to enhance one's own security causes reactions that, in the end, can make one less secure. Cooperation among states to mute these competitions can be difficult because someone else's "cheating" may leave one in a militarily weakened position. All fear betrayal.

Often, statesmen do not recognize that this problem exists: They do not empathize with their neighbors; they are unaware that their own actions can seem threatening. Often, it does not matter if they know of this problem. The nature of their situation compels them to take the steps they do.

The security dilemma is particularly intense when two conditions hold. First, when offensive and defensive military forces are more or less identical, states cannot signal their defensive intent—that is, their limited objectives—by the kinds of military forces they choose to deploy. Any forces on hand are suitable for offensive campaigns. For example, many believe that armored forces are the best means of defense against an attack by armored forces. However, because armor has a great deal of offensive potential, states so outfitted cannot distinguish one another's intentions. They must assume the worst because the worst is possible.

A second condition arises from the effectiveness of the offense versus the defense. If offensive operations are more effective than defensive operations, states will choose the offensive if they wish to survive. This may encourage preemptive war in the event of a political crisis because the perceived superiority of the offensive creates incentives to strike first whenever war appears likely. In addition, in the situation in which offensive capability is strong, a modest superiority in numbers will appear to provide greatly increased prospects for military success. Thus, the offensive advantage can cause preventive war if a state achieves a military advantage, however fleeting.

The barriers to cooperation inherent in international politics provide clues to the problems that arise as central authority collapses in multiethnic empires. The security dilemma affects relations among these groups, just as it affects relations among states. Indeed, because these groups have the added problem of building new state structures from the wreckage of old empires, they are doubly vulnerable.

In this chapter, it is argued that the process of imperial collapse produces conditions that make offensive and defensive capabilities indistinguishable and make the offense superior to the defense. In addition, uneven progress in the formation of state structures will create windows of opportunity and vulnerability. These factors have a powerful influence on the prospects for conflict, regardless of the internal politics of the groups emerging from old empires. Analysts inclined to the view that most of the trouble lies elsewhere, either in the specific nature of group identities or in the short-term incentives for new leaders to "play the nationalist card" to secure their power, need to understand the security dilemma and its consequences. Across the board, these strategic problems show that very little nationalist rabble-rousing or nationalistic combativeness is required to generate very dangerous situations.

The Indistinguishability of Offense and Defense

Newly independent groups must first determine whether neighboring groups are a threat. They will examine one another's military capabilities to do so. Because the weaponry available to these groups will often be quite rudimentary, their offensive military capabilities will be as much a function of the quantity and commitment of the soldiers they can mobilize as the particular characteristics of the weapons they control. Thus, each group will have to assess the other's offensive military potential in terms of its cohesion and its past military record.

The nature of military technology and organization is usually taken to be the main factor affecting the distinguishability of offense and defense. Yet, clear distinctions between offensive and defensive capabilities are historically rare, and they are particularly difficult to make in the realm of land warfare. For example, the force structures of armed neutrals such as Finland, Sweden, and Switzerland are often categorized as defensive. These countries rely more heavily on infantry, which is thought to have weak offensive potential, than on tanks and other mechanized weaponry, which are thought to have strong offensive potential. However, their weak offensive capabilities have also been a function of the massive military power of what used to be their most plausible adversary, the former Soviet Union. Against states of similar size, similarly armed, all three countries would have considerable offensive capabilities—particularly if their infantries were extraordinarily motivated—as German and French infantries were at the outset of World War I, as Chinese and North Vietnamese infantries were against the United States, and as Iran's infantry was against Iraq.

Ever since the French Revolution put the first politically motivated mass armies into the field, strong national identity has been understood by both scholars and practitioners to be a key ingredient of the combat power of armies.[2] A group identity helps the individual members cooperate to achieve their purposes. When humans can readily cooperate, the whole exceeds the sum of the parts, creating a unit stronger relative to those groups with a weaker identity. Thus, the "groupness" of the ethnic, religious, cultural, and linguistic collectivities that emerge from collapsed empires gives each of them an inherent offensive military power.

The military capabilities available to newly independent groups will often be unsophisticated; infantry-based armies will be easy to organize, augmented by whatever heavier equipment is inherited or seized from the old regime. Their offensive potential will be stronger the more cohesive their sponsoring group appears to be. Particularly in the close quarters in which these groups often find themselves, the combination of infantry-based, or quasi-mechanized, ground forces with strong group solidarity is likely to encourage groups to fear each other. Their capabilities will appear offensive.

The solidarity of opposing groups will strongly influence how each group assesses the magnitude of the military threat of the others. In general, however, it is quite difficult to perform such assessments. One expects these groups to be "exclusive" and, hence, defensive. Frenchmen generally do not want to turn Germans into Frenchmen, or the reverse. Nevertheless, the drive for security in one group can be so great that it produces near-genocidal behavior toward neighboring groups. Because so much conflict has been identified with "group" identity throughout history, those who emerge as the leaders of any group and who confront the task of self-defense for the first time will be skeptical that the strong group identity of others is benign.

What methods are available to a newly independent group to assess the offensive implications of another's sense of identity?[3] The main mechanism that they will use is history: How did other groups behave the last time they were unconstrained? Is there a record of offensive military activity by the other? Unfortunately, the conditions under which this assessment occurs suggest that these groups are more likely to assume that their neighbors are dangerous than not.

The reason is that the historical reviews undertaken by new groups rarely meet the scholarly standards that modern history and social science hold as norms (or at least as ideals) in the West. First, the recently departed multiethnic empires probably suppressed or manipulated the facts of previous rivalries to reinforce their own rule; the previous regimes in the Soviet Union and Yugoslavia lacked any systemic commitment to truth in historical scholarship. Second, the members of these various groups no doubt did not forget the record of their old rivalries; it was preserved in oral history. This history was undoubtedly magnified in the telling and was seldom subjected to critical appraisal. Third, because their history is mostly oral, each group has a difficult time divining another's view of the past. Fourth, as central authority begins to collapse and local politicians begin to struggle for power, they will begin to write down their versions of history in political speeches. Yet, because the purpose of speeches is domestic political mobilization, these stories are likely to be emotionally charged.

The result is a worst-case analysis. Unless proven otherwise, one group is likely to assume that another group's sense of identity, and the cohesion that it produces, is a danger. Proving it to be otherwise is likely to be very difficult. Because the cohesion of one's own group is an essential means of defense against the possible depredations of neighbors, efforts to reinforce cohesion are likely to be undertaken. Propagandists are put to work writing a politicized history of the group, and the mass media are directed to disseminate that history. The media may either willingly, or under compulsion, report unfolding events in terms that magnify the threat to the group. As neighboring groups observe this, they do the same.

In sum, the military capability of groups will often be dependent on their cohesion, rather than their meager military assets. This cohesion is a threat in its own right because it can provide the emotional power for infantry armies to take the offensive. A historical record of large-scale armed clashes, much less wholesale mistreatment of unarmed civilians, however subjective, will further the tendency for groups to see other groups as threats. They will all simultaneously "arm"—militarily and ideologically—against each other.

The Superiority of Offensive over Defensive Action

Two factors have generally been seen as affecting the superiority of offensive over defensive action—technology and geography. Technology is usually treated as a universal variable, which affects the military capabilities of all the states in a given competition. Geography is a situational variable, which makes offense particularly appealing to specific states for specific reasons. This is what matters most when empires collapse.

In the rare historical cases in which technology has clearly determined the offense–defense balance, such as World War I, soldiers and statesmen have often failed to appreciate its impact. Thus, technology need not be examined further, with one exception: nuclear weapons. If a group inherits a nuclear deterrent, and its neighbors do as well, "groupness" is not likely to affect the security dilemma with as much intensity as would be the case in nonnuclear cases. Because group solidarity would not contribute to the ability of either side to mount a counterforce nuclear attack, nationalism is less important from a military standpoint in a nuclear relationship.

Political geography will frequently create an "offense-dominant world" when empires collapse. Some groups will have greater offensive capabilities because they will effectively surround some or all of the other groups. These other groups may be forced to adopt offensive strategies to break the ring of encirclement. Islands of one group's population are often stranded in the sea of another. Where one territorially concentrated group has "islands" of settlement of its members distributed across the nominal territory of another group (irredenta), the protection of these islands in the event of hostile action can seem extremely difficult. These islands may not be able to help one another; they may be subject to blockade and siege, and by virtue of their numbers relative to the surrounding population and because of topography, they may be militarily indefensible. Thus, the brethren of the stranded group may come to believe that only rapid offensive military action can save their irredenta from a horrible fate.[4]

The geographic factor is a variable, not a constant. Islands of population can be quite large, economically autonomous, and militarily defensible. Alternatively, they can have large numbers of nearby brethren who form a powerful state, which could rescue them in the event of trouble. Potentially, hostile groups could have islands of another group's people within their states; these islands could serve as hostages. Alternatively, the brethren of the "island" group could deploy nuclear weapons and thus punish the surrounding group if they misbehave. In short, it might be possible to defend irredenta without attacking or to deter would-be aggressors by threatening to retaliate in one way or another.

Isolated ethnic groups—ethnic islands—can produce incentives for preventive war. Theorists argue that perceived offensive advantages make preventive war more attractive: If one side has an advantage that will not be present later and if security can best be achieved by offensive military action in any case, then leaders will be inclined to attack during this "window of opportunity."[5] For example, if a surrounding population will ultimately be able to fend off relief attacks from the home territory of an island group's brethren, but is currently weak, then the brethren will be inclined to attack sooner rather than later.

In disputes among groups interspersed in the same territory, another kind of offensive advantage exists—a tactical offensive advantage. Often the goal of the disputants is to create ever-growing areas of homogeneous population for their brethren. Therefore, the other group's population must be induced to leave. The Serbs have introduced the term "ethnic cleansing" to describe this objective, a term redolent with the horrors of 50 years earlier. The offense has tremendous tactical military advantages in operations such as these. Small military forces directed against unarmed or poorly armed civilians can generate tremendous terror. This has always been true, of course, but even simple modern weapons, such as machine guns and mortars, increase the havoc that small bands of fanatics can wreak against the defenseless. Consequently, small bands of each group have an incentive to attack the towns of the other in the hope of driving people away.[6] This is often quite successful, as the vast population of war refugees in the world today attests.

The vulnerability of civilians makes it possible for small bands of fanatics to initiate conflict. Because they are small and fanatical, these bands are hard to control. (This allows the political leadership of the group to deny responsibility for the actions those bands take.) These activities produce disproportionate political results among the opposing group—magnifying initial fears by confirming them. The presence or absence of small gangs of fanatics is thus itself a key determinant of the ability of groups to avoid war as central political authority erodes. Although almost every society produces small numbers of people willing to engage in violence at any given moment, the rapid emergence of organized bands of particularly violent individuals is a sure sign of trouble.

The characteristic behavior of international organizations, especially the United Nations (UN), reinforces the incentives for offensive action. Thus far, the United Nations has proven itself unable to anticipate conflict and provide the credible security guarantees that would mitigate the security dilemma. Once there is politically salient trouble in an area, the

United Nations may try to intervene to "keep the peace." However, the conditions under which peacekeeping is attempted are favorable to the party that has had the most military success. As a general rule, the United Nations does not make peace: It negotiates cease-fires. Two parties in dispute generally agree to a cease-fire only because one is successful and happy with its gains, while the other has lost, but fears even worse to come. Alternatively, the two sides have fought to a bloody stalemate and would like to rest. The United Nations thus protects, and to some extent legitimates, the military gains of the winning side, or gives both a respite to recover. This approach by the international community to intervention in ethnic conflict, helps create an incentive for offensive military operations.

Windows of Vulnerability and Opportunity

Where central authority has recently collapsed, the groups emerging from an old empire must calculate their power relative to each other at the time of collapse and make a guess about their relative power in the future. Such calculations must account for a variety of factors. Objectively, only one side can be better off. However, the complexity of these situations makes it possible for many competing groups to believe that their prospects in a war would be better earlier, rather than later. In addition, if the geographic situation creates incentives of the kind discussed earlier, the temptation to capitalize on these windows of opportunity may be great. These windows may also prove tempting to those who wish to expand for other reasons.

The relative rate of state formation strongly influences the incentives for preventive war. When central authority has collapsed or is collapsing, the groups emerging from the political rubble will try to form their own states. These groups must choose leaders, set up bureaucracies to collect taxes and provide services, organize police forces for internal security, and organize military forces for external security. The material remnants of the old state (especially weaponry, foreign currency reserves, raw material stocks, and industrial capabilities) will be unevenly distributed across the territories of the old empire. Some groups may have had a privileged position in the old system. Others will be less well placed.

The states formed by these groups will thus vary greatly in their strength. This will provide immediate military advantages to those who are farther along in the process of state formation. If those with greater advantages expect to remain in that position by virtue of their superior numbers, then they may see no window of opportunity. However, if they expect their advantage to wane or disappear, then they will have an incentive to solve outstanding issues while they are much stronger than the opposition.

This power differential may create incentives for preventive expropriation, which can generate a spiral of action and reaction. With military resources unevenly distributed and perhaps artificially scarce for some because of arms embargoes, cash shortages, or constrained access to the outside world, small caches of armaments assume large importance. Any military depot will be a tempting target, especially for the poorly armed. Better armed groups also have a strong incentive to seize these weapons because this would increase their margin of superiority.

In addition, it matters whether or not the old regime imposed military conscription on all groups in society. Conscription makes arms theft quite easy because hijackers know what to look for and how to move it. Gains are highly cumulative because each side can quickly integrate whatever it steals into its existing forces. High cumulativity of conquered resources has often motivated states in the past to initiate preventive military actions.

Expectations about outside intervention will also affect preventive war calculations. Historically, this usually meant expectations about the intervention of allies on one side or the other, and the value of such allies. Allies may be explicit or tacit. A group may expect itself or another to find friends abroad. It may calculate that the other group's natural allies are temporarily preoccupied, or a group may calculate that it or its adversary has many other adversaries who will attack in the event of conflict. The greater the number of potential allies for all groups, the more complex this calculation will be and the greater the chance for error. Thus, two opposing groups could both think that the expected behavior of others makes them stronger in the short term.

A broader window-of-opportunity problem has been created by the large number of crises and conflicts that have been precipitated by the end of the Cold War. The electronic media provide free global strategic intelligence about these problems to anyone for the price of a shortwave radio, much less a satellite dish. Middle and great powers, and international organizations, are able to deal with only a small number of crises simultaneously. States that wish to initiate offensive military actions, but fear outside opposition, may move quickly if they learn that international organizations and great powers are preoccupied momentarily with other problems.

CROATS AND SERBS
Viewed through the lens of the security dilemma, the early stages of Yugoslavia's disintegration were strongly influenced by the following

factors. First, the parties identified the reemerging identities of the others as offensive threats. The last time these groups were free of constraint, during World War II, they slaughtered one another with abandon. In addition, the Yugoslav military system trained most men for war and distributed infantry armament widely across the country. Second, the offensive appeared to have the advantage, particularly against Serbs "marooned" in Croatian and Muslim territory. Third, the new republics were not equally powerful. Their power assets varied in terms of people and economic resources, access to the wealth and military assets of the previous regime, access to external allies, and possible outside enemies. Preventive war incentives were consequently high. Fourth, small bands of fanatics soon appeared on the scene. Indeed, the political and military history of the region stressed the role of small, violent, committed groups: the resistance to the Turks, the Ustashe in the 1930s, and the Ustashe state and Serbian Chetniks during World War II.

Serbs and Croats both have a terrifying oral history of each other's behavior. This history goes back hundreds of years, although intense Croat–Serb conflict is only about 125 years old. The history of the region is quite warlike: The area was the frontier of the Hapsburg and Turkish Empires, and Croatia had been an integral part of the military apparatus of the Hapsburg Empire. The imposition of harsh Hungarian rule in Croatia in 1868; the Hungarian divide-and-conquer strategy that pitted Croats and Serbs in Croatia against each other; the rise of the independent Serbian nation-state out of the Ottoman Empire, formally recognized in Europe in 1878; and Serbian pretensions to speak for all south Slavs were the main origins of the Croat–Serb conflict. When Yugoslavia was formed after World War I, the Croats had a very different vision of the new state than the Serbs. They hoped for a confederal system, while the Serbs planned to develop a centralized nation-state.[7] The Croats did not perceive themselves to be treated fairly under this arrangement, and this helped stimulate the development of a violent resistance movement, the Ustashe, which collaborated with the fascist powers during the 1930s.

The Serbs had some reasons for assuming the worst about the existence of an independent Croatian state, given Croatian behavior during World War II. Ustashe leadership was established in Croatia by Nazi Germany. The Serbs, both communist and noncommunist, fought the Axis forces, including the Croats, and each other. (Some Croats also fought in Josip Broz Tito's communist partisan movement against the Nazis.) Roughly a million people died in the fighting—some 5.9 percent of Yugoslavia's prewar population.[8] The Croats behaved with extraordinary brutality toward the Serbs, who suffered nearly 500,000 dead—more than twice as many dead as the Croats.[9] (Obviously, the Germans were responsible for many Serbian deaths as well.) Most of these were not killed in battle; they were civilians murdered in large-scale terrorist raids.

The Croats themselves suffered some 200,000 dead in World War II, which suggests that depredations were inflicted on many sides. (The noncommunist, "nationalist" Chetniks were among the most aggressive killers of Croats, which helps explain why the new Croatian republic is worried by the nationalist rhetoric of the new Serbian republic.) Having lived in a pre- and postwar Yugoslavia largely dominated by Serbs, the Croats had reason to suspect that the demise of the Yugoslav Communist Party would be followed by a Serbian bid for hegemony. In 1971, the Croatian Communist Party had been purged of leaders who had favored greater autonomy. In addition, the historical record of the Serbs during the past 200 years is one of regular efforts to establish an ever larger centralized Serbian national state on the Balkan Peninsula. Thus, Croats had sufficient reason to fear the Serbs.

Serbs in Croatia were scattered in a number of vulnerable islands; they could only be "rescued" by offensive action from Serbia. Such a rescue, of course, would have been enormously complicated by an independent Bosnia, which in part explains the Serbian war there. In addition, Serbia could not count on maintaining absolute military superiority over the Croats forever: Almost twice as many Serbs as Croats inhabit the territory of what was once Yugoslavia, but Croatia is slightly wealthier than Serbia.[10] Croatia also has some natural allies within former Yugoslavia, especially Bosnian Muslims, and seemed somewhat more adept at winning allies abroad. As Croatia adopted the trappings of statehood and achieved international recognition, its military power was expected to grow. From the Serbian point of view, Serbs in Croatia were insecure and expected to become more so as time went by.

From a military point of view, the Croats probably would have been better off postponing their secession until after they had made additional military preparations. However, their experience in 1971, more recent political developments, and the military preparations of the Yugoslav army probably convinced them that the Serbs were about to strike and that the Croatian leadership would be rounded up and imprisoned or killed if they did not act quickly.

Each side not only had to assess the other's capabilities, but also its intentions, and there were plenty of signals of malign intent. Between 1987 and 1990, Slobodan Milosevic ended the administrative autonomy within Serbia that had been granted to Kosovo and Vojvodina in the 1974 constitution.[11] In August 1990, Serbs in the Dalmatia region of Croatia held a cultural autonomy referendum, which they defended with armed roadblocks against expected Croatian interference.[12] By October, the

Yugoslav army began to impound all of the heavy weapons stored in Croatia for the use of the territorial defense forces, thus securing a vast military advantage over the nascent armed forces of the republic.[13] The Serbian window of opportunity, already large, grew larger. The Croats accelerated their own military preparations.

It is difficult to tell just how much interference the Croats planned, if any, in the referendum in Dalmatia. However, Croatia had stoked the fires of Serbian secessionism with a series of ominous rulings. In the spring of 1990, Serbs in Croatia were redefined as a minority, rather than a constituent nation, and were asked to take a loyalty oath. Serbian police were to be replaced with Croats, as were some local Serbian officials. No offer of cultural autonomy was made at the time. These Croatian policies undoubtedly intensified Serbian fears about the future and further tempted them to exploit their military superiority.

It appears that the Croats overestimated the reliability and influence of the Federal Republic of Germany as an ally due to some combination of World War II history, the widespread misperception created by the European media and by Western political leaders of Germany's near-superpower status, the presumed influence of the large Croatian émigré community in Germany, and Germany's own diplomacy, which was quite favorable to Croatia even before its June 1991 declaration of independence.[14] These considerations may have encouraged Croatia to secede. Conversely, Serbian propaganda was quick to stress the German–Croatian connection and to speculate on future German ambitions in the Balkans.[15] Fair or not, this prospect would have had an impact on Serbia's preventive war calculus.

RUSSIA AND UKRAINE

Through the lens of the security dilemma, several important factors in Russian–Ukrainian relations can be identified that suggest that the potential for conflict is not as great as for Yugoslavia. First, the propensity of Russians and Ukrainians to view one another's cohesion as an offensive military threat is slight. A principal stabilizing factor here is the presence of former Soviet nuclear forces in both Russia and Ukraine, which provides each republic with a powerful deterrent. Second, each side's perception of the other's "identity" is comparatively benign. Third, settlement patterns create comparatively less pressure for offensive action. These three factors reduce the pressure for preventive war.[16]

The nuclear forces of the former Soviet Union—both those clearly under Commonwealth (effectively Russian) control and those with a more ambiguous status in Ukraine—have probably helped stabilize Russian–Ukrainian relations. This is because nuclear weapons make it dangerous for either to launch a campaign of violence against the other. Mutual deterrence prevails. In a clash of wills between two nuclear-armed states about attacks on minority populations, the state representing the interests of the victims would have more credibility; it would be the defender of the status quo. The potential military consequences of each side's "groupness" is thus muted.

Most of the Soviet nuclear forces came under the control of the Russian Republic, thereby rendering large-scale anti-Russian violence in Ukraine very risky. The presence of large numbers of nuclear weapons on Ukrainian soil gives Ukraine a nuclear "threat that leaves something to chance." Although these weapons are believed to remain under the technical control of the Commonwealth (Russian) command structure, military action by Russians against Ukraine could precipitate a Ukrainian attempt to seize these weapons. Given the significant representation of Ukrainians in the Soviet officer and noncommissioned officer corps, it is quite likely that there are many Ukrainians who know a lot about nuclear weapons, making their seizure quite plausible. This would be a novel kind of nuclear crisis, but it would probably be enough of a crisis to produce the prudent behavior among nuclear powers that existed during the Cold War. An overt nationalist political campaign in Russia for action against Ukraine could also provoke Ukrainian seizure of these weapons.

Russian and Ukrainian histories of each other, as well as their past relations, are less terrifying than those found among groups within the former Yugoslavia. There is no record of large-scale Russian–Ukrainian military rivalry and no clear, salient incident of nationalist bloodletting. However, one dangerous historical episode could play a significant role in the development of an anti-Russian, Ukrainian history: The communist war on independent farmers and its concomitant famine in 1930–1932 killed millions.[17] If Ukrainians begin to blame the famine on Russians, this would be quite dangerous politically. If, instead, the famine continues to be blamed on a Communist Party headed by a renegade Georgian psychopath, then this experience will cause less trouble. Ukrainian President Leonid Kravchuk, in his public utterances, tends to portray the Bolsheviks, not the Russians, as the culprits.[18]

That the famine has not played a large role in Ukrainian nationalist rhetoric is a good sign, but this event provides potential tinder. Russian nationalists should therefore be very careful how they portray future Russian–Ukrainian relations. If they project a subordinate status for Ukraine, then Ukrainian nationalists will have a strong incentive to portray the famine as a Russian crime in their effort to build cohesion to resist Russian domination. *Izvestia* reports that Sergei Baburin, leader of the Russian Unity bloc in the Russian parliament, informed the Ukrainian ambassador that "either Ukraine reunites again with Russia or there will be war."[19] Such statements will be heard and acted upon in Ukraine.

It is difficult for Ukrainian nationalists to argue convincingly that they were exploited by Russia.[20] Ukrainians seem to have achieved at least proportional representation in the Soviet governing and military apparatus.[21] They produced a share of Soviet gross national product (GNP) more than proportional to their share of population, and the kinds of goods they produced suggest that Ukraine enjoyed a fair share of industrial investment.[22] Ukrainian nationalists assert, however, that the Soviet Union extracted substantial economic resources from Ukraine—perhaps as much as half of Ukrainian GNP.[23]

Of greater importance, Ukrainian nationalists believe and many scholars agree that both the Russian Empire and the later Soviet Union did everything possible to retard the growth of an independent Ukrainian identity and to russify Ukraine. This experience led to the reassertion of Ukraine's cultural and political identity.[24] Alarmingly, Rukh, the main pro-independence party in Ukraine, has apparently drifted toward a more virulent nationalism, one that portrays Russia and Russians as the enemy.[25]

These worrisome signs must be put into context, however. In general, ethnic hatred has not played a great role in Ukrainian efforts to define their state. Initially, both of the large political parties in Ukraine tried to accommodate all groups in the country. There is no record of Ukrainian persecution of resident Russians. The Ukrainians and the Russians living in the eastern part of the country have had amicable relations for a great many years. A majority of Russians voted for Ukrainian independence. There are no reports of Ukrainian nationalist gangs operating against Russians.[26]

The history of relations between Russians and Ukrainians is thus conducive to peace. Neither has strong reasons to assume that the other's "groupness" constitutes a strong offensive threat to its survival. That said, Russian–Ukrainian political history is conducive to Ukrainian mistrust, and the famine is a singular historical episode that could prove problematic.

The security situation between the two republics is favorable from a stability standpoint. The 12 million Russians in the Ukraine (who constitute 21 percent of the population) are not settled in small vulnerable islands; many of the areas of settlement are proximate to each other and to the Russian border. Others are proximate to the Black Sea coast, which may help explain the intensity of the dispute about the ultimate disposition of the Black Sea Fleet. Large numbers of Russians are still to be found in the armed forces of the newly independent Ukraine, complicating any Ukrainian state action against resident Russians. The expulsion of Russians from eastern Ukraine would thus be a tough job for the Ukrainians. Russia is also a nuclear power and thus in a position to make credible threats to protect the safety of its own. In addition, the proximity of many Ukrainian Russians to the border of the Russian Republic would facilitate a conventional rescue operation, should that prove necessary. The fact that Russia has at least three times the population, wealth, and probable conventional combat power of Ukraine would favor such a rescue. In sum, Russia is not being forced to take offensive conventional action to protect its nationals in Ukraine. Because Russians can probably protect their brethren in the Ukraine later, they have only limited incentives to solve the problem now.

To say that the Russians can protect their brethren, however, is not to say that military intervention in Ukraine would be cheap or safe. The Ukrainians inherited ample stocks of armaments from the Soviet Union; the Ukrainian presence in the Soviet military made fatuous any Russian thoughts of spiriting away this vast quantity of military equipment and guarantees that the Ukrainian military will know how to use the weaponry in its possession.[27] Efforts to coerce Ukraine would likely precipitate Ukrainian efforts to seize the nuclear weapons now within its territory. Thus, although Russia clearly has the power to protect Ukrainian Russians in the event of oppression, lacking such a provocation, Russian nationalists would have great difficulty convincing their compatriots that Ukraine is ripe for the picking.

Finally, unlike Yugoslavia, external factors reinforce restraint in Russian–Ukrainian relations. Because they are quite close to Western Europe and heavily armed, it is reasonable for Russians and Ukrainians to assume that conflict between the two republics would be condemned by outside powers. Each side has reason to fear being branded the aggressor in such a conflict because the United States and the Europeans lack any deep organic ties to either Russia or Ukraine. Thus, Western diplomacy should encourage evenhandedness toward the two parties. Thus far, the West has shown a tendency to patronize the Ukrainians and dote on the Russians; this is a mistake. It would be better for both to believe that whoever was labeled the aggressor in a Russian–Ukrainian conflict could end up earning the enmity of the wealthiest and most powerful coalition of powers in the history of the world.

In sum, although there are some danger signs in Russian–Ukrainian relations, the security dilemma is not particularly intense in this case. To the extent that Western powers have an interest in peace between these two powers, efforts should be made to preserve this favorable state of affairs.

COMPARISON SUMMARY

A brief review of these two cases highlights factors that favored war in Yugoslavia and that still favor peace in Russian–Ukrainian relations. This comparison also identifies some early warning indicators that should be monitored regarding Russia and Ukraine.

In Yugoslavia, Croats and Serbs found each other's identity a threat because of the primitive military capabilities they could field and the terrible record of their historical relationship. In the Russia–Ukraine case, nuclear weapons mute the conventional competition, making group cohesion less of a military asset. If Ukraine eliminates its nuclear arsenal, as it has pledged to do, it will increasingly come to rely on nationalism to strengthen an army that will only be able to stand against Russia through superior motivation. Eliminating Ukraine's nuclear arsenal will therefore make Russia stronger and Ukraine more nationalistic. This could prove dangerous.

In Yugoslavia, Serbs in Croatia were militarily vulnerable, and Serbs in Serbia had only one way to defend them—a speedy, powerful offensive. Russians in Ukraine are less geographically isolated and can be protected in several ways: Russians in Ukraine may be able to defend themselves by virtue of their numbers and their presence in the Ukrainian army, Russia itself could make nuclear threats, and the Russian army will probably maintain a markedly quantitative superiority over Ukraine, which would facilitate a rescue operation, should one be needed. Systematic de-russification of the Ukrainian armed forces, accompanied by a precipitate decline in Russia's military capabilities, would therefore be a sign of trouble in Russian–Ukrainian relations.

Although Ukrainians and Russians in the eastern Ukraine do live together, no violent bands have emerged and begun to engage in communal terror. In Yugoslavia, such bands emerged early in the dissolution process. It may be that the Russian presence in the Ukrainian army has helped discourage such developments, or it may be that there are enough lawless places in the former Soviet Union to absorb those prone to violence. Aspiring Croatian and Serbian thugs had no other outlet for their violent inclinations. The appearance of small Russian or Ukrainian terrorist groups could have a powerful incendiary effect on relations between the two republics and would thus indicate trouble.

In Yugoslavia, the Serbs had many incentives for preventive war. They outnumbered the Croats by only two to one and enjoyed no economic advantage. The Croats were likely to find allies within the former Yugoslavia. They were also likely to find allies abroad. Serbia was less well placed. Serbia enjoyed privileged access to the spoils of Yugoslavia, so it was initially much more powerful militarily than Croatia. The combination of dependence on an offensive to protect brethren in Croatia, and a temporary but wide military advantage, proved to be too large a temptation to resist.

The Russians have few incentives for preventive war. With three times the human and material resources of Ukraine, it is unlikely that the balance of military power will soon shift against them, nor does it seem likely that Ukraine will be better than Russia at finding allies abroad. Ukrainian pledges to become a nonnuclear state make it attractive even for nationalist Russians to postpone aggression until later; making war now would be a risky proposition. If Ukraine's economy recovers much more quickly than Russia's, or if Ukraine finds powerful allies abroad while Russia finds itself isolated, or if Russia begins to fear that endless border wars will tie down many of its forces in the future, Russians might begin to think more about preventive action against Ukraine.

Even if many of the factors that currently favor peace change, Russia's possession of nuclear weapons should continue to mute its incentives for defensively motivated, preventive conventional war. It should be noted, however, that nuclear powers had a tendency to solve security problems conventionally—when they could—during the Cold War.

CONCLUSION

Three main conclusions follow from the preceding analysis. First, the security dilemma and realist international relations theory more generally have considerable ability to explain and predict the probability and intensity of military conflict among groups emerging from the wreckage of empires.

Second, the security dilemma suggests that the risks associated with these conflicts are quite high. Several of the causes of conflict and war highlighted by the security dilemma operate with considerable intensity among the groups emerging from empires. The kind of military power that these groups can initially develop and their competing versions of history will often produce mutual fear and competition. Settlement patterns, in conjunction with unequal and shifting power, will often produce incentives for preventive war. The cumulative effect of conquered resources will encourage preventive grabs of military equipment and other assets.

Finally, if outsiders wish to understand and perhaps reduce the odds of conflict, they must assess the local groups' strategic view of their situation. Which groups fear for their physical security and why? What military options are open to them? By making these groups feel less threatened and by reducing the salience of windows of opportunity, the odds of conflict may be reduced.

Because the international political system as a whole remains a self-help system, it will be difficult to act on such calculations. Outsiders rarely have major material or security interests at stake in regional disputes. It is difficult for international institutions to threaten credibly in advance to intervene, on humanitarian grounds, to protect groups that fear for the future. Vague humanitarian commitments will not make vulnerable groups feel safe and will probably not deter those who wish to repress them. In some cases, however, such commitments may be credible because the conflict has real security implications for powerful outside actors.

Groups drifting into conflict should be encouraged to discuss their individual histories of mutual relations. Competing versions of history should be reconciled if possible. Domestic policies that raise bitter memories of perceived past injustices or depredations should be examined. This exercise need not be managed by an international political institution; nongovernmental organizations could play a role. Discussions about regional history would be an intelligent use of the resources of many foundations. A few conferences will not, of course, easily undo generations of hateful, politicized history, bolstered by reams of more recent propaganda. The exercise would cost little, however, and therefore should be tried.[28]

In some cases, outside powers could threaten not to act; this would discourage some kinds of aggressive behavior. For example, outside powers could make clear that if a new state abuses a minority and then gets itself into a war with that minority and its allies, the abuser will find little sympathy abroad if it begins to lose. To accomplish this, however, outside powers must have a way of detecting mistreatment of minorities.

In other cases, it may be reasonable for outside powers to provide material resources, including armaments, to help groups protect themselves. However, this kind of hard-bitten policy is politically difficult for liberal democratic governments now dominating world politics to pursue, even on humanitarian grounds. In addition, it is an admittedly complicated game in its own right because it is difficult to determine the amount and type of military assistance needed to produce effective defensive forces, but not offensive capabilities. Nevertheless, considerable diplomatic leverage may be attained by the threat to supply armaments to one side or the other.

Nonproliferation policy also has a role to play. In some cases, nuclear weaponry may be an effective way of protecting the weak from the strong. Russia may behave with considerable restraint toward Ukraine as long as some nuclear weapons remain on Ukrainian territory, vulnerable to

Ukrainian seizure. However, once the last weapon is gone, Russian nationalists may become much more assertive.

The future balance of power between Ukraine and Russia is less conducive to good relations than the current one, which is the reason Ukrainians have sought Western security guarantees as a quid pro quo for ratifying the Strategic Arms Reduction Treaty (START), for adhering to the Nuclear Non-Proliferation Treaty, and for ridding themselves of nuclear weapons. Absent such guarantees and the measures needed to render them credible, Ukrainians can be expected to prolong the "transition" phase to the nonnuclear status that they have promised.[29] It would be politically difficult for the United States to reverse the arms control initiatives already launched, but it is reasonable to stretch out their implementation. Recent suggestions to accelerate the denuclearization of Ukraine (and Belarus and Kazakhstan), therefore, have it exactly backward.[30] The West should hold Ukraine to a steady, proportional withdrawal schedule over the longest period consistent with the prescribed outline of the START agreement. Some of the benefits of nuclear deterrence could thus be secured during the coming difficult political and economic transition in Russia and Ukraine.

It will frequently prove impossible, however, to arrange military assets, external political commitments, and political expectations so that all neighboring groups are relatively secure and perceive themselves as such. War is then likely. These wars will confirm and intensify all the fears that led to their initiation. Their brutality will tempt outsiders to intervene, but peace efforts originating from the outside will be unsuccessful if they do not realistically address the fears that triggered the conflicts initially. In most cases, this will require a willingness to commit large numbers of troops and substantial amounts of military equipment to troubled areas for a very long time.

Acknowledgments

I would like to thank Robert Art, John Mearsheimer, Steve Meyer, Harvey Sapolsky, Jack Snyder, and Steve Van Evera for comments. Daryl Press served ably as my research assistant. The 1992 annual summer conference of Harvard University's Olin Center for Strategic Studies provided the first opportunity to present these ideas. The Carnegie Corporation of New York funded release time.

Notes

[1] The following realist literature is essential for those interested in the analysis of ethnic conflict: Kenneth Waltz, *Theory of International Politics* (Reading, Mass.: Addison Wesley, 1979), chapters 6 and 8; Robert Jervis, "Cooperation under the Security Dilemma," *World Politics*, no. 2, January 1978, pp. 167–213; Robert Jervis, *Perception and Misperception in International Politics* (Princeton, N.J.:

Princeton University Press, 1976),
chapter 3; Thomas C. Schelling, *Arms
and Influence* (New Haven, Conn.: Yale
University Press, 1966), chapters 1 and
6.

[2] See Carl von Clausewitz, *On War*
(Princeton, N.J.: Princeton University
Press, 1984), pp. 591–592; Robert
Gilpin, "The Richness of the Tradition
of Political Realism," in Robert E.
Keohane, *Neorealism and its Critics*
(New York: Columbia University Press,
1986), pp. 300–321, especially pp. 304–
308.

[3] This problem shades into an assessment of "intentions," another very
difficult problem for states in international politics. This issue is treated as a
capabilities problem because the
emergence of anarchy forces leaders to
focus on military potential, rather than
on intentions. Under these conditions,
every group will ask whether
neighboring groups have the cohesion,
morale, and martial spirit to take the
offensive if their leaders call on them to
do so.

[4] It is plausible that the surrounding
population will view irredenta in their
midst as an offensive threat by the
outside group. They may be perceived
as a "fifth column," that must be
controlled, repressed, or even expelled.

[5] See Stephen Van Evera, "The Cult of
the Offensive and the Origins of the
First World War," *International Security*, vol. 9, no. 1, Summer 1984, pp.
58–107.

[6] Why do they not go to the defense of
their own, rather than attack the other?
Here, it is hypothesized that such groups
are scarce relative to the number of
target towns and villages, so they cannot
"defend" their own with any great
confidence.

[7] James Gow, "Deconstructing Yugosla-
via," *Survival*, vol. 33, no. 4, July–
August 1991, p. 292; J.B. Hoptner,
Yugoslavia in Crisis 1934–1941 (New

York: Columbia University Press,
1962), pp. 1–9.

[8] Ivo Banac, "Political Change and
National Diversity," *Daedalus,* vol. 119,
no. 1, Winter 1990, pp. 145–150,
estimates that 487,000 Serbs; 207,000
Croats; 86,000 Bosnian Muslims; and
60,000 Jews died in Yugoslavia during
the war.

[9] Aleksa Djilas, *The Contested Country*
(Cambridge, Mass.: Harvard University
Press, 1991), pp. 103–128. See chapter
4, "The National State and Genocide:
The Ustasha Movement, 1929–1945,"
especially pp. 120–127, which vividly
describes the large-scale Croatian
murders of Serbs, as well as Jews and
Gypsies; however, Djilas does not
explain how 200,000 Croats also died.

[10] See Sabrina Ramet, *Nationalism and
Federalism in Yugoslavia 1962–1991,*
2nd ed. (Bloomington, Ind.: Indiana
University Press, 1992), appendix 2, p.
286.

[11] Gow, "Deconstructing Yugoslavia," p.
294. Vojvodina contains the only
petroleum and gas in Yugoslavia
proximate to Serbia, so this act probably
had a strategic motive; see Central
Intelligence Agency, *Atlas of Eastern
Europe* (Washington, D.C.: US Government Printing Office, August 1990), p.
10.

[12] International Institute for Strategic
Studies, *Strategic Survey 1990–1991*
(London: Brassey's for the IISS, 1991),
p. 167.

[13] Gow, "Deconstructing Yugoslavia," p.
299.

[14] See John Newhouse, "The Diplomatic
Round," *The New Yorker,* August 24,
1992, especially p. 63. See also John
Zametica, *The Yugoslav Conflict,*
Adelphi Paper 270 (London: Brassey's
for the IISS, 1992), pp. 63–65.

[15] Ramet, *Nationalism and Federalism,*
p. 265.

[16] Untangling the strategic from the
purely nationalist aspects of the dispute

about Crimea is difficult. It is doubtful that Russian nationalists fear for the safety of Russians in Crimea because they are the clear majority there, and Crimea is quite defensible. Russian nationalists want it because the conquest of Crimea from the Turks is seen as a major Russian national achievement. It is likely that Ukrainians want to keep Crimea because they fear that concessions on this point will lead to new Russian demands for territorial adjustments. Strategic elements are likely salient in both sides' calculus. Control of Crimea and the Black Sea Fleet would give Russia military dominance of the Ukraine's seaborne trade from Odessa.

[17] Norman Stone, "The Mark of History," *The National Interest,* vol. 27, Spring 1992, p. 37 gives a figure of 8 million dead in the famine.

[18] See interviews with Ukrainian President Leonid Kravchuk in *Le Figaro,* January 23, 1992, as quoted in Foreign Broadcast Information Service (hereafter FBIS), January 27, 1992, and in *Der Spiegel,* February 3, 1992, as quoted in FBIS, April 2, 1992.

[19] Quoted in Roman Solchanyk, "The Crimean Imbroglio: Kiev and Moscow," *Radio Free Europe/Radio Liberty Research Report,* vol. 1, no. 40, October 9, 1992.

[20] Abraham Brumberg, "Not so Free at Last," *New York Review of Books,* October 22, 1992, p. 62, suggests that many Ukrainians believe that Moscow always views Ukraine as "a colony to be exploited."

[21] Ukrainians made up roughly one-quarter of the Soviet officer corps and were also well represented in the Communist Party. See Brian Taylor, "Red Army Blues: The Future of Military Power in the Former Soviet Union," *Breakthroughs,* vol. 2, no. 1, Spring 1992, pp. 1–8; Adrian Karatnycky, "The Ukrainian Factor,"

Foreign Affairs, vol. 71, no. 3, Summer 1992, p. 107.

[22] Ukraine had about 18 percent of Soviet population and is said to have produced, "33 percent of televisions, 25 percent of computation and automation equipment, 22 percent of tractors, 31 percent of harvesters." See Karatnycky, "Ukrainian Factor," pp. 96–97. Julian Cooper suggests that some 17.5 percent of defense workers in the Soviet Union were to be found in the Ukraine in the mid-1980s, and some 13.7 percent of defense firms. See Tables 5 and 7 in "Reconversion industrielle," *La Décomposition de l'Armée Soviétique,* Dossier No. 45 (Paris: FEDN, April 1992), pp. 151, 153.

[23] Valeriy Semivolos, "An Army for Ukraine," *Vecherniye novosti,* July 20, 1991, p. 3 (as translated in *Commonwealth of Independent States, A Journal of Selected Press Translations,* vol. 2, no. 2, Spring 1992, pp. 33–34). Semivolos suggests that 100 billion rubles out of a Ukrainian GNP of 218.5 billion went to Moscow.

[24] Brumberg, "Not so Free at Last," p. 60.

[25] Ibid., pp. 59–60.

[26] The appearance of self-styled Cossacks, however, is a cause for concern, but so far they have not revealed specific anti-Russian tendencies.

[27] Taylor, "Red Army Blues," p. 3, suggests there were 20 divisions based in Ukraine and 4,000 nuclear warheads. There were 28 air bases and 2–4 naval bases. Ostensibly, the ground- and air-launched tactical nuclear weapons are gone, leaving somewhat more than 1,200 strategic nuclear warheads associated with ballistic missiles and strategic bombers. The status of the Black Sea Fleet's nuclear weapons is unclear.

[28] See Stephen Van Evera, *Managing the Eastern Crisis: Preventing War in the Former Soviet Empire* (Cambridge,

Mass.: MIT Defense and Arms Control Studies Program, January 6, 1992), p. 12.

[29] Security guarantees are an unlikely substitute for an independent Ukrainian deterrent. Recall the endless arguments about the credibility of the US nuclear guarantee to Germany, in which the United States stationed more than 300,000 troops and thousands of tactical nuclear warheads. The US guarantee to Germany was credible, but mainly due to the elaborate measures taken to make it so.

[30] See Steven Miller, "Western Diplomacy and the Soviet Nuclear Legacy," *Survival*, vol. 34, no. 3, Autumn 1992, pp. 21–22, especially footnote 57.

Chapter 7

Beyond Nationalism and Internationalism: Ethnicity and World Order

Pierre Hassner

The terms "ethnicity" and "world order" have one important thing in common: Nobody knows what they mean. Their ambiguity goes beyond the essentially contested character of all political concepts. Both contain a mythical element that tempts one to interpret them ironically or cynically. All political ethnicity is, in a sense, a "fictional identity" or an "imagined community" that creates confusion about family and political ties.[1] In a politically divided world, the temptation to substitute the term "world disorder" for "world order" is at least as legitimate as using the latter when referring to an agreement between a few great powers and an international organization controlled by them. The terms "ethnicity" and "world order" have nonetheless emerged at the center of the international debate in the aftermath of the Cold War. This is testimony to the sudden disappearance of the international community's conceptual and institutional bearings.

BREAKDOWN AND BREAKUP

When empires collapse, when alliances wither away, and when nation-states are in crisis, two contrasting phenomena emerge: the "politics of the soil" and the "politics of the satellite."[2] The former is grounded in the community of the small, face-to-face group—the family or the tribe, the clan or the gang. The latter refers to the growing importance attached to global issues—the fate of the planet, economic and ecological interdependence, mass communications. However, neither the small community nor the world constitute viable, self-sustaining political units. Only intermediate institutions—regions, nations, and, above all, states and international organizations—can function as true international actors and be endowed with legitimate power.

Both their legitimacy and power become suspect, however, when these structures no longer satisfactorily meet the needs of the community or the constraints of interdependence. Yet, who will define these needs and these constraints? US secretaries of state have often asked in exasperation: "Who speaks for Europe?" It is just as fair to ask: "Who speaks and acts for the people or the community? Who can speak and act in the name of world order?" Both these questions are as old as politics. However, they become particularly dramatic and urgent with the emergence of ethnic conflict following the decline of communism and with international attempts to override the traditional barriers of sovereignty through humanitarian intervention and peace enforcement.

The bipolar era severely limited the sovereignty and the freedom of states (particularly within the Soviet sphere), as well as cultural and economic cooperation (at least across the Iron Curtain). Thus, it was natural that communism's decline would encourage the rebirth of nations and increase their openness to external influences. What was unclear was whether the future would feature a new bipolar cleavage (this time based on a North–South confrontation), a new multipolar equilibrium, or global cooperation based on interdependence and a growing sense of international solidarity. The surprise is that, although indications in the direction of each model have emerged, their course has been troubled, distorted, and, in some respects, dominated by another more powerful development—political decomposition and anarchy.

First, there has been the breakdown of communist multinational entities. This occurred in a horrifically bloody and systematic way in Yugoslavia, in a peaceful and hesitant way in Czechoslovakia, and in a disorderly, and only occasionally violent, way in the Soviet Union. Although economic interdependence among former associates remains inevitable, political separation is in the ascendant.

This leads to a second observation: Within and between newly independent nations, conflict is more likely than cooperation. Two factors are decisive in this respect, and this is the heart of the problem of ethnic conflict. First, the Eastern concept of nationhood is an ethnic one (based on common culture defined in terms of race, language, tradition, or religion), rather than a constitutional one (based on state, territory, citizenship, and political principles) as in the West. This is reinforced by a second consideration: Political evolution in the East has been arrested, and ethnic identity has been repressed by decades of ideological and external domination. This explains the aspiration many have to create ethnically homogeneous political entities.

Fulfilling this aspiration is made impossible by the characteristics of the modern world, which make borders more permeable, and by the inextricable overlapping and intertwining of populations within virtually all multinational states. In some cases, this intermingling is a remnant of the ethnic heterogeneity that used to exist throughout Eastern Europe—a heterogeneity that was drastically reduced in Central Europe during and after World War II by the murder of Jews and the expulsion of Germans and that has persisted in the Balkans and the former Soviet Union.

Above all, this intermingling can be traced back to the policies of communist rulers, who moved peoples and borders and generated innumerable irrational enclaves: sometimes through a Machiavellian desire to divide and rule (as in the case of Josef Stalin); sometimes through shortsighted impulsiveness (as in in the case of Nikita Khruschev's gift of Crimea to Ukraine); sometimes through an attempt to counterbalance the dominant national group, while preventing the secession of the others (as in the case of Josip Broz Tito). The existence of large numbers of Krajinas, Sandjaks, Nagorno-Karabakhs, and Dniestrians—of minorities within minorities, each playing the role of victim and oppressor, with the victim's victim appealing to its oppressor's oppressor—makes the attainment of ethnic homogeneity impossible. Any attempt to create it will inevitably be intolerable to minorities and to their neighboring brethren.

In short, ethnic homogeneity is desired, but impossible; heterogeneity is inevitable, but generally rejected—sometimes by all concerned. Provisions for minority rights are usually recommended by external mediators and international organizations. They tend to satisfy neither minority groups, who want independence or union with ethnically related states, nor majority groups, who suspect that steps toward local autonomy will lead to this very result and who want to realize their own hegemonic visions of political unity. The acceptance of ethnic diversity under common laws requires a strong central government, a common ideological bond, or a tradition of tolerance and respect for individual rights. Ideally, all three conditions will be met. All three are lacking in the postcommunist world, hence opening the door to violent conflict.

These problems are not limited to postcommunist states, of course. India attempted with some success to be a model secular state, but with the Congress Party's decline and the rise of Hindu fundamentalism, the prospect that a civil war will develop along religious lines has increased. In Afghanistan, the victory over Soviet forces was only a preface to the war between primarily ethnic and religious factions. The sanctity of Africa's postcolonial boundaries, however arbitrary and however contrary to the ethnic map of the continent, was respected for many years, but here, too, a Pandora's box has been opened, and Ethiopia is now in the process of splitting into ethnically based political entities.

That said, ethnicity is not always the source of anarchic violence. Although in Sudan the ongoing genocide is based on race and religion, in the case of Somalia, it was one of the only true nation-states on the continent, and most of its leaders belong to the same ethnic clan. As in Liberia, the conflict that has erupted in Somalia resembles gang warfare as much as tribalism.

Directly or indirectly, ethnic conflict will not spare the West, however much Western nations may be favored by history, geography, and economic prosperity, if only because of the growing refugee problem. When majorities and minorities cannot live together, the result is the displacement of borders, people, or both. For those who practice "ethnic cleansing," the creation of large numbers of refugees is, in fact, an explicit goal. The result is that the victims of war and ethnic persecution now constitute a third category of refugees, together with political and economic refugees. A new phenomenon in postwar Europe, their plight merges with the great movement of frustrated, hungry, and homeless masses from the East and the South that are knocking at the door of the developed West. Together, they constitute one of the most dramatic phenomena of the current period: a return to great migrations. Unfortunately, this is occurring at a time when the nations of the West are in the throes of both an economic and an identity crisis, the latter provoked by international interdependence and by the impersonal characteristics of modern society. Hence, Western nations tend to limit immigration; they fear, much the same as communist countries, the destabilizing consequences of opening their societies. Economic selfishness, xenophobia, racism, and hatred born of fear of the unknown all work in the direction of exclusion.

Democratic states feel assaulted, both from within and from outside, by demands they feel unable to fulfill. They can satisfy neither their citizens' quest for security and community, nor the cries for help made by newcomers and the victims of war and oppression. The conflicting pressures for opening and closing result in a mixture of paralysis and chaos, a chaos in which displaced persons, stranded between a world that allows or forces them out and one that does not let them in, are only one element. Others include transnational flows, actors (ranging from communication media to financial speculators), and networks of arms and drug dealers. This is a chaos that states seem more and more unable to overcome, even when they are engaged in a common enterprise, such as European integration.

RETURN TO THE MIDDLE AGES?

Historically, every chaotic or anarchic situation has raised a call for some kind of order. The calling into question of sovereignty and state effectiveness is bringing forth demands for supranationality, as well as demands for subnational retrenchment. It is not only the order of Yalta (bipolarity and the Cold War) and the order of Versailles (the borders and states that emerged from the Ottoman and the Austro-Hungarian Empires) that are being challenged. The order of Westphalia—the idea of a system based on territoriality and the sovereignty of states—is also being called into question.

To be sure, the order of Westphalia was a nonegalitarian one in which the great powers took it upon themselves to decide the fate of small nations. However, it was also horizontal in that it did not recognize any authority above the states themselves. States enjoyed a monopoly on the legitimate use of violence within their borders, and they retained a right to use force outside their borders. Today, civil wars and social violence challenge the domestic monopoly, and interdependence, nuclear weapons, democracy, and the evolution of international values raise doubts about the legitimacy of interstate war. Most important, the great achievement of the modern state—the establishment of a neutral authority that ensures the primacy of common citizenship over privileges based on bloodlines and over religious divisions—is being jeopardized both by the trend toward transnational de-territorialization and by the trend toward national, subnational, and ethnic re-territorialization.

The multiplication of different types of actors, loyalties, and conflicts leads to a return in some respects to the sixteenth century, to the power of merchant towns and religious wars. In others respects, it is a return to the Middle Ages when, in contrast to the modern nation-state and its monopoly of violence, order was based on a variety of actors; of authorities, territorial and not territorial; of loyalties; and of rivalries. To some, this holds the promise of more flexibility and tolerance; to others, it evokes memories of the Inquisition and of witch-hunts, of bands of beggars and robbers, of wandering knights and pirates.[3]

If the international community is returning to the Middle Ages, it will be doing so without a pope and without an emperor. In other words, the system will lack a spiritual authority respected by all and capable of inspiring both truces and crusades. The system will also lack a temporal authority capable of putting the sword at the disposal of this inspiration or of arbitrating, in its own name, the innumerable rivalries of a heterogeneous world.

An ambivalent emperor of sorts—the United States—does exist, and there is an aspiring pope and church—the United Nations (UN). Both have enjoyed new preeminence since the end of the bipolar era. Yet, the United States and the United Nations, not unlike most of their medieval predecessors, have insufficient material resources and enjoy insufficient legitimacy, not least from each other, to impose order on the system as a whole.[4] They will be unable to fulfill the functions of a world government or a world federation, which would seem necessary, given the problems of the postnational and postinternational age.

This is most clearly illustrated by the nuclear issue. During the Cold War, the nuclear problem involved, above all, the issue of deterrence, which reinforced the sovereignty of nuclear states and led to a balance that had comparatively little impact on society. The antinuclear protests of the 1980s and the Chernobyl catastrophe, however, began to break down the wall between nuclear issues and society. Moreover, the dissolution of the Soviet Union elevates the problem of nuclear proliferation as an issue that is bound to affect and be affected by domestic anarchy, economic crises, ethnic conflict, religious fanaticism, civil war, the international arms trade, and terrorism. Solutions to the proliferation problem will not be found primarily in a new strategic balance. Effective solutions would require a level of control over societies and transnational flows that would logically mean the need for world government. At a minimum, it would involve the establishment of an international authority capable of controlling and punishing delinquents, such as Iraq.

What are the broader implications of the Iraqi case? On the one hand, a criminal regime has survived a defeat at the hands of a coalition led by the only superpower, the United States, after commiting an act of aggression condemned by the only international authority, the United Nations. On the other hand, it has been subjected to an international embargo, been forced to reveal and dismantle its nuclear installations, and been forced to accept on its territory a zone where foreign powers protect a minority group Iraq has been persecuting.

This paradoxical situation can be interpreted in at least four ways. It can be seen as an anomaly that originated out of a unique constellation of the dominant power's economic and strategic interests. Alternatively, it can be seen as a breakthrough in the evolution of the rule of international law and the development of a true international authority, the United Nations. Possibly it can be seen as a return to the colonial and neocolonial practices of the nineteenth century and the interwar period: the resurrection of practices such as humanitarian intervention and institutions such as the mandate and the protectorate.[5] Finally, it could be seen as a sign that the international community has entered (for the foreseeable future) into a "permanent transition" in which—from the standpoint of functional effectiveness, legitimacy, and power—the national, regional, and global levels will coexist—sometimes in harmony, sometimes in conflict. In this case, ethics and law, politics and economics, humanitarian and military action could be distinguished analytically, but in practice would be inseparable, as would private and public, domestic and foreign, national and international.

International actions in Cambodia, Somalia, and the former Yugoslavia demonstrate that what happened in Iraq cannot be explained solely in terms of US interests. Similarly, neither "rule of law" nor the "neocolonial" interpretation offers a complete explanation of what is occurring in international affairs. To avoid capitulating to confusion, as in the fourth and most tempting interpretation, a few distinctions about the basic dilemmas that now exist will be developed.

INTERPENETRATION AND IDENTITY

What emerges from this discussion is that the international roles of particular types of units—be they nations, regions, ethnic communities, or federations—cannot be judged in the abstract. Their prospects depend on local conditions, historical and geographical, although these in turn are deeply modified by general or global trends. The issue here is the relation between the size and viability of political units, on the one hand, and the impact of factors such as a state crisis, economic recession, migration, mass communications, and the general cultural contradictions of the modern world, on the other.

Earlier observations about ethnicity (homogeneity being desired, but unattainable, and heterogeneity being inevitable, but unacceptable) and about neomedievalism (the ambiguous effects of multiple allegiances) reflect a deeper tension between unity and diversity, which is the signature of current history. Individual and collective selves are divided among multiple allegiances, aspirations, and pressures, yet long for unity. The modern world has a powerful homogenizing influence, particularly in cultural terms, through the revolution in communications; yet, the need for diversity and separation, for distinguishing among "us," "we," and "the others" is felt ever more strongly. In the words of Michael Ignatieff:

> The more evident our common needs as a species become, the more brutal becomes the human insistence on the claims of difference. The centripetal forces of need, labor, and science which are pulling us together as a species are counterbalanced by the centrifugal forces, the claims of tribe, race, class, section, region, and nation, pulling us apart. . . .The economy in which our needs are now satisfied has become global while the polity in which we try to control the pace and development of these needs remains national. Economy has broken away from the reins of polity.[6]

Two theoretical formulations help clarify this insight. Karl Deutsch defined international relations in terms of "the gap between interdependence and control."[7] States have never been able to control the international environment. What is new is, first, that they control it less and less, while being more and more constrained by it; second, that they are less and less capable of controlling their domestic environment, the social groups, or the national minorities that are supposed to be subject to their authority; and, finally, that their plight is shared, with a vengeance, by international authorities such as the United Nations or the European Community (EC). In a forthcoming book, Ole Waever and Barry Buzan focus on the notion of "societal security" or, given present trends, "the social construction of societal insecurity."[8]

These ideas can be further developed by asking what is meant by "interdependence" and "societal." It is useful to distinguish among the interaction of strategies (particularly diplomatic and military), the interdependence of interests (particularly economic), and the interpenetration of societies. Although "the gap between interdependence and control" is felt at all three levels, it is most acute at the third. The interpenetration of societies is the driving force behind many current conflicts, and this interpenetration is fed, of course, by its economic and strategic consequences.

The interpenetration of societies can be seen in the flow of money and goods, but even more so in terms of people, communications, and cultural models. Whose security or whose identity is threatened by this interpenetration? Here it is useful to consider the distinction between community (*Gemeinschaft*) and society (*Gesellschaft*).

Society is essentially a network of relations of exchange, competition, and cooperation between individuals and institutions. It is increasingly assuming a global character, as Ignatieff points out. A community, being based on family or familylike ties, aspires to identity, unity, and autonomy. Hence, it feels threatened by modern society with its constant flow of people, goods, and messages, with its bureaucratic and technological constraints, with its economic and cultural appeals. In turn, defensive and aggressive reactions threaten the normal functioning of an open society, as well as the freedom and mobility of its individuals.

The nation-state represents a compromise between ethnic communities and societal requirements. Through its language, its education, its shared memories and myths, it retains some relation to its roots and some elements of warmth and community. Yet, through its bigger size, its impersonal laws, and its bureaucratic organization, it comes closer to fulfilling the requirements of modern society. When the nation-state leans too much in the latter direction, it contributes to the revival of ethnicity. It is clear that the European Community, its name notwithstanding, is more of a society; it is based on individualism, instrumental rationality, and cooperation and lacks the myths, symbols, and affectivity of a community. Conversely, ethnic and national groups struggling for unification or independence are, or aspire to be, communities; they lack the dimensions, institutions, and, above all, the degree of socialization found in societies.

Issues of nationalism, regionalism, and internationalism have to be seen in terms of this distinction. Regional solutions are positive if the societies concerned emphasize integration and the development of cross-border economic, social, and cultural ties between individuals and groups. European integration may be threatening to the nation-state, but it has contributed to Western liberal political culture—a culture based on peace and trade, compromise and cooperation. It has contributed to the devaluation of historical and territorial quarrels and to a proliferation of personal, cultural, and economic ties involving individuals, firms, and regions. It has made war among member-states inconceivable.

Conversely, regionalizing the Yugoslav war would almost certainly mean broadening the war, not ending it through the efforts of neighboring states. In short, regionalization is stabilizing when it extends, encourages, and builds upon networks of cooperative ties; it is destabilizing when it extends, encourages, and builds upon traditional, national, territorial, or cultural cleavages, alignments, and conflicts.

It is tempting to see the economically developed, liberal Western center and, particularly, the European Community as a society, dominated by the postnational, posthistorical logic of peaceful integration, economic interdependence, and societal interpenetration, while viewing the less-developed, post-totalitarian, or predemocratic periphery, particularly the Balkans, as being composed of antagonistic communities dominated by the nationalistic logic of violent disintegration. This corresponds to Ernest Gellner's notion of "federal affluence." Gellner argues that nationalism declines in regions in which nationality has acquired a safe home base, and economic inequalities are reduced; it is exacerbated in places in which people feel insecure in their cultural identity, are threatened, or are still nation-building and state-building through war, genocide, and ethnic cleansing.[9]

Although largely true, this view is too simple. No region of the world, particularly Europe, is entirely dominated either by cooperation or by conflict. In Western Europe, the recession has created economic inequalities, psychological insecurity, and a search for scapegoats. The prospect of open-ended integration and interdependence has led to a retrenchment and reaffirmation of ethnic ties in ways not unlike what one sees elsewhere in Europe. At the same time, Eastern Europe is part of the modern, interdependent world. Examples of attempted and successful economic cooperation are found side by side with intense ethnic conflicts. Even conflict-ridden regions, such as the Balkans and the Caucasus, are involved in the cooperative Black Sea initiative being promoted by Turkey. Most important, Western and Eastern Europe have a great deal of influence on each other. The processes of Western integration and Eastern disintegration are linked in many paradoxical ways, and they may lead to a no less paradoxical result: a mixture of interpenetration and convergence, on the one hand, separation and mutual rejection on the other.

In the long run, the only solution is the progressive integration of the center and the periphery. This has already taken place in Asia with Japan and, later, the newly industrialized countries becoming active and essential parts of the international capitalist system. In Europe, the most important contribution the European Community can make to peaceful development in its eastern and southern peripheries is to allow its European neighbors free access to EC markets and to hold out the prospect of full membership for those who have reached the required threshold in terms of market economy and political pluralism.

In the meantime, the expansion of relations between East and West, as illustrated by the case of German reunification, is likely to be destabilizing. Integrating economically advanced sectors of the periphery into the center will contribute to the disintegration of the periphery and of its constituent units, particularly when they include great regional disparities. The sudden opening of Eastern economies to Western competition has, more often than not, brought them close to economic collapse. At the social, cultural, and political levels, former Soviet President Mikhail Gorbachev's opening to the West, which was supposed to revitalize the Soviet system, was a powerful contributor to its demise.

In the East, the opening of borders, increased economic hardship, and violent ethnic conflicts, encouraged by the breakdown of supranational empires and dictatorships, have produced a flood of emigrants and refugees surging toward the West. These population movements, in turn, exacerbate societal insecurities in the West, both in practical terms (competition for jobs or housing) and in terms of intangible fears about losing ethnic or cultural identities. This can lead to xenophobia and violence, as seen in Germany, thus creating moral anxieties and divisions in society. In addition, the mood of national retrenchment and the absence of European and Western solidarity in handling the refugee and migration problems have adverse consequences for European integration, as shown by various reactions to the Maastricht Treaty. In the West and the East, at the center and the periphery, cultural identity and societal security have become central themes of political attitudes and conflicts. The consequence is mutual resentment. If this process gets out of control, the two halves of Europe might be tempted to turn their backs on each other.

Isolationism, however, is no more a solution at the regional and global levels than at the ethnic and national levels. Short of applying Federal Republic of Yugoslavia (Serbia and Montenegro) President Dobrica Cosic's rationale for ethnic cleansing—"the only way we can stand each other is by putting borders between us"[10]—or rebuilding the Iron Curtain, there is no alternative to trying to manage refugee and migration problems. Cooperation between home and host countries and efforts to remedy the root causes of these problems, both economic and political, are needed. Various instruments should be employed, ranging from economic assistance and encouraging pluralistic tolerance to military intervention against states whose practices most disrupt regional security. In the final analysis, societal security cannot exist in a vacuum: It is inseparable from state security, from economic security, and, last but not least, from individual security.

This is not to say that these various dimensions of security necessarily work in harmony. In particular, one important development in modern societies is the increasing divergence between political and cultural identities. The preferred solution is the preservation of national cultures and identities within a common, postnational political framework. It is possible, however, that the homogenizing forces of modern society would dominate national cultures; it is precisely their insecurity about the resilience of their real cultural identity that leads nations and ethnic groups to invent mythical ones and to define themselves with respect to equally mythical enemies. Extreme nationalism, in fact, is very often a reaction to national decline.

A reasonable compromise between those two visions would be Anthony Smith's idea of nurturing "families of cultures."[11] European nations would maintain their respective cultural identities, but would increasingly emphasize their common features. However, what has not been examined in this context are the political consequences of this proximity, both among European nations and between Europe and the rest of the world. Would the idea of a European family of cultures lead to retrenchment, confrontation (for example, with Islam), or to a new sense of mission toward the East and South? The danger here is that it might exacerbate the very tensions it is meant to mitigate.

INTERPENETRATION AND INTERVENTION

The effects of interpenetration on the demand for, and the chances of, intervention in foreign conflicts are paradoxical: Interpenetration strengthens the demand for intervention, while making diplomatic and military action more difficult.

The demands are strengthened by the fact that the revolution in mass communications and the declining significance of physical distances due to modern technological advances have had the effect of bringing different cultural, psychological, and historical worlds into more frequent collision. Prosperous, peaceful societies cannot ignore the horrors of hunger and genocide that occur in nearby regions, which are relayed by television every night, nor can they accept the relaxed cynicism of diplomats and historians, for whom these horrors are seen as inevitable in some regions (such as the Balkans) and as an unavoidable part of the nation-building process. Western societies cannot help interpreting these horrors in terms of their own historical experiences (in particular, with the racist doctrines and crimes of the Nazis) and with regard to their global and individualistic ideals. In addition, the parties to these violent conflicts insist that they be considered an integral part of the European and international communities.

However, the qualities of Western societies that lead to public pressure to "do something" also put severe limits on Western abilities to translate words into practice. First, Western cultures based on relativism and compromise find it hard to understand codes of behavior based on fanaticism, machismo, and paranoia, as well as political structures based on ethnic loyalties. Consequently, Western societies find it difficult to adapt expectations, threats, and promises to the conditions at hand. Between dealing with members of other cultures or followers of other ideologies as if they were Western democrats and simply dismissing them as crazy and unpredictable, there is often very little middle ground. As a result, the West rarely deals effectively with leaders such as the Ayatollah Khomeini, Slobodan Milosevic, and Saddam Hussein.

Second, democracy, individualism, and the economic (rather than military) orientation of Western societies make military intervention against nondemocratic states difficult, especially if military operations promise to be lengthy and costly. Seeing concentration camps on television screens often galvanizes an interest in punishing war criminals, but seeing Western soldiers die almost always leads to revulsion, no matter how popular or morally justified the original intervention. As a result, the West consistently overestimates the value of economic sanctions and is extremely reluctant to make military threats. In turn, this provokes contempt and possible miscalculation on the part of foreign leaders, who often boast of their disregard for human life, and may cause them to discount the West's ability to accept sacrifices, to suffer pain, and to take risks.

Third, because the West is not inclined to embark on colonial adventures again (attempting to establish military domination over the poor and underdeveloped), yet also finds inaction in the face of barbarity and chaos unacceptable, military intervention is seen as a last resort and the provisional interlude in a long-range task that is essentially civilian—that is, pacification through integration. Whether to make intervention unnecessary or to limit its damage, a policy of assistance aimed at integration is needed. Intervention without integration leads either to chaos or permanent military occupation. Employing a combination of intervention and integration was one of the great strengths of empires. Nation-states have much more difficulty doing this, especially when they are relatively prosperous, but are suffering from economic and identity crises (and, therefore, are worried about jobs and national unity).

The only way to avoid unilateral intervention, immediate integration, or a relapse into anarchy is to shift the task of protecting and administering troubled areas to the international community. This means a return to a system of protectorates (as practiced under the Concert of Europe), mandates (as practiced under the League of Nations), and trusteeships (perhaps using the UN Trusteeship Council). The difference between earlier efforts and the current situation is that it would now be difficult to grant single states mandates or trusteeships over others. Only the United Nations can play this role, which it is already trying to do in Cambodia with very limited success. The United Nations, however, lacks the resources, both financial and human, and the independent authority to carry out such tasks. Even if reformed and considerably strengthened, the United Nations cannot be expected to control and run Bosnia, Kosovo, Somalia, Nagorno-Karabakh, and all the other trouble spots where one or more parties have asked for protection.[12]

In most cases today, only the United States can organize and carry out military interventions on a grand scale, only the European Community can employ conditional integration, and only the United Nations (or, less plausibly, the Conference on Security and Cooperation in Europe) can give legitimacy either to military interventions or to the establishment of protectorates in chaotic regions. Although each of these three actors faces great problems in doing their share, because of both internal weaknesses and the intractable nature of the conflicts they face, they have even more trouble in agreeing on a division of tasks and areas of competence.

LEGITIMACY AND POWER

This leads to the final contradiction between the growing popularity of the idea of "world order," on the one hand, and the growing fragmentation of the world itself, on the other: To find legitimacy, military intervention must be based on universal principles, while its implementation depends on a particular constellation of power and interest.

The legitimacy of international military intervention is no longer denied, as it once was, because it challenges state sovereignty or the principle of noninterference in internal affairs. Only a few years ago, the only justification for international military actions (other than wars of liberation and independence) was self-defense; Vietnam's intervention against Pol Pot and Tanzania's against Idi Amin Dada were presented to the international community as responses to aggression. Recently, however, there has been the passage of UN resolutions calling for free access to victims (43/131), the establishment of humanitarian corridors (45/100), military action to repel Iraq's aggression against Kuwait (678), international action to protect Iraq's Kurds (688), and military measures "to restore as soon as possible conditions of safety for humanitarian relief operations in Somalia" (794).

Today, the prevailing international consensus accepts that intervention may be legitimate in three types of cases: in cases in which aggression is committed against an internationally recognized state (the Iraqi invasion of Kuwait); in cases in which states massacre their own citizens, whether for ideological or ethnic reasons (Cambodia); and in cases in which a breakdown in law and order leads to anarchy and massive suffering (Somalia). The former Yugoslavia fits all three categories. The issue now is less whether intervention is legitimate (although means, costs, and risks remain controversial), than who should do it and to what regional or international end.

After the fall of communism ended the bipolar confrontation, there was a happy coincidence, at least on paper, between international power and international legitimacy. The international power structure has been dominated by a great-power concert, led by the United States. Decisions about the legitimacy of international actions were supposed to be made by the international community, represented by the United Nations, which itself was represented by the Security Council. This coincidence, which was exploited extensively by US President George Bush and perhaps even more so by French President François Mitterrand—ever prone to speak of the commands of international law and the UN mandate—is likely to be short lived. Russia and China are not going to forego the veto forever. Indeed, Russia has already been exercising de facto veto-power over UN and American policies on Bosnia. Challenges to US leadership, from Russia, China, or other powers, are bound to multiply with the passage of time. Moreover, given the present composition of the Security Council, its present resources, and its present rules of engagement, the United Nations is not particularly credible or effective. Finally, the previous and current secretary-generals of the United Nations have not seemed particularly enthusiastic about US initiatives any more than the United

States has been about UN Secretary-General Boutros Boutros-Ghali's *Agenda for Peace.*

A parting of the ways, leading to a two-track approach to world order, is therefore likely and perhaps desirable. In some cases, Western democracies, including new democracies ready to act in concert with the West, may have to take action without waiting for UN authorization. In cases such as these, collective actions would be preferable. Even then, if it is to avoid a replay of the nineteenth century, the West would need to find a way to legitimate its actions by some universal authority.

For the second track, the United Nations would have to be thoroughly remolded: in its Security Council permanent membership to include Germany, Japan, and some powers from the developing world; in its institutional mechanisms; in its finances; and through the creation, as proposed by Boutros-Ghali, of standing or preassigned military forces capable of carrying out peace-enforcement missions. Unless this process leads to the establishment of world government, the UN decision to use force will still be controlled by member-states. As a result, the decision to use force will inevitably bear the mark of parochial interests, as well as universal principles.

This is particularly true because these universal principles are too general and too contradictory to provide specific answers to the problems of ethnicity and world order. Previous architects of the European order thought they had discovered answers to these problems. For Klemens von Metternich and the Vienna Congress in 1815, it was dynastic legitimacy. For Woodrow Wilson at Versailles in 1918, it was the right to self-determination. Both architects had the power to redraw the map of Europe according to these principles. The victors of the Cold War do not have this power, nor do they have answers to some of the following critical questions: What is a nation? Which groups have the right to form nation-states? How should the international community arbitrate between conflicting claims of historical legitimacy, self-determination, economic viability, or regional security? How should border modifications and population transfers be decided?

The new concert of powers, acting in the name of the international community, can indicate a strong preference for negotiation and opposition to the unilateral use of force. It can and should rule out certain evils (such as genocide) and the use of certain means (such as nuclear war). The compromises it will have to make between principles and the commands of peace and justice will be hard to reach, however. In addition, it will often be hard-pressed to explain why it is acting in some cases and not others.

Because it is not possible to intervene whenever intervention can be justified or is desirable, one should not draw the conclusion that intervention should never be practiced, nor should one conclude that the international community can afford to stop paying attention to precedents and the consequences of its actions. The deterrent or demonstration effects of actions should not be discounted.

This only underlines the fragmented and contradictory character of the international system today. First, problems—and often solutions—are increasingly global, although power continues to belong to particular actors and will continue to do so for the foreseeable future.

Second, international affairs are increasingly complex and multidimensional, but international authorities and institutions are (and will continue to be) limited and, more often than not, one-dimensional. For example, an international agency under UN auspices can manage nuclear energy, but this agency would not be prepared to meet the diffuse and complex challenge of managing nuclear proliferation, which involves transnational society at every level. The same is true for international institutions in charge of refugees and minority problems.

During the Cold War, most conflicts tended to be seen through the prism of East–West confrontation. Today, principles are much more universal—and universally accepted—but conflicts are more idiosyncratic. Notions such as "collective security" and "humanitarian assistance" are constantly open to suspicion and to the charge of hypocrisy. This is not surprising. The international order is not immune from the tension between universal rules and particular cases, between absolute duties and relative interests.

Acknowledgments

Parts of this article draw on "Par delà le National et l'Internationale la Dérision et l'Espoir," *Universalia 1993* (Paris: Encyclopaedia Universalia, *forthcoming*).

Notes

[1] See E. Balibar and I. Wallerstein, *Race—Nation—Classe: Les Identités Ambigües* (Paris: La Découverte, 1988); Benedict Anderson, *Imagined Communities: Reflections on the Origin and Spread of Nationalism* (London: Verso Press, 1983).

[2] See N. Gardels, "Two Concepts of Nationalism: An Interview with Isaiah Berlin," *New York Review of Books,* November 21, 1991, p. 22.

[3] On neomedievalism, see O. Waever, "Territory, Authority, and Identity: The Late Twentieth Century Emergence of Neo-Medieval Political Structures in Europe," Paper presented at the first General Conference of the European Peace Research Association (EUPRA), Florence, November 8–10, 1991. See also the special issue, "Empire et Nations," of *Commentaire*, vol. 15, no. 57, Spring 1992, especially the contribution by A. Winkler, "L'Empire Revient," p. 17.

4 See Leslie Gelb, "Tailoring US Role at the UN," *International Herald Tribune*, December 2–3, 1991.

5 See Ghassan Salame, "Un Retour aux Mandates?" Paper presented at the New Strategic Debate Conference, organized by the French Ministry of Defense, Paris, September 29, 1992.

6 Michael Ignatieff, *The Needs of Strangers* (London: Hogarth Press, 1984), pp. 130–131.

7 Karl Deutsch, *The Analysis of International Relations* (New Haven, Conn.: Yale University Press, 1965).

8 Ole Waever, Barry Buzan, et al., *Identity, Migration, and the New Security Agenda in Europe* (London: Frances Pinter, 1993).

9 Ernest Gellner, "A Year in the Soviet Union," *Contention,* Winter 1992, pp. 115–116.

10 Quoted by Milos Vasic in *The Independent,* May 19, 1992.

11 Anthony D. Smith, *National Identity* (London: Penguin Books, 1992), pp. 171–176.

12 For more detailed discussion, see Adam Roberts, "The United Nations and International Security," chapter 11 in this volume.

Chapter 8

Ethnic Conflict and Refugees
Kathleen Newland

There are millions of people in the world today who have been driven from their homes because they belong to a particular ethnic group. Ethnic diversity does not automatically produce conflict, and ethnic conflict does not automatically produce violence. Ethnic violence, however, very often produces refugees. The total number of refugees worldwide has grown dramatically in the 1980s and early 1990s: from about 8 million at the end of the 1970s to more than 18 million in 1993—and this does not include an even larger number of internally displaced people. At a time when many of the ideologically inspired conflicts that produced refugees in the Cold War era are winding down, there is great concern that ethnic conflict will generate large and growing numbers of refugees. Is this concern well founded? An examination of the relationship between ethnic conflict and coerced population movements may help to answer the question.

This article will proceed in five sections. The first will clarify some terms and discuss ways of understanding both "refugees" and "ethnicity," as well as the connection between the two. The second will examine the impact of ethnic conflict on refugee movements. The third section will look at the recent growth of refugee populations generated by ethnic conflict and assess the prospects for the immediate future. Section four will review the international mechanisms for responding to ethnic conflict. The final section will evaluate some recommendations for international actions to address these problems.

DEFINITIONS
The definition of a refugee included in the 1951 United Nations (UN) Convention Relating to the Status of Refugees is the most widely recognized legal formulation; in practice, however, many states and international organizations operate with a wider understanding of the term. According to the 1951 convention, a refugee is a person who "owing to a well-founded fear of being persecuted for reasons of race, religion, na-

tionality, membership of a particular social group, or political opinion, is outside the country of his nationality and is unable or, owing to such fear, unwilling to avail himself of the protection of that country."[1] The Organization of African Unity's 1969 Convention on Refugee Problems in Africa accepts the UN criteria, but also recognizes as a refugee a person who has had to flee his or her country "owing to external aggression, occupation, foreign domination, or events seriously disturbing public order. . . ."[2]

In 1984, the Central American nations, along with Mexico and Panama, adopted a declaration that built upon the Organization of African Unity (OAU) definition, adding to it the additional criteria of "massive violation of human rights."[3] Although not a legally binding instrument, the Cartagena Declaration has become the basis for refugee policy in that region. The United Nations respects the OAU and Cartagena definitions when working in these regions, and some argue that the enlarged definitions have achieved some status in customary international law. The UN General Assembly and the secretary-general have, on an ad hoc basis, frequently asked the office of the UN High Commissioner for Refugees (UNHCR) to concern itself with groups of people who are not covered by the narrower definition of the 1951 convention, including even some groups who have not left their own countries, but are internally displaced.

The definitional issue is important because, as political scientists Aristide Zolberg, Astri Suhrke, and Sergio Aguayo have written, "Refugee status is a privilege or entitlement, giving those who qualify access to certain scarce resources or services outside their own country, such as admission into another country ahead of a long line of claimants, legal protection abroad, and often some material assistance from public or private agencies."[4] They identify three groups who are likely to become refugees: dissidents, target minorities, and victims of violence. A fourth category, the victims of massive human rights abuses, can be added. The first two of these are covered by the 1951 convention as victims of persecution, the third was codified in the OAU Convention, and the fourth was identified in the Cartagena Declaration. What people in all four groups have in common, and what sets them apart from other kinds of migrants, is that they cannot rely on the protection of their own governments.

Although the 1951 convention requires people to have crossed an international border in order to avail themselves of the protection and assistance to which refugee status entitles them, in practice, it is becoming increasingly common for people to be assisted within the territory of their own states, as seen today in Bosnia-Herzegovina, northern Iraq, and Sri Lanka. In some cases (Sri Lanka and Bosnia), international assistance is rendered with the consent of the government of origin; in others, assistance is given in areas effectively detached from the sovereignty of the state (northern Iraq); in still others, the state does not hold sway over large swaths of territory (Sudan). In the most extreme cases, such as Somalia, the state has ceased to exist in functional terms.

James Hathaway argues that the drafters of the 1951 convention had specific and limited aims. They did not intend to try to protect people against every form of serious harm, but concerned themselves with the risks that people face when the state to which they belong cannot or will not fulfill the basic duty of protection it owes to its own population. In that situation, refugee law is designed to substitute the protection of the international community for national protection. It is a "response to disenfranchisement from the usual benefits of nationality."[5]

It is this relationship between the refugee and the state in which the refugee claims nationality that makes ethnicity such a salient factor in refugee problems: In many cases, ethnicity is used to define who is entitled to nationality.

Ethnicity itself is an imprecise concept. Generally, ethnic groups are identified, by their own members or by others, primarily in cultural terms such as language, religion, national origin, social organization, tribe, or race.[6] Few of these criteria are immutable. Groups assimilate or differentiate over time, with cultural markers acquiring or losing significance in response to changing circumstances. Different ways of thinking about ethnicity lead to different conclusions about the nature of ethnic conflict. Rudolfo Stavenhagen identifies three approaches:

- Ethnicity is an inherent, primordial affiliation responding to a deep psychological need for a sense of belonging and security within a community. Different, often hostile, rules of behavior apply to the "other" outside the group. In this view, latent conflict is inherent in ethnic diversity and is only kept in check by external authority.
- Ethnicity is a framework of social organization through which people relate to members of their immediate communities and to those outside. The boundaries of ethnic affiliation are defined by society and may be quite flexible. Ethnic conflicts are conflicts among different types of social organization.
- Ethnicity is a political and economic resource, a major factor in the distribution of power and wealth. A group may emphasize its ethnicity when it is useful and downplay it when it is seen as a handicap. Ethnic conflict is usually defensive or opportunistic, a tool for political mobilization aimed at preserving or capturing resources.[7]

In examining the relationship between ethnic conflict and refugees, the third approach is the most useful, for it emphasizes that ethnicity can be an important determinant of privilege and entitlement.

THE IMPACT OF ETHNIC CONFLICT
ON REFUGEE MOVEMENTS

The position that the state and the government of the day take on ethnic issues does much to establish the extent to which ethnicity can be used as a resource. A strong emphasis on an inclusive national identity that transcends ethnic particularism may devalue ethnicity as a political currency, particularly if it is coupled with effective antidiscrimination provisions in law. However, even in these cases, ethnic affiliations remain potentially powerful tools for the mobilization of political support for governments or for specific parties or politicians. Particularly when control of the state is contested, exploitation of the ethnic factor often proves irresistible. When struggles for power degenerate into violence, supporters of particular contenders identified by their ethnic affiliation may be targeted for persecution or violent attack—and flee as a result.

The relationship between states and ethnic groups is central to the consideration of the role of ethnic conflict in generating refugee movements because refugees are defined by their relationship to the state of which they are citizens (or, if stateless, in which they normally reside). Refugees are people who, for the reasons discussed above, cannot assume protection by their own states. In many refugee crises of the modern era, ethnicity has been one, if not the major, criterion according to which people have been denied the protection of their own governments. Three patterns stand out.

In an ethnocratic state, members of groups other than the dominant one are exposed to discrimination at best and to forced assimilation, persecution, expulsion, or violence at worst. In these situations, the state may not acknowledge a responsibility to protect those whom it defines as nonnationals. In other cases, the mechanisms of the state are captured by a single ethnic group (or a coalition), which uses them to further its own interests at the expense of others. Ethnic conflict is likely to result when the efforts of subordinate groups to gain access to power and resources meet with resistance from the dominant group. In still other situations, the state fails to mediate conflict among ethnic groups because it is incapable of, or uninterested in, doing so or because it is in sympathy with one of the contenders.

It is important to distinguish between the unwillingness of a state to protect its citizens and its inability to do so. Either may entitle those who flee to "substitute protection" provided under refugee law; however, "unwillingness" should subject the state to the approbation of the international community, while "incapacity" should lead to assistance rather than sanction.

Helsinki Watch, the monitoring group set up in 1978 to track compliance with the human rights provisions of the Helsinki Accords among the
signatory countries, offers an example of the manipulation of the ethnic
factor in its description of Slobodan Milosevic's policies in Yugoslavia:

> After his rise to power as president of Serbia in 1987, President
> Milosevic embarked on a series of moves to extend his power through-
> out Yugoslavia, with little regard for the human rights of non-Serbs or
> those Serbs opposed to his policies. Milosevic's dogmatic communism
> gave way to strident nationalism. Through an incessant propaganda
> campaign in the press in the late 1980s and early 1990s, the Serbian
> government repeatedly manipulated the patriotism of its people and
> exaggerated the scope and nature of human rights abuses against Serbs
> in Kosovo, Croatia, and Bosnia-Herzegovina . . . . The exaggeration
> and misrepresentation of human rights abuses against Serbs was used
> by Milosevic to stir up national passions and thereby to consolidate or
> extend his power in Kosovo, Croatia, and Bosnia-Herzegovina.[8]

Milosevic's campaign, supposedly designed to protect Serbs, ultimately
had the opposite effect. When hostilities commenced, Milosevic's policies were cited to justify the persecution of Serbian minorities in various
parts of Yugoslavia.

It is fundamental to the idea of sovereignty that the state is the protector
of the rights of its citizens and that only citizens have full rights within the
state. The idea of the state as the protector of the rights of citizens, in
combination with the ideology of ethnic nationalism (in which ethnicity
defines nationality), leads to the denial of state protection for ethnic
minorities. For example, one current justification offered by Serbian
nationalists for their denial of rights to ethnic Albanians in Kosovo—
rights that they insist should be accorded to ethnic Serbs in Croatia—is
that Serbs in Yugoslavia are a nation, whereas Albanians are merely a
minority group.[9] Minorities have no right in international law (or Yugoslav law) to self-determination. It is then but a short step to deny them any
rights at all. Needless to say, this kind of logic inspires secessionism
among minority groups, so that they too can claim nationally guaranteed
rights in their own nation-states.

Zolberg, Suhrke, and Aguayo identify four main types of ethnic conflict, each associated with distinct refugee problems.[10]

The Explosion of Ethnic Hierarchies

In this pattern, social class and ethnic affiliation coincide in one of two
forms: either a ruling minority or a trading minority. The first exploits its
privilege to extract resources from the ruled; the second acts either as an

exploitative bourgeoisie or an unpopular intermediary between rulers and peasants. This type of conflict often has a revolutionary character and involves the elimination of the dominant minority group through massacre, forced expulsion, or coerced flight. The overthrow of the Tutsi in Rwanda and the Buganda in Uganda, and the attacks against the Arabs in Zanzibar and the ethnic Chinese in Indonesia, fall into this category. South Africa holds out the prospect of a violent overthrow of white minority rule if efforts at constitutional reform fail.

Target Minorities

Certain ethnic groups may be seen as an obstacle to nation-building, incapable of being part of a newly constructed, unitary national identity. The Jews in Nazi Europe are the prime historical example, but other groups—the Armenians in the Ottoman Empire of the late nineteenth and early twentieth centuries, Gypsies in Nazi Europe, ethnic Turks in Bulgaria, and Bahais in Iran—are among those who have been "defined out" of citizenship. Also at risk are indigenous peoples, although they have not often become refugees in large numbers.

Communal Conflict

Groups involved in communal conflict are not necessarily hierarchically related. Recurrent conflict between them may have to be mediated by the central government. If the government is not willing to do so or is too weak, "ethnic cleansing" or other forms of coerced separation of populations may be the result, sometimes leading to refugee flows on a massive scale—as in Palestine and Punjab in 1948, and Bosnia-Herzegovina today.

Separatism

Attempts to secede are likely to arise when large groups are regionally concentrated, and central power is perceived to be working against the interest of their members. Eritrea, southern Sudan, northern Sri Lanka, East Bengal, and Biafra are examples. If the central government is insensitive to the grievances of a regional ethnic grouping, and resistant to the idea of mediation and redress, armed conflict often results. Refugees may flee the violence of secessionist wars or the aftermath of a failed secessionist move if they become target minorities as a result.

Ethnicity is an important factor, not only in causing people to flee, but also in determining their choice of, and reception in, countries of asylum. People compelled to leave their own homes will seek refuge in regions populated by ethnically related peoples if possible. Moreover, receiving countries are often more receptive to asylum-seekers of their own ethnicity. As Gil Loescher points out, "In the Third World, the remarkable receptivity provided to millions of Afghans in Pakistan and Iran, to ethnic kin from Bulgaria in Turkey, to Ethiopians in the Sudan, to Ogadeni Ethiopians in Somalia, to southern Sudanese in Uganda, to Issaq Somalis in Djibouti, and to Mozambicans in Malawi has been facilitated by the ethnic and linguistic characteristics that they share with their hosts."[11] The same might be said of the more than 200,000 Burmese Muslim refugees from Arakan Province who have fled to neighboring Bangladesh, or the Krahn tribespeople from Liberia who have found asylum in Côte d'Ivoire.

There are important exceptions to the generalization of welcoming neighbor countries, however, particularly if the ethnic affiliations spanning a border concern a disaffected minority group in the receiving country (for example, the Kurds in Turkey) or if a delicate balance among ethnic groups in the receiving country risks becoming unbalanced by an influx of people from one of its constituent groups. This, in part, explains the unwillingness of Malaysia to accept Sino-Vietnamese refugees. The only country in the region that freely accepted Vietnamese refugees in 1979–1980 was China, when 260,000 ethnic Chinese crossed the northern border. Indeed, some countries attach such importance to common ethnicity that they do not regard ethnic compatriots fleeing from other countries to the "home" country as refugees. Germany, for example, offers citizenship to all ethnic Germans who wish to return (although it is now contemplating a tightening of eligibility), as does Israel to all Jews. Ethnic Russians who leave other republics that were once part of the Soviet Union have the automatic right of citizenship in Russia.

The discussion thus far has focused on the role that ethnic conflict plays in generating refugees. However, it is also worth noting the role that refugees play in sustaining, if not creating, ethnic conflict. Sometimes, refugee–warrior communities actively engage in cross-border hostilities (sometimes with the compliance of host governments) that continue the conflict that caused their group to leave. Refugee camps themselves occasionally see fighting between rival ethnic groups: for example, as seen between Gari and Borana tribespeople from Ethiopia in camps along the Kenyan border.

THE GROWTH OF REFUGEE POPULATIONS GENERATED BY ETHNIC CONFLICTS

The list of ethnic conflicts that generate substantial numbers of refugees has grown in recent years. It now includes conflicts in Armenia, Azerbaijan, Bhutan, Burma, Ethiopia, Georgia, Iraq, Sri Lanka, Sudan, and, of course, former Yugoslavia. This list is far from comprehensive. It is, however, important to recall that ethnic dynamics are not the primary cause of the most serious refugee crises of the past 20 years: Somalia, Vietnam's second wave of "boat people," Cambodia, Central America, Afghanistan, and Haiti.

There are forces at work in contemporary world politics contributing to both the growth and the decline of refugee-producing ethnic conflicts. It is difficult to predict which will predominate. Forces that contribute to the growth of refugee-producing ethnic conflicts include the breakup of the Soviet empire and increased competition for economic resources.

Waves of state formation typically follow the disintegration of empires, as aspiring nationalities attempt to seize a historic opportunity to create their own nation-states. Ethnic conflict is common when boundaries are redrawn, and, as discussed in the previous section, the consolidation of national identities that follows is often exclusive, leaving minority groups exposed. The former Soviet Union has tremendous potential for ethnic conflict: It contained some 200 ethnic groups, 15 republics, and 38 autonomous regions. Stalinist policies—russification and forced relocation of various national groups—left many vulnerable minorities. One estimate is that as many as 65 million people were residing outside the areas of their ethnic origin at the time the Soviet Union ceased to exist.[12]

The ways in which successor states deal with nationality issues, citizenship, and minority rights will largely determine whether or not ethnic conflicts develop—and whether those that do develop descend into persecution and violence, sending frightened people across borders to seek protection. A number of refugee-producing conflicts are already under way. Most notably, the struggle between Armenia and Azerbaijan over the enclave of Nagorno-Karabakh has displaced more than 500,000 people. The entire Azeri population of Armenia has fled, as have about 300,000 Armenians who used to live in Azerbaijan. In neither case have the refugees been forced to rely on the international community for protection, however, because the governments of the two republics have established refugee affairs offices to help with resettlement. Although their legal status is not in doubt, the assistance aspect of their plight is serious because the economies of both Azerbaijan and Armenia are in grave difficulty.[13]

Ethnic violence in Georgia has displaced 100,000 South Ossetians (most have gone to Russia's North Ossetia Autonomous Republic) and 18,000 Georgians. Meskhetian Turks once resident in Uzbekistan have been forced to flee, mostly to Azerbaijan. Other hot spots where tensions along ethnic lines are simmering include the Dniestr Republic and the Chechen-Ingush Autonomous Republic.[14]

In general, citizens of the former Soviet Union have fewer opportunities to gain refugee status than they did during the Cold War period. In most cases, they are now subject to the normal determination procedures that other asylum-seekers face. An exception applies to Jews, ethnic Germans, Greeks, and Armenians, who are able to take advantage of "right of return" conventions in Israel, Germany, Greece, and Armenia. Approximately 160,000 ethnic Germans left for Germany in 1991 and 167,000 Jews for Israel. The United States still accepts some former Soviet citizens for resettlement under its refugee admissions program, mostly Jews or Evangelical Christians.[15]

The former communist states of Eastern Europe also have a volatile ethnic mix, with a strong potential for displacement; this potential has already been realized most spectacularly in the former Yugoslavia. More than 3 million people were displaced within the borders of the former Yugoslav territories at the beginning of 1993, and another 600,000 had sought refuge in other countries.[16] The largest number of those affected are Muslims from Bosnia-Herzegovina, the second largest group is made up of Croatians, and the third largest is comprised of Serbs. The potential for displacement in former Yugoslavia is far from exhausted, however. Ethnic tensions are high in the former autonomous province of Kosovo following Serbia's brutal revocation of its autonomy. Kosovo has a population that is 78 percent Albanian and 15 percent Serb and Montenegrin. People in the province of Vojvodina are also tense; the 22 percent of its population that is ethnic Hungarian fears that it, too, could become the target of an ethnic cleansing campaign by the Serbian majority. Montenegro and Macedonia both have Muslim minorities of about 13 percent and Serbian minorities of about 3 percent.[17] Other minority groups in Central and Eastern Europe feel themselves to be at risk. They include the following: the Hungarian minorities in Slovakia and Romania, as well as Serbia; ethnic Turks in Bulgaria; Gypsies in Romania; and Russians in the Baltic states, as well as within other non-Russian republics of the Commonwealth of Independent States.

The second factor contributing to ethnic tensions in many regions is economic decline. Disputes about economic benefits become more fiercely contested when economies are in decline—conditions that are widespread and acute in the developing world and Eastern Europe, but are also known in the Western industrialized countries. Making scapegoats of refugees and asylum-seekers, particularly those easily identifiable as belonging to different ethnic groups, has been an ugly feature of the resurgence of right-wing populism in both Germany and France. Too often, the governments' response has been to look for ways to reduce asylum applications, rather than to reduce xenophobic reactions to them.

In subsistence economies, violent conflict disrupts food production and distribution and the often-precarious conditions of daily life; famine and disease are often greater threats to the well-being of the general population than violence itself. A number of the ethnic conflicts that have erupted into violence and generated refugees in the developing world can be characterized as resource wars, in which battle lines reflect ethnic or tribal affiliations. Some begin as disputes about grazing, water, or agricultural rights, as population pressures or droughts impel people to move beyond the areas they traditionally inhabited.

Although state formation and economic decline threaten to fan ethnic conflict, the end of the Cold War and a strengthening of international mechanisms for humanitarian action and mediation should work to dampen conflict—or at least keep it below the threshold at which people feel compelled to flee.

The end of Cold War has reduced, although not eliminated, the likelihood that outside forces will exploit ethnic cleavages, aggravate them, or raise the level of violence by arming different factions. The argument is made with some frequency that the Cold War "kept the lid" on ethnic tensions and that the end of superpower conflict is releasing long-suppressed rivalries, thereby contributing to refugee flows. There is little evidence for this. The arguments in favor of such a theory commonly confuse the effects of the end of Soviet empire, accounted for above, with the effects of the end of superpower confrontation. In fact, the Cold War aggravated or even created ethnic tensions by disrupting historical balances between groups; by artificially strengthening the position of client groups by arming them, arranging sanctuaries, and providing diplomatic support for them; and by coopting certain groups to act as proxies (for example, the Hmong in Laos or the Miskito in Nicaragua), thereby exposing them to retribution later on. Local impulses toward accommodation or reconciliation were sometimes submerged by the superpower patron's interest in continuing the conflict.[18] Refugee populations themselves became pawns in disputes remote from their immediate concerns.

The Cold War also encouraged refugee flows from the Eastern bloc by motivating receiving countries to suspend normal refugee determination procedures. Anyone leaving a communist country could expect automatic refugee status in the West, regardless of his or her motivation for leaving or the objective conditions of life in the country of origin. The end of the East–West confrontation has thus radically changed the dynamics of refugee movements. Its most positive effects have been on the protracted and bitter conflicts driven by superpower rivalry in southern Africa, Central America, Southeast Asia, and Afghanistan. Many of the refugees who fled from these conflicts now have the prospect of returning to their home countries.

A second factor that is working to restrain ethnic conflict and refugee-producing violence is heightened international concern about the human rights policies of various countries. Issues that until this decade tended to be regarded as internal matters are now increasingly being defined as matters of international concern, in particular because they threaten to inundate other countries with refugees. As the number of refugees surpassed 18 million, international organizations and their member-states have begun to consider preventive measures—not to prevent people from crossing borders to seek refuge, but to prevent conditions from deteriorating to the point at which people feel they must flee. This necessarily turns attention to developments in the countries from which refugees originate and has given rise to a greater willingness to intervene in domestic disputes on humanitarian grounds. Of the two most dramatic examples to date, northern Iraq and Somalia, the first was explicitly carried out to allow a refugee population composed of a persecuted ethnic minority to return home. In both cases, the international intervention was remedial rather than preventive, however. The idea of strengthening peacekeeping and human rights regimes to prevent violence and persecution has great potential, but little has yet been accomplished.

A final historical trend that influences the growth of ethnically driven refugee movements is democratization. Its impact is ambiguous. Without a firm structure of protection for minority rights, democratization can heighten the insecurity of minorities, at least in the short run. This is particularly the case in "winner-take-all" electoral systems in which ethnic differences are exaggerated and used as a tool for mobilizing political support. The temptation to exploit ethnic problems for political gain is powerful, as is the impulse to build a power base from within one's own ethnic group, and then reward its members for their support in a way that gives them a disproportionate share of power, patronage, and opportunities for economic gain. The promotion of multiparty politics in Africa may encourage ethnic conflicts to emerge in sharper relief as parties coalesce along tribal lines. The results of the 1993 elections in Kenya, for example, reinforce this concern.[19] Other countries that should be monitored for potential outbreaks of violent confrontation during the course of political liberalization include Nigeria, Chad, Guinea, Mali, and Malawi. On the other hand, it is only through participatory political structures that multiethnic societies can, in the long run, ensure that constituent groups within them have nonviolent means to resolve conflicts, press claims, and seek redress of grievances.

THE EFFECTIVENESS OF INTERNATIONAL INSTITUTIONS

There are very few preventive actions that are specific to the problems of refugees. As a result, the prospects for improving international performance in this area lie in the more general areas of institutional development; democratization and participatory government; economic opportunity; mechanisms for redress of grievances; and protection of human rights. In the case of refugee flows arising from ethnic conflict, the protection of minority rights is particularly important.

Before World War I and in the interwar period, the assumption that ethnically homogeneous states were the best vehicles for the protection of citizens' rights was widely held. Flowing from this assumption, there was greater willingness to consider redrawing borders and exchanging populations as ways of creating more homogeneous states. Thus, for example, an international treaty provided for an involuntary exchange of populations between Greece and Turkey in the 1920s.[20] In situations in which exchanges were not possible, international treaties securing guarantees of minority rights were seen as necessary and appropriate, not as unwarranted intrusions into domestic affairs. However, the minority treaties negotiated after World War I had catastrophic consequences. Not only did they increase resentment of minorities, they became the pretext under which Germany later invaded surrounding territories, ostensibly to protect German minority populations. This experience discredited the whole notion of international legal instruments to protect minorities.[21]

The approach that took hold after World War II relied almost entirely on the promotion of universal human rights. If the rights of each member of an ethnic minority could be secured, it would not be necessary to worry about the rights of groups. However, simple provisions for nondiscrimination, as included in the Universal Declaration of Human Rights, tend to be seen by members of ethnic or religious minorities as prescriptions for assimilation.[22] The International Covenant on Civil and Political Rights is a bit more specific about minority rights, but is still primarily defensive.[23]

In December 1992, the UN General Assembly passed a Declaration on the Rights of Persons Belonging to National or Ethnic, Religious, and Linguistic Minorities, a document that is more assertive than previous UN instruments. It was first introduced in 1978—ironically, by Yugoslavia. It contains no definition of minorities, leaving some room for ambiguity. (Some would argue that its provisions should be applied to sociological, as well as numerical, minorities to be applicable to subordinate groups that are numerically superior, such as the black majority in South Africa or the indigenous population in Guatemala.)

The declaration enjoins states not just to prevent discrimination against minorities, but to protect and promote their identity and rights. Article 1 states that "States shall protect the existence and the national or ethnic, cultural, religious, and linguistic identity of minorities within their respective territories, and shall encourage conditions for the promotion of that identity. States shall adopt appropriate legislative and other measures to achieve those ends." Article 4.1 reads: "States shall take measures where required to ensure that persons belonging to minorities may exercise fully and effectively all their human rights and fundamental freedoms without any discrimination and in full equality before the law." Other articles go on to confirm, inter alia, rights of political and economic participation, education, free association (including contact with other members of the minority, even across national borders), and to assert that "national policies and programs shall be planned and implemented with due regard for the legitimate interests of persons belonging to minorities" in Article 5.1.[24]

Like other UN human rights instruments, there are no enforcement or implementation measures attached to the declaration. However, it does reaffirm the treatment of minorities as a legitimate concern of the international community. More important, it creates some hope that the United Nations may take a more active role in the monitoring and protection of minority rights, thus helping to prevent situations from deteriorating to a point at which members of certain groups become refugees.

The UN human rights regime as it stands, centered on the Human Rights Commission, is weak. Roberta Cohen notes, "early attempts by the Subcommission on Prevention of Discrimination and Protection of Minorities to focus on minority issues were essentially rebuffed by higher UN bodies. As a result, neither the subcommission nor the commission has ever conducted an in-depth study of a specific minority or made recommendations about how to protect a group at risk. Nor have UN bodies created machinery to address the concerns of racial, ethnic, religious, and linguistic groups."[25] However, greater assertiveness on the part of minority groups and the unavoidable recognition that they are key players in the preservation or disruption of international peace and security has persuaded the United Nations to become more engaged.

The secretary-general has shown greater willingness to use his good offices to raise human rights issues with governments, send fact-finding missions, appoint special rapporteurs, and draw public attention to abuse. There is also greater, although still not very systematic, attention given to the need for "early warning" of developments that could produce refugees. Nonetheless, the focus on conditions in countries of origin remains an uncomfortable one for the United Nations, where many member-states are unwilling to acknowledge the growing international consensus on human rights standards, much less to subject themselves to international scrutiny.[26]

The office of the UN High Commissioner for Refugees is placing a greater emphasis in its work on prevention—again, focusing on the circumstances that force people to flee. This inevitably draws it deeply into issues of human and minority rights. The high commissioner addressed this connection in a presentation to the UN Commission on Human Rights in 1992:

> It is broadly accepted that human rights form the overall basis for protection and assistance to refugees, and can be the key to finding solutions to refugee problems. Human rights violations are a major cause of refugee flows, although the immediate cause of most refugee movements today is armed conflict or serious internal disturbance. Human rights violations, combined with severe economic deprivation, usually lie at the root of the conflict or aggravate it. In situations where fear of persecution is the basis of flight, then the link between human rights violations and refugee flows is even clearer.[27]

The UNHCR is promoting the deployment of human rights monitors in volatile areas in which minorities are at risk and is working with officials in new states to formulate national legislation and administrative structures that are consistent with international standards.[28]

The UN system is not the only international institution concerned with ethnic conflict and refugees, however. Other players include the International Committee of the Red Cross (ICRC); regional organizations, such as the OAU and the Conference on Security and Cooperation in Europe (CSCE); nongovernmental organizations, such as Amnesty International, the Minority Rights Group, and the regional Human Rights Watch organizations; and the international news media. Space precludes a detailed examination of their roles here, but they have often been most effective in drawing attention to the plight of ethnic groups at risk of displacement and in assisting and mediating on behalf of groups affected by conflict. The ICRC, in fact, has a clearer mandate than any other institution concerning the protection of noncombatants in times of armed conflict. However, enforcement of humanitarian law is not the task of the ICRC, but of the states party to the Geneva conventions and their protocols; many of the same problems that apply to UN enforcement apply here as well.

It is worth mentioning one recent initiative of the CSCE, in which a high commissioner for national minorities was appointed in December 1992 in response to the tragedy of former Yugoslavia and the possibility of other ethnic crises developing in Eastern Europe. The Helsinki Final Act of 1975 recognized the obligation of European states to respect the right of minorities to full equality before the law and the right of minorities to enjoy the full panoply of human rights and fundamental freedoms. The CSCE went further in 1990 by recognizing the right of minority peoples to develop their own identities and not be subject to forcible assimilation. In 1991, it went further still and asserted that minority rights are legitimate subjects of international concern and "do not constitute exclusively an internal affair of the respective state."[29] In July 1992, it showed its seriousness about the observance of the declared standards by suspending the participation of the rump Federal Republic of Yugoslavia (Serbia and Montenegro) for "clear, extensive, and in many cases irreparable violations of commitments arising from membership in the CSCE."[30]

Ironically, it was Yugoslavia that pushed the issue of minorities onto the CSCE agenda and that of the United Nations. Yugoslavia under Josip Broz Tito was, legislatively, a model of ethnic accommodation. The special rapporteur of the UN Subcommission on the Prevention of Discrimination and Protection of Minorities noted in July 1992 that "the solutions found in Yugoslavia were very sophisticated, comprehensive, and aimed at a degree of national and ethnic pluralism unparalleled anywhere in the world." He also observed that "it would be excessively legalistic and naive simply to compare national legislation with regard to minorities on the assumption that perfect models could be found which could prevent the eruption of violent conflict."[31]

It is common to attribute the breakdown of the national policy of ethnic pluralism in Yugoslavia to the end of authoritarian communist rule, losing sight of the fact that the hardest of hard-line communists and the most authoritarian of authoritarians, Milosevic, became the champion of ethnic nationalism at the expense of other ethnic groups. The significant change in Yugoslavia was not the end of a communist regime, but the end of a regime credibly committed to ethnic pluralism and the protection of minority rights. The high rate of intermarriage among ethnic groups in postwar Yugoslavia is testament to the mutability of supposedly immutable ethnic hatred. (There are estimated to be 1.5 million marriages between Serbs and Croats alone—more than 20 percent of the adult population of those two groups.) The coming to prominence of politicians willing to resuscitate ethnic animosities and exploit the results for political gain set the stage for conflict; the opportunism that made them communists in the Tito era led them to embrace ethnic nationalism thereafter.

The Yugoslav experience has been one of almost total frustration from the standpoint of international institutions that deal with ethnic conflict and refugees. The level of violence has grown along with international involvement. It is not too early to try to draw some lessons from this experience.

RECOMMENDATIONS

There are both optimists and pessimists among those who recommend ways to reduce the number of people violently uprooted by ethnic conflict. The former espouse solutions focused on protection of human and minority rights; democratization with a commitment to pluralism; legal mechanisms for the redress of grievances; and political representation and power-sharing. According to this view, the role for the international community is to foster strong domestic institutions and procedures, negotiate human rights guarantees, reinforce moderate pluralists, and, if necessary, impose sanctions on those who promote discrimination or violent ethnonationalism.

Pessimists, on the other hand, look for ways to arrange for the peaceful and orderly separation of conflicting groups, whether through negotiated secession, partition, exchanges of populations with compensation for lost property, and, in the extreme, the evacuation of target groups. The role of international institutions, according to this view, is to help negotiate the terms of separation in as civilized a manner as possible, on the assumption that conflictual relations between groups cannot be repaired.

Institution-building in states in which legal, judicial, electoral, and administrative services have shown themselves unable to protect the rights of ethnic groups can be strengthened through international technical assistance and training. The UNHCR, for example, has been providing advisory and mediation services to some of the newly independent states of the former Soviet Union, working with local officials to draft inclusive nationality laws that will not leave minorities stateless or vulnerable to discrimination or forced assimilation. The ICRC has long been active in acquainting military personnel with international humanitarian law. Many nongovernmental organizations and bilateral programs offer training, advice, and mediation. There is enormous scope for more activity of this sort at all levels, specifically aimed at the resolution, or at least the moderation, of ethnic tensions before they escalate into violent conflict.

Human rights monitoring performs a protective function and provides an early warning system, both of which are valuable for prevention. The presence of external witnesses may itself deter some abuse. If deterrence fails, the monitors can alert the government (if it is unaware of the problem) and the international community to the need for action. Human rights monitoring is an integral part of UN peacekeeping operations in El Salvador, Cambodia, and Namibia; elsewhere, the most active monitoring is carried out by nongovernmental organizations. They are freer than the United Nations to denounce government abuse. In some places, they operate at considerable personal risk, lacking the protection afforded by official status. Their reports are also easier for governments to ignore, however. Human rights monitoring by the United Nations and regional intergovernmental organizations should be strengthened. Optimists are likely to have more faith in the preventive effect of monitors, but optimists and pessimists alike agree on the importance of an early warning system. Of course, early warning itself is useless unless it is linked to some form of response.

Both internationally and bilaterally, officially and unofficially, there needs to be an intense effort to consider possible forms of coercion short of military intervention, and even short of economic sanctions. The repertoire of actions—such as diplomatic pressure, culture boycotts, unofficial embargoes on selected products, and public exposure—needs to be systematically and intelligently expanded. Anthropologists, linguists, theologians, and psychologists should be enlisted along with economists, political scientists, and strategists, to analyze what forms of pressures and reward might be effectively deployed in different cultures to reinforce support for human rights and minority rights and discourage inter-ethnic conflict.

Exchanges of populations to separate ethnic groups are again being seriously discussed as a way of solving intractable conflicts. Pessimists argue that it is better for the international community to supervise such exchanges to ensure that they are peaceful and orderly and that fair compensation is made for assets left behind. Otherwise, exchanges may go on, but in a context of violence, expropriation, and terror.

Proponents of this course of action disagree about whether or not the international community should participate in population exchanges that are not purely voluntary. The argument against such exchanges is that forced movement is a violation of fundamental human rights. There are also practical objections. The potential for equal or near-equal exchanges of population is limited because symmetrical minorities are rare. If exchanges are not equal, the country that receives a disproportionately large number may face serious problems. It may expect—or demand—compensation, thereby generating new international tensions. The case in favor of involuntary exchange is utilitarian: It may prevent more injury than it causes.

The international community is becoming more open to the idea of redrawing international borders as a possible outcome of protracted negotiations of the sort that led to the separation of the Czech and Slovak republics, is in train for Eritrean independence, and may yet lead to the separation of Quebec from English-speaking Canada. The United Nations and regional bodies should be prepared to offer their good offices to facilitate the negotiation of "velvet divorces" if separation offers a practical alternative to continuing ethnic conflict. It must be recognized, however, that there are relatively few cases in which new borders offer a solution to ethnic conflict; ethnic geography is seldom tidy. Moreover, the international community should insist that nationalistic movements that initiate violent struggles for separation (in which other ethnic groups are targeted for abuse) severely prejudice their chances for recognition as legitimate authorities.

A recommendation less draconian than new borders or population exchanges involves the creation of "safety zones" for vulnerable ethnic groups. The creation of safety zones has been the subject of some disagreement between the ICRC and UNHCR in Yugoslavia. The UNHCR has expressed reservations that evacuation from zones of conflict (except in cases of special vulnerability or medical need) or the establishment of safety zones could contribute inadvertently to the consolidation of ethnic cleansing. It has taken the position that "efforts should concentrate first on bringing safety to people, rather than people to safety."[32] The ICRC maintains that this consideration must be secondary to the purely humanitarian consideration of how best to relieve suffering.

Optimists and pessimists can agree without difficulty on a number of recommendations. The importance of developing better early warning capabilities has already been mentioned. Both human rights monitors and special rapporteurs can be used for early warning. More generally, continuing efforts are being made within the UN system to collect and assess information, as well as to use it to improve preparedness. Nongovernmental organizations and national governments should continue to increase their support for such efforts.

Another important area of agreement is on recommendations for humanitarian access to victims of conflict. Provisions for access exist in international humanitarian law, at least under conditions of armed conflict, but are routinely violated as starvation and persecution of civilian populations are used as weapons of war. As the president of the ICRC observed in mid-1992,

> . . . over this past year of conflict, the ICRC has been forced to recognize that breaches of international humanitarian law and of hu-

man rights have become almost commonplace, especially as regards the civilian population, despite numerous public appeals and confidential approaches at all levels and to all the parties. There is no doubt that the vicious circle of hatred and reprisals erodes basic humanitarian values more and more each day, although these values are universally recognized . . . as we all know, it is first and foremost up to the states and their governments to respect and ensure respect for the basic rules of humanitarian law.[33]

Ensuring respect for humanitarian law is a responsibility that governments should undertake more actively and consistently. States party to the Geneva conventions have the authority to conduct war crime trials independently. Such trials should be pursued in egregious cases, although in a collective forum.

The international community should also withhold full recognition of new states until they present a plan for the protection of minority rights. Trial memberships in international organizations should perhaps be contemplated. The withdrawal of recognition (as with the Franco government in Spain after World War II) should certainly be part of the international community's repertory of options; new states should not be the only ones subject to assessment of their conduct. In addition, withholding multilateral aid from states that pursue policies likely to generate refugees is an option that should be pursued more aggressively.

Zolberg and his colleagues point out that "external mechanisms can support, but not substitute for internal efforts to develop mutual restraint and tolerance . . . this places responsibility on minorities as well as majorities."[34] The same human rights and humanitarian standards that are applied to governments should also be expected of subnational groups. Through such practices, the idea should be reinforced that the legitimacy of a government and, indeed, a state depends on its willingness to secure core human rights for its entire population.

Ethnicity is one of the major fault *lines along which societies fracture under pressure. However, this does not mean that they fracture because they are ethnically diverse, or that lack of diversity guarantees stability. Somalia, for example, is an ethnically homogeneous country that has fragmented more comprehensively than many polyethnic societies. The economic and political strains that lead to violent conflict will often break societies apart along ethnic lines and force large numbers of people to flee. However, in most cases, it is misleading to present ethnic diversity as the cause of fracture, rather than the element that determines its topography.

Notes

[1] Article I. A. 2, UN Convention Relating to the Status of Refugees, 1951.

[2] Article 1.2, OAU Convention on Refugee Problems in Africa, 1969.

[3] Conclusion 3, Cartagena Declaration on Refugees, *Colloquio sobre la Proteccio Internacional de los Refugiados en America Central, Méjico y Panamá: Problemas Juridicos y Humanitarios*, November 19–22, 1984.

[4] Aristide R. Zolberg, Astri Suhrke, and Sergio Aguayo, *Escape from Violence: Conflict and the Refugee Crisis in the Developing World* (Oxford: Oxford University Press, 1989), p. 3.

[5] James C. Hathaway, "'Fear of Persecution' and the Law of Human Rights," *Bulletin of Human Rights,* vol. 91, no. 1, March 1992, pp. 99, 101–102.

[6] Rudolfo Stavenhagen, *The Ethnic Question* (Tokyo: United Nations University Press, 1990), pp. 2–3. Stavenhagen notes that "Race may at first glance appear not to be cultural at all but biological . . . but it is also true that certain biological features such as skin color or eye shape are quite unimportant by themselves and only become important in human relationships when a given society attributes cultural and social significance to them. This is why race also serves to denote an ethnic group, and some authors speak of 'social races' in contrast to the usually perceived 'biological races'."

[7] Ibid.

[8] Helsinki Watch, *Yugoslavia: Human Rights Abuses in Kosovo 1990–1992,* October 1992.

[9] Ibid.

[10] Zolberg, Suhrke, and Aguayo, *Escape from Violence,* pp. 236–245.

[11] Gil Loescher, *Refugee Movements and International Security*, Adelphi Paper 268 (London: Brassey's for the IISS, Summer 1992), p. 42.

[12] Roger P. Winter, "Chips Off the Old Bloc: Displacement in a Disintegrating USSR," in UN Committee for Refugees, *World Refugee Survey 1992* (Washington, D.C.: US Committee for Refugees, 1992), p. 19.

[13] Ibid., p. 78.

[14] Ibid., p. 79.

[15] Ibid.

[16] Statement by the UNHCR at the Meeting of the Humanitarian Issues Working Group of the International Conference on former Yugoslavia, Geneva, Switzerland, December 4, 1992.

[17] All figures represent the population distribution at the time of the outbreak of fighting in the former Yugoslavia. See Bill Frelick, *Yugoslavia Torn Asunder: Lessons for Protecting Refugees from Civil War* (Washington, D.C.: US Committee for Refugees, February 1992).

[18] This argument is more fully developed in K.C. Soedjatmoko, "Patterns of Armed Conflict in the Third World," in Oyvind Osterud, ed., *Studies in War and Peace* (Oslo: Norwegian University Press, 1986). See also Kathleen Newland and K.C. Soedjatmoko, eds., *Common Humanity: Selected Writings of Soedjatmoko* (Hartford, Conn.: Kumarian Press, 1993).

[19] Julian Ozanne, "Moi's Cabinet Fails to Reassure International Observers," *Financial Times,* January 14, 1993, p. 5.

[20] Zolberg, Suhrke, and Aguayo, *Escape from Violence,* p. 14.

[21] Astri Suhrke, "Towards a Comprehensive Refugee Policy: Conflict and Refugees in the Post-Cold War World," Unpublished Paper presented to the Joint ILO–UNHCR Meeting on "International Aid as a Means to Reduce the Need for Emigration," Geneva, Switzerland, May 1992.

[22] "Everyone is entitled to all the rights and freedoms set forth in this declaration, without distinction of any kind, such as race, color, sex, language, religion, political or other opinion,

national or social origin, property, birth, or other status." See Article 2, Universal Declaration of Human Rights, Adopted by Resolution 217A (III) of the UN General Assembly, December 10, 1948.

[23] "In those states in which ethnic, religious, or linguistic minorities exist, persons belonging to such minorities shall not be denied the right, in community with the other members of their group, to enjoy their own culture, to profess and practice their own religion, or to use their own language." See Article 27, International Covenant on Civil and Political Rights, Adopted by Resolution 2200 (XI) of the UN General Assembly, December 16, 1966.

[24] Draft Declaration on the Rights of Persons Belonging to National or Ethnic, Religious, and Linguistic Minorities, Adopted by the UN Commission on Human Rights as Resolution 1992/16.

[25] Roberta Cohen, *Human Rights and Humanitarian Emergencies: New Roles for UN, Human Rights Bodies* (Washington, D.C.: Refugee Policy Group, September 1992), p. 15.

[26] For example, the Chinese Premier Li Peng made the following statement to the UN Security Council Summit in 1992: "The issue of human rights falls within the sovereignty of each country and should not be judged in disregard of its history and national conditions. It is neither workable nor appropriate to demand that all countries measure up to the human rights criteria or models of one or a small number of states. China is opposed to using human rights as an excuse for interference in the internal affairs of other countries." Cited in W.B. Ofuatey-Kodjoe, "Human Rights and Humanitarian Intervention," in A. Legault, C.N. Murphy, and W.B. Ofuatey-Kodjoe, *The State of the United Nations: 1992*, Academic Council on the United Nations System (ACUNS) Reports and Papers 1992, No. 3 (Providence, R.I.: ACUNS, 1992), p. 37.

[27] Sadako Ogata, Statement to the Forty-eighth Session of the Commission on Human Rights, February 20, 1992.

[28] Ibid.

[29] Edward Mortimer, "Grievous National Harm," *Financial Times*, December 16, 1992, p. 13.

[30] Statement by vice-minister of foreign affairs of the Czech and Slovak Federal Republic, Martin Palous, at the International Meeting on Humanitarian Aid for Victims of the Conflict in the former Yugoslavia, Geneva, Switzerland, July 29, 1992.

[31] Mortimer, "Grievous National Harm," p. 13.

[32] UNHCR, Working Document for the Humanitarian Issues Working Group of the International Conference on the former Yugoslavia, Geneva, Switzerland, December 4, 1992.

[33] Statement by Cornelio Sommaruga, president of the ICRC, International Meeting on Humanitarian Aid for Victims of the Conflict in former Yugoslavia, held under the auspices of the UNHCR, Geneva, Switzerland, July 29, 1992.

[34] Zolberg, Suhrke, and Aguayo, *Escape from Violence,* p. 264.

Chapter 9

International Mediation of Ethnic Conflicts

Jenonne Walker

Efforts by outsiders to mediate ethnic tensions within states, especially those involving secessionist demands, are few and far between. Successful mediation efforts are scarcer still. For most of the postwar era, few questioned the prevailing consensus that international borders were sacrosanct and that the way governments behaved at home was essentially their own concern. Successive United Nations (UN) resolutions defined "self-determination" as limited to the right of colonial peoples in the Third World to achieve independence from their European overlords. The accompanying principle of "freedom from interference in the internal affairs of states" was taken to mean that outsiders were not to meddle in what happened in these countries once independence was achieved. Nowhere was this view more ardently embraced than in Africa, where the borders left behind by colonial empires often made little ethnic, economic, or even geographic sense, but where rulers of most of the created states agreed that attempts to change borders would invite chaos.

That, of course, does not mean that outside powers have been absent from involvement in internal conflicts since World War II. Support for a government confronting domestic opposition, whether stemming from ethnic grievances or otherwise, has not been considered "interference." Both Moscow and Washington also supported antigovernment forces in various parts of the world as their global rivalry unfolded. Others, usually, but not only, former colonial powers sometimes also played that game. At different times, for example, French President Charles de Gaulle pronounced the Biafrans of Nigeria and the Quebecois of Canada to be distinct nations worthy of statehood. However, taking sides, whether militarily or diplomatically, openly or covertly, is a far cry from mediation.

Guarantees of minority rights, usually for whites who chose to remain in newly independent black states, and power-sharing arrangements among black tribes sometimes formed part of independence settlements. However, the colonial government transferring power saw itself (and was seen) more as an active party in the negotiations than an outside mediator and, in any case, usually had special leverage in influencing the terms of independence.

The only postcolonial attempts by outside states to mediate ethnic quarrels, including those regarding territory or statehood, have come after fighting. The most notable examples are Washington's long-running efforts to promote Arab–Israeli agreements and to find a solution to the Cyprus problem, both of which began only after land had been taken and was being held by force. Russian troops (sometimes operating under a Commonwealth of Independent States umbrella, sometimes in ad hoc arrangements with one or more other former Soviet republics) currently are trying to arrange and police shaky cease-fires in Georgia, Moldova, Tajikistan, and Nagorno-Karabakh. The Conference on Security and Co-operation in Europe (CSCE) has been attempting for nearly a year to get a peace conference under way on Nagorno-Karabakh.

The same general rule has applied to other efforts to settle civil conflicts whose source is more a struggle about ideology or power than a conflict between ethnic communities. The Economic Community of West African States (ECOWAS) organized a military intervention force, and Central American states began diplomatic efforts, but only after civil wars were raging in Liberia and El Salvador, respectively. Some of these cases scarcely deserve to be called "mediation" efforts; in the former Soviet Union and Liberia, the near-term hope is that exhaustion of the combatants, the threat of a superior outside force, or some combination of the two, will finally make a cease-fire stick.

Both the European Community (EC) and the United States intervened before fighting began in the former Yugoslavia, but by taking sides and urging continued unity of the federal state. Later, when it became clear that a split was inevitable, the EC tried to mediate the peaceful separation of Slovenia and Croatia. However, both Croatia's Franjo Tudjman and Serbia's Slobodan Milosevic had staked their political survival on nationalism before mediation efforts began, and the West's clearly stated preference for preserving the federal Yugoslav state may have encouraged Milosevic to believe he was being given a free hand to use force to do so.

At times, private groups have been more willing to try their hand at mediation than governments. In the early 1970s, when neither the Organization of African Unity (OAU) nor any individual government dared involve itself in Sudan's civil war lest it be blamed for intervening in Sudanese affairs, the World Council of Churches and the All African Conference of Churches worked to bring the contending parties to the negotiating table. That, too, happened only after fighting in Sudan was raging.

In short, raising the question of how outsiders can mediate ethnic conflict before it turns violent takes the international community into uncharted waters. The favored solution of most Westerners to civic quarrels is free and fair elections, whose results all contending parties agree to accept. However, that is inadequate when an ethnic minority's objection to rule by the majority, with which it shares a state, is itself the root of the problem. Similarly inadequate are traditional efforts to devise effective compromises when the heart of a conflict is less a dispute about concrete, quantifiable interests (land, resources, economic or political power) than about identity. Power and material benefits can be shared. In the eyes of many, a conflicting sense of identity is irreconcilable.

As the newly freed states of Central and Eastern Europe now so vividly demonstrate, a brutally suppressed sense of cultural identity and belonging can result in fury when freed. One can believe that Latvians, for instance, are harming their own long-run self-interest by making it hard for their country's large Russian minority to obtain the full rights of citizenship. Yet, the resentment against lifelong Russian residents, who refused even to learn the Latvian language, runs deep.

This chapter addresses the issue of what steps the international community can and should take once fighting begins between ethnic communities within a state. Its main purpose, however, is to explore what the international community can do to keep violence from starting in the first place.

LESSONS FROM THE PAST

To begin, this chapter will examine some general guidelines for policymakers, drawing on lessons from the partial and inadequate efforts that have been made to date to ease ethnic tensions within states.

The first guideline is to beware of general guidelines. The international community can and should devise better tools for mitigating and mediating ethnic conflict, and some will be sketched out in this chapter. However, the wise application of general principles will vary from case to case. Abstract principles are no substitute for understanding the complex political, economic, social, cultural, psychological, and personal forces at play in particular situations.

The second, and closely related, guideline to keep in mind is that there is no substitute for good judgment about individual situations. Experts in most Western foreign ministries warned that the Yugoslav Federation could not survive communism's demise. Their political leaders, believing (rightly) that Serbia would not allow republics to leave the federation peacefully, refused to face the inevitable until passions were high and both Serb and Croatian leaders had staked their political survival on irreconcilable positions.

The third guideline, which follows from the first two, is that the earlier the efforts to mediate ethnic quarrels begin, the better are their chances for success. Indeed, they are most likely to be effective if they begin well before there is a concrete "dispute" to mediate. Thus, the West should consider not only what might be called "hard" mediation—efforts to find specific solutions to specific disputes—but also "soft" mediation—the broader question of what outsiders can legitimately and usefully do to ease tensions among ethnic groups who share the same state or between states across whose borders ethnic communities spill. Efforts to create better relations between communities may help prevent specific conflicts that later require hard mediation from developing, as well as contribute to an atmosphere that facilitates their resolution once they do occur.

A fourth guideline is that international efforts at soft mediation should not stop when a specific dispute is resolved or an election has been monitored. Remaining behind to facilitate dialogue and prevent small incidents from becoming big ones is also important.

The fifth, and perhaps most important, guideline is that neither hard nor soft mediation is likely to be successful if it only consists of diplomats proposing solutions and urging reasoned compromise. Mediation efforts must be supported by a combination of political, economic, and military muscle that promises (or threatens) an effective mix of pain and gain.

In theory, this should be easier to do in Europe where, through a variety of regional organizations, governments already have given each other impressive rights to "interfere" in domestic affairs when human rights are being violated. Latin America—where few internal conflicts are primarily ethnic in nature—may be moving in a similar direction by proclaiming, within the Organization of American States (OAS), a common responsibility for ensuring democratic governments in OAS members. Africa and Asia, both rife with actual and potential ethnic conflicts, still resist the notion of international oversight of internal affairs (the OAU Charter for the Protection of Human and Peoples' Rights notwithstanding). This chapter, therefore, pays particular attention to Europe (also the area in which ethnic tensions currently seem most dangerous), but also explores the way tools being developed in Europe might—or might not—be applicable elsewhere.

SOFT MEDIATION

In one important sense, the territorial map of Central and Eastern Europe, including the former Soviet Union, is similar to that of Africa: Borders were imposed by outside powers with little regard for geography, shared history, or ethnic ties. As in Africa, although virtually every state or ethnic group has some claim to somebody else's territory, most leaders agree that trying to redraw the map would be disastrous for all.

In marked contrast to Africa, however, Europeans are trying to create a regional system to oversee how governments behave at home toward minority and other human rights issues. Their efforts include the following: a variety of procedures designed to apply pressure on states to comply with the norms of behavior subscribed to by all European states, Canada, and the United States in the CSCE; using the desire of Central and East European states for membership in the Council of Europe and the EC as a source of influence over their domestic laws and practices; and efforts by both the Council of Europe and the CSCE to broaden acceptance of judicial review or at least some form of third-party involvement in all disputes about compliance with minority and other human rights agreements. The spectrum of European regional arrangements thus encompasses both soft and hard mediation. Often the distinction between the two is blurred.

The overall aim of the efforts now under way in Europe is twofold. The first is to assure minorities that they can appeal for the redress of grievances beyond the rule of government officials in their own countries. The hope is that this will temper the desire for secession and provide an alternative form of minority protection from intervention by "big brother" states. This could, for example, help democratic forces in Russia counter the suggestion, increasingly heard in both civilian and military circles, that the protection of human rights for the 25 million ethnic Russians in other republics will provide a new mission for the Russian army.

The second thing that regional organizations and arrangements can do is to decrease the importance of borders that now divide Europe's ethnic groups. Opposition of South Tyrol's German-speakers to their incorporation in Italy seems to have been overcome not only by the specific rights guarantees they have won, but also by Austria's growing closeness to the EC, which makes the border between Austria and Italy less important. Other arrangements, such as the Visegrad grouping of Poland, Hungary, and the Czech and Slovak Republics, have similar goals. Still other projects—among Baltic, Black Sea, Danubian, and trans-Carpathian states—aim in part to promote social, economic, and cultural, as well as political, cooperation to lessen the importance of borders that divide the various ethnic groups.

Providing international guarantees for minority rights and making Europe's borders more porous are big jobs. They are unlikely to be completed soon, if indeed ever. However, working toward them should be the main goal of security policy in Europe today.

The Council of Europe (COE) plays an important role in this process because it is open only to functioning democracies (and has a track record of suspending a member that ceases to be democratic)[1] and because its Court of Human Rights renders binding judgments about its members' compliance with the European Convention on Human Rights.[2] Moreover, COE membership has become a tacit precondition (necessary, if not sufficient) of membership in the EC. In assessing applications for membership, the COE conducts intensive examinations not only of a country's constitution and laws, but also of the conduct of national and local officials. It also provides a range of educational programs to make private citizens, as well as officials, aware of their rights and obligations under the Human Rights Convention and Court. An important part of the message is that there is more to democracy than majority rule; protection of the numerically or economically weak is also essential.

There is encouraging, if anecdotal, evidence that several Central and East European states have made concrete changes in their domestic policies in pursuit of COE membership. Bulgaria, for example, took steps to demonstrate that it had stopped the forced assimilation of ethnic Turks. Czechoslovakia adopted a Charter of Fundamental Rights and Freedoms patterned largely on the European Human Rights Convention. Poland changed its electoral laws.

Within the CSCE, all the European states, as well as the United States and Canada, have made even more specific commitments about human rights safeguards, some of which explicitly address minority rights. The CSCE relies almost entirely on moral suasion, but is taking potentially important steps to increase its political leverage: Human rights rapporteurs can be dispatched to any member-state if any other six members so request; ad hoc steering groups or special representatives of the chairman-in-office can monitor specific situations; the CSCE has begun sending missions of long duration to areas of great tension; a new high commissioner for national minorities will play a continuous monitoring and early warning role; provisions have been established for emergency meetings of senior officials to call governments to account for possible noncompliance with minority and other human rights guarantees.

The first job of any CSCE mission is to make its presence known, to show that the international community is watching and that an international presence is available to hear grievances. The round tables they organize with ethnic communities—separately and, if possible, jointly—

can serve to vent these grievances. In some cases, they have been able to negotiate useful, concrete agreements. CSCE officials believe, for example, that the efforts of their Mission of Long Duration in Kosovo has helped prepare the ground for the possible reopening of Albanian elementary schools there. The mission in Nagorno-Karabakh facilitated a prisoner exchange agreement between Armenia and Azerbaijan.[3] These are good examples of the ways that "soft" mediators, if alert, can do "hard" mediating work.

Europeans, of course, did not invent the idea that international bodies should try to improve the situation of minorities or other disadvantaged groups. UN peacekeepers and international relief workers have been doing this for years. In Cyprus, UN peacekeepers investigate and try to resolve complaints of criminal activity that have an intercommunal angle, and the UN development program's "Nicosia Master Plan" has helped that city's Greek and Turkish communities cooperate on a range of practical urban problems. The International Committee of the Red Cross also has a long history of gaining better treatment for sick and wounded prisoners and of intervening to protect the rights of prisoners.[4]

Indeed, the UN's efforts at what political scientists sometimes call "prenegotiations" or "supplementary negotiations" is expanding as its peacekeeping, humanitarian, and even government-making (for example, in Cambodia) activities grow. Deputy Secretary-General for Humanitarian Affairs Jan Eliasson notes that he sometimes is allowed into countries that would not permit a visit by the UN deputy secretary for political affairs. Once in, he can sometimes reach agreements that have political, as well as humanitarian, payoffs. These have included cease-fires to facilitate the safe delivery of humanitarian supplies.[5]

In Somalia, Robert Oakley, the US special ambassador accompanying its humanitarian relief effort, used meetings with clan leaders about the rebuilding of roads and bridges, over which food must be transported, to urge them to settle their deep-seated differences. The two main warlords met under his auspices and talked about disarming their troops. To discuss broader political issues, he also used town meetings of clan leaders, elders, clerics, women, and officials—ostensibly organized to prepare for the arrival of US troops and the humanitarian supplies they escorted.

The OAS has been especially inventive in this regard. Its election monitors in Nicaragua remained to help resettle former guerrilla factions that were returning to their homes in rural areas and, later, to help build low-cost housing, supported in part by an EC grant. With the housing project enabling it to remain in the country, the OAS has also had the opportunity to defuse subsequent incidents and promote reconciliation.

This stands in marked contrast to the situation in Haiti in which the OAS election monitors departed after the election of Father Jean-Bertrand Aristide, leaving no international presence to help resolve subsequent problems when they arose.

Several private groups are also involved in the soft mediation of ethnic conflicts. The Hebrew University of Jerusalem's "Project on Prenegotiation" aims to help residents of the ethnic communities in that divided city to begin thinking together about ways to manage health care, sanitation, water, economic development, and cultural issues. They hope this will eventually improve the prospects for resolution of their more fundamental differences.[6] The Kettering Foundation in the United States has a project to encourage teams from Lebanon's various ethnic and religious communities to write joint issue papers on similar kinds of problems.

Only in Europe is an international presence in states with ethnic or other internal problems becoming routine, however. There should be a continuing effort to reinforce this principle in Europe and to extend it to other parts of the world. Missions representing either the United Nations or some regional body could provide a monitoring capability that might help ease tensions in potentially volatile situations, render objective judgments about alleged mistreatment of minorities, and be alert to opportunities to mediate specific issues. To be most effective, such missions should include a military component, not only to help monitor the local military's activities, but also because military officers often talk (and listen) best to brother officers.

In Europe, mixed civilian–military teams might be especially useful in states with a substantial Russian minority and where Russian soldiers remain against the wishes of the host government. A willingness to accept such missions might even be made a condition for international recognition. (The acceptance of short-term human rights fact-finding missions was a condition for the admission of new states into the CSCE following the Soviet Union's breakup, but short visits cannot accomplish much.)

It might also be possible to win a priori agreement to accept military monitors and human rights fact-finding teams when a state's alleged infractions of minority rights are subject to the CSCE's procedures for the peaceful settlement of disputes. Such teams could provide impartial judgments about alleged abuse and try to ensure that no party disrupts mediation efforts by resorting to force. Better still might be an agreement to accept a long-term mission whenever requested by any six CSCE members. (This is now the requirement for brief visits from human rights fact finders.)

Other international institutions are also in the soft mediation business. The International Monetary Fund (IMF) reportedly made Slovak leaders aware that democratic institutions and nondiscrimination against their Hungarian minority were tacit conditions for continued financial support. Germany's bilateral treaties with its eastern neighbors include special rights for ethnic Germans in the latter, in tacit return for the German economic benefits those treaties confer. The European Community made a Czech–Slovak customs union a precondition for continued association. Both the EC and the Visegrad grouping of Poland, Hungary, and the Czech and Slovak Republics hope that incorporation of the last two in broader arrangements will facilitate accommodation between the newly independent Slovak state and its Hungarian minority. Other arrangements or aspirations also can help to improve the lot of ethnic groups and transcend state borders. These include the Black Sea Economic Cooperation arrangement among Turkey, Greece, Albania, Bulgaria, Romania, Russia, Moldova, Georgia, Azerbaijan, Armenia, and Ukraine and the proposed Euro-Carpathian group of Poland, Hungary, the Czech and Slovak Republics, Ukraine, and Romania.

Security policy and arms control have also become venues for soft mediation in Europe. The CSCE's Forum for Security Cooperation is less concerned with negotiating force reductions than with establishing a continuing dialogue on security perceptions and policies, not least the military's role in a democracy. High on its agenda is the negotiation of a code of conduct that would prescribe limits on a government's use of force on its own territory, even in cases involving secessionist movements.

The plethora of efforts under way, both bilaterally and in various multilateral organizations, to establish working links between those midlevel military and civilian officials in both Eastern and Western Europe dealing with security, judicial, police, local government, and other issues also constitutes a type of soft mediation. They are all part of a process designed to transmit Western values, attitudes, and methods to Eastern Europe and the former Soviet Union. They also provide congenial opportunities for leaders in the eastern half of Europe to dispel suspicions about each other's intentions. The presence of Western officials can facilitate discussion between, for example, Hungary and Romania about Bucharest's treatment of its Hungarian minority.

The mediation of human rights issues is different in Latin America, however, which is not surprising given the region's history and political circumstances. No court has made binding judgments about compliance with the Inter-American Human Rights Commission (IAHRC). During most of the OAS's life span, so many of its most powerful members have been dictatorships that the reports of its Human Rights Commission were rarely even debated at annual assemblies. Nonetheless, the commission continued to press the limits of the politically possible and contributed to a few significant successes.

Early on, the commission established its right to hold hearings within the territory of a state with a questionable human rights record and, in the process of taking testimony from prisoners, dissidents, and others, has sometimes been able to win small improvements in their treatment. The commission has also used its right to "place itself at the disposition" of parties seeking a friendly settlement to a dispute. For example, it was able to respond to a request from the government of Nicaragua in 1982 to make contact with that country's Miskito Indians and help devise a partial solution to their grievances.

In contrast to the CSCE, the IAHRC's work on "norm setting" has proceeded incrementally, through specific investigations, rather than by meetings of senior officials who reach broad agreements on principles. As a result, although the commission could assert that certain hemispheric norms had been identified, governments felt little need to pay attention. The efficacy of the commission's work depended largely on publicity, its main source of leverage being governmental interest in avoiding or limiting bad publicity. Nicaraguan dictator Anastasia Somoza claimed that a commission report had been partly responsible for his downfall.[7] When US economic pressure finally forced the Argentinian junta to accept a visit from the IAHRC in 1979, disappearances and other human rights abuses sharply declined in an attempt to elicit a less critical report on the appalling human rights situation then prevailing.

The high point of the IAHRC's success to date came during the US presidency of Jimmy Carter, when economic and military assistance were linked to a country's human rights performance. Many right-wing governments that had depended on US help were willing to make changes in their human rights policies—some big, some small—to retain such aid. The effectiveness of the IAHRC declined sharply under the Reagan administration, however, when it became clear that it was only interested in criticizing human rights abuses perpetuated by communist governments.

More recently, however, the establishment of democracy in many of Latin America's most powerful states has created new opportunities for action. At its June 1991 general assembly meeting in Santiago, the OAS established a procedure to call emergency meetings in which a decision could be taken on collective action "in the case of any event giving rise to the sudden or irregular interruption of the democratic political process or of the legitimate exercise of power by the democratically elected government in any of the organization's member-states."[8] The "Santiago procedure" has been used twice—to impose economic and diplomatic sanctions on Haiti following the coup in that country and to extract from Peru's Alberto Fujimori a promise to hold elections rather than face similar sanctions.[9]

Most internal conflicts in Latin America are not based on ethnic divisions and so, strictly speaking, are beyond the scope of this chapter. Anything that broadens acceptance of the principle that domestic behavior, including the respect for democratic principles and individual freedom, is a matter of legitimate concern to the international community will in time create pressure on those countries that have resisted "outside interference" in how governments treat people.

Ideally, of course, norm setting, monitoring, and enforcement activities would be conducted on a universal basis by the United Nations. The continued resistance of many African, Asian, and Middle Eastern governments to any "interference" in their domestic affairs makes this unrealistic at present. However, the UN's role in these areas has expanded in ways that would have been inconceivable even a few years ago. It is virtually administering Cambodia and played a significant role in running Angola, in anticipation of elections in both countries. By continuing to develop the UN's role along these lines, while using regional organizations where possible to "push the edge of the envelope," it may be possible over time to strengthen the international community's role in guaranteeing minority rights.

HARD MEDIATION

All members of the Council of Europe accept hard mediation—binding judgments of the Court of the Human Rights with respect to their compliance with the Human Rights Convention—as a matter of course. The council now includes Poland, Hungary, and Bulgaria. (Czechoslovakia also was a member, but both the Czech and Slovak Republics must reapply and undergo a new vetting process.) The COE may soon add a protocol to its Human Rights Convention specifically dealing with minority rights. On the whole, however, those countries that meet the COE's criteria for full membership are long-established democracies in which ethnic tensions are unlikely to lead to war.

Both the COE and CSCE are looking for ways to strengthen their hands in Central and Eastern Europe. Lord Owen, cochairman of the UN's peace conference on Bosnia-Herzegovina, has suggested that as part of an eventual settlement, a human rights court should be established with a mixture of judges from the European Human Rights Court and Bosnia-Herzegovina's ethnic communities.[10] COE officials would like to expand this idea, providing assistance to human rights panels that might be established by other regional groups, ideally including some or all of the members of the Commonwealth of Independent States.

In addition to its long-running (and so far unavailing) efforts to convene a peace conference on Nagorno-Karabakh and its hope that its Mission of Long Duration in South Ossetia can go beyond monitoring and begin mediating the dispute among ethnic Ossetians and the Georgian and Russian governments under which they live, the CSCE agreed at its December 1992 Stockholm Summit to establish a court of conciliation (for advisory opinions) and arbitration (for binding judgments).[11] Membership will be optional, and even those who join can place some limits on the court's jurisdiction. Although the court will deal only with disputes between participating states, possible cases might include one brought by Russia against Latvia, for example, alleging infringement of the human rights of ethnic Russians living in the latter, or one by Hungary against Romania for the mistreatment of ethnic Hungarians there. If all European governments with minority problems accept the court's jurisdiction, it would extend at least some aspects of its judicial review on minority rights issues to countries that do not meet the Council of Europe's democratic criteria for full membership.

This may seem an idle dream. It may be unrealistic to expect that the governments that most need international supervision of their treatment of minorities would subject themselves to such judgments. However, the COE's new and aspiring Central and East European members are among the most ardent advocates of adding a minority rights protocol to the Human Rights Convention. There is reason to hope that concern about the fate of their ethnic brethren in other countries will lead many of them to accept oversight of their own behavior. The opportunity to test fully their apparent willingness to do so should not be missed.

Binding arbitration regarding anything as sensitive, subjective, and fraught with emotion as ethnic quarrels is a risky business. As noted at the outset of this chapter, such disputes are often matters of identity rather than of quantifiable, concrete interests to which compromise judgments are applicable, much less acceptable. Land, resources, even political power can be divided or shared. It is far harder to compromise conflicting senses of identity. It is important for minorities to know that the international community offers a reliable means of redressing their grievances. However, it is equally important to know when something less formal than a judicial hearing is better—when an opportunity to test suggestions and try out ideas may prove more fruitful. Thus, although the new court can do useful work, governments will need to use discretion and good sense about when to use it and when the other, less formal means that the

CSCE, for example, is developing to provide the good offices of third parties should be used instead.

CARROTS AND STICKS

Even "binding" judgments of a Court of Human Rights or arbitration panel, in the end, depend upon the willingness of member governments to comply. Only in exceptional cases will punitive actions be taken against recalcitrant states. Thus, even court rulings should perhaps be considered more a form of political and moral suasion than international "enforcement."

Moral suasion is effective in Europe, especially in countries in which large segments of the elite are eager for acceptance into what former Soviet President Mikhail Gorbachev used to call the "common European home." However, this alone will not always be sufficient to prevent or halt abuse. Western governments, regional organizations, corporations, and other involved individuals should be far more imaginative in the use of carrots and sticks to influence how governments treat their people. In the United States, for example, only a very small percentage of the Bush administration's economic assistance to Central and Eastern Europe went to projects that might be described as "democracy building"—training of national and local government officials, lawyers, journalists, educators, human rights activists, nongovernmental organizations, and others so vital to a civil society. Private Western investors can help by providing equal employment opportunities for ethnic groups. Western governments might even link small business loans in areas that have substantial minorities to compliance with such principles.

Some economic assistance could be earmarked for projects designed by two or more neighbors (who often share the same ethnic groups). Using economic inducements to promote Hungarian cooperation with Slovakia or Romania, or Ukrainian cooperation with Moldova, or one day among the former Yugoslav republics, or even between Armenia and Azerbaijan, would be an updated application of the Marshall Plan principle that helped get France and Germany working together after World War II.

All the ideas suggested in this chapter are modest. They could help ease some tensions some of the time. However, the desire for acceptance into the European club, judicial oversight (whose effectiveness depends on the consent of the overseen), and economic inducements cannot keep all Europe's ethnic problems from turning violent. US and European leaders once hoped that the European Community's role as Yugoslavia's chief trading partner and aid donor—and the desire of all Yugoslav republics for EC membership—would enable the European Community to negotiate a settlement of that country's ethnic disputes and secure a relatively peaceful breakup when disintegration seemed inevitable. Yet, Milosevic and his followers cared more about Greater Serbia than the good opinion of Western Europe or even Serbia's immediate economic well-being. They gambled (rightly, it now seems) that they could get away with aggression and ethnic cleansing to attain their objectives.

The international community, therefore, must also have at its disposal—and be willing to use—means of real enforcement: both economic sanctions and military options. The point is not just that stronger measures might be needed if both soft and hard mediation fail. Having these options will help make mediation work. Mediation is far more likely to succeed if a credible economic or military threat lurks in the background. It took US economic pressure to get the Argentinian junta to accept a visit from the Inter-American Human Rights Commission, and it took the threat of military action to get Somalia's warlords to talk to each other. Similarly, the contending factions in Angola's largely tribal-based civil war became amenable to outside mediation only when their respective US and Soviet backers withdrew military support. The "outside intervention" that finally proved decisive in Eritrea's long struggle for freedom from Ethiopia was Moscow's decision to cut off the latter's military supplies.

The tools that are most likely to be effective obviously will vary from case to case. However, the international community needs to have in its repertory the ability to impose and enforce economic sanctions without the consent of the target state, as well as the ability to use military force when egregious violations of minority or other human rights take place. In Europe, this may mean changing the CSCE's rules to allow the imposition of economic sanctions by a large majority, rather than by the consensus of its membership. It could also mean having military units organized and trained to operate in a variety of multilateral frameworks—UN, CSCE, North Atlantic Treaty Organization (NATO), Western European Union (WEU), or ad hoc coalitions acting under UN or CSCE mandates—to do a variety of jobs. Those jobs could include enforcing embargoes, ensuring delivery of humanitarian supplies, establishing safe havens for refugees, or placing peacekeeping forces along the borders of states whose neighbors are threatening to intervene on behalf of conationals. In cases in which multilateral intervention on the ground is deemed too costly, military retaliation against aggressor states should be an option.

It cannot be emphasized too strongly that the credible threat of economic or military action should be an aid to mediation, not an alternative to it. Ideally, ethnic tensions should be defused before they explode into open conflict. Escalation should be discouraged and, where necessary, deterred. However, military forces that are unlikely to be used are also unlikely to deter. By allowing Serbia's Milosevic to demonstrate that aggression and ethnic cleansing can succeed, the international community is sending precisely the wrong signal to potential troublemakers and aggressors everywhere, not least those in parts of Russia and elsewhere in the former Soviet Union.

TOOLS AND THE WILLINGNESS
TO USE THEM

None of the arrangements or other tools discussed in this chapter will be effective if governments are perceived to be unwilling to use them. The European Community established an independent judicial panel that devised strict criteria for recognition of former Yugoslav republics, including minority rights guarantees. For political reasons it then ignored them in recognizing Croatia, which the panel said failed to meet the criteria, but not Macedonia, which passed every test. Just when West Europeans were telling Romania that its willingness to enforce economic sanctions against Serbia would be a factor in its relations with the West, the WEU let Bucharest into its consultative forum, despite the former's failure to crack down on sanctions-busters. The Council of Europe suspended Greek membership when Athens fell under military rule, but did not do the same when Turkey came under the sway of the military, due in part to Turkey's perceived strategic importance to the West. Finally, Turkish–Cypriot leader Rauf Denktash has been able to reject the UN's ideas for a settlement because a substantial Turkish military force protects Turkey's gains on the island, and the West is loath to press Ankara on the point, in part lest Turkey stop providing the bases from which the Iraqi Kurds are supplied. This is not to say that outside governments are always wrong to give other concerns priority over the resolution of internal conflicts among ethnic groups. Governing means having to make imperfect compromises among competing goals, each of which may be admirable in itself.

What the development of regional or international tools can do is change expectations about the way governments will behave. The growing body of agreements about the way governments are expected to deal with their own people, including minorities, can establish and steadily raise the conditions for acceptance into the democratic club and for favorable international relations, including economic interactions. Equally important, the evolution of agreed standards and arrangements for collective oversight of compliance with them creates expectations about how other members of the international community will respond to important violations. Politicians will always find excuses for not acting if they are so determined. If the idea of joint responsibility for ensuring compliance with agreed norms takes root and if better tools are available for meeting these responsibilities, at least some of the excuses governments used for inaction on Yugoslavia will be denied them.

Acknowledgments

Jennone Walker wrote this chapter as part of a project on European Regional Organizations and Ethnic Conflict funded by the John D. and Catherine T. MacArthur Foundation.

Notes

[1] Greece was suspended in 1969, and Turkey's rights were curtailed in 1981.
[2] The European Convention on Human Rights ostensibly deals only with individual human rights, but has been used in cases involving minority issues, such as the right to French language education for francophone children in Flemish areas of Belgium and Britain's denial of free and fair trial in Northern Ireland.
[3] Author interviews with CSCE officials, Vienna, Austria, October 1992.
[4] See David P. Forsythe, "Humanitarian Mediation by the International Committee of the Red Cross," in F. Toaval and I. William Zartman, eds., *International Mediation in Theory and Practice* (Boulder, Colo.: Westview Press, 1985), pp. 233–247.
[5] Author interview with Jan Eliasson, Washington, D.C., December 1992.
[6] Jay Rothman, "The Human Dimension in Israeli–Palestinian Negotiations," *The Jerusalem Journal of International Relations*, vol. 14, no. 3, 1992, pp. 69–81.
[7] A. Somoza, with J. Cox, *Nicaragua Betrayed* (Boston, Mass.: Western Islands Press, 1980).
[8] Resolution No. AG/RES 1080, adopted June 5, 1991, by the Twenty-first General Assembly of the Organization of the American States.
[9] In deference to Latin American sensitivities about US intervention in their domestic affairs, the OAS term for mediation, whether soft or hard, is "facilitation."
[10] Lord Owen, Speech to the Parliamentary Assembly of the Council of Europe, Strasbourg, France, October 3, 1992.
[11] Decisions of the Stockholm Summit of the CSCE, December 1992.

Chapter 10

Outside Intervention in Ethnic Conflicts
Robert Cooper and Mats Berdal

Ethnic problems are widespread. In perhaps half the states of the world, a majority is oppressing a minority, or vice versa. When ethnic oppression does not turn into ethnic conflict, it is most often because of the weakness of the oppressed. Ethnic problems become ethnic conflicts as the power of the state weakens. It may be that the ethnic problems themselves weaken the state, or it may be that, as the state disintegrates for some other reason, people return to older, more traditional loyalties. It is when conflict begins that outside powers, acting unilaterally or in concert, are likely to become engaged.

This chapter examines the particular difficulties associated with outside military intervention in conflicts originating from and sustained by ethnic tension. This will be done by examining four historic cases—Cyprus, Sri Lanka, Bangladesh, and Lebanon—and, more briefly, by examining the current experience of outside intervention in the former Yugoslavia, the former Soviet Union, and Liberia. Although these cases differ in several important respects, they point to some general characteristics of ethnic conflict that have a bearing on any deliberations about outside military intervention. Thus, although recognizing that each case of ethnic conflict is unique in origin, course, and effect, this chapter will develop some guidelines for policymakers faced with the prospect of intervening in an ethnic conflict.

For the purposes of this chapter, "ethnic" groups are defined not merely in terms of race, but are also taken to include cases in which group identity is provided by factors such as religion, language, association with a specific territory, and the "myth of common descent."[1] Similarly, although the main focus of this enquiry is the use or threat of force, this does not exclusively mean coercive interference. For reasons that will be explored, it is also necessary to consider other types of collective intervention legitimized by the international community—through the United

Nations (UN) or regional bodies—and aimed at assisting in the resolution of ethnic conflicts. Such interventions may, as in the case of peacekeeping operations, involve military deployments based on an agreement between the parties in a dispute. At the other extreme, they may be coercive.[2]

The subject of outside intervention in ethnic conflict is important for several reasons. At the broadest level, it is intimately linked to changes in thinking about the nature of state sovereignty. In addition, three related developments have placed the issue of intervention in ethnic conflict firmly on the agenda of national policymakers and international organizations.

The first of these is the passing of the Cold War. This has led to the removal of impediments to intervention that existed throughout the East–West confrontation. As long as the character of the international political system was shaped by superpower bipolarity, the dangers of unilateral intervention and the tendency for peripheral conflicts to acquire an East–West dimension militated against overt involvement by the major powers. Similarly, the absence of consensus in the UN Security Council meant that the scope for collective operations was also limited. These problems no longer exist. Yet, they also point to a central paradox of the end of the Cold War: The system of bipolarity contained elements of order whose disappearance has not only altered the context within which military intervention is considered, but has also increased the potential for violent ethnic conflict within the system as a whole.[3]

Second, the collapse of communism and the ideological victory of democracy has led to ethnic conflicts. The collapse of communism was as much a collapse of legitimacy as of anything else. Authoritarianism does, however, have the merit of dampening ethnic issues; if ethnic problems do occur, they can easily be suppressed. Democracy, on the other hand, requires the identification of a political community to which everyone belongs; voluntary acceptance of majority decisions implies a strong sense of a common destiny. If people are allowed to choose who governs them, many feel that they should also choose who is to be governed. Thus, it is not an accident that the sudden overthrow of authoritarian regimes and the arrival of democracy have been accompanied by ethnic tensions and secessionist movements. This is true in Africa—where the end of the Cold War also removed the legitimacy ascribed to one-party rule—as it is in Europe.

Third, in the field of human rights there has been, throughout the past three years, an increasing acceptance of the concept of "human rights enforcement."[4] One should be careful about overemphasizing the precedence of Security Council Resolution 688 in April 1991, which provided the basis for Western governments and nongovernmental organizations to intervene in support of the Kurdish population in northern Iraq. Nonetheless, it is clear that, within the community of states, outside intervention in the case of gross human rights violations and widespread suffering caused by war and ethnic repression is now more acceptable.[5] The US-led intervention in Somalia in December 1992 sought to establish a secure environment for humanitarian relief operations. It thereby points to a broadening of the category of events considered "threats to international peace and security," which provides the basis for action under Chapter VII of the UN Charter.[6]

Whether or not these developments are to be welcomed, they all suggest the need for a more careful analysis of the specific problems posed by outside military intervention in ethnic conflicts.

CYPRUS

There have been three main outside interventions since the Cyprus dispute changed from an anticolonial campaign to an ethnic conflict.[7] First, there was a British and subsequent UN peacekeeping effort. Second, there was a series of fairly overt Greek interventions. These included the presence on Cyprus of Greek officers beyond agreed numbers and close connections between the Greek army and the Cyprus National Guard, culminating in the Greek-led coup against the Makarios government. This precipitated the third intervention, the Turkish invasion of July 1974.

Cyprus became independent in 1960 under arrangements that allowed Britain to retain sovereignty of two base areas and allowed Greece and Turkey to station limited numbers of troops on the island for the purposes of providing common defense and of training Cypriot forces. The Cypriot constitution was guaranteed by Britain, Greece, and Turkey. By 1963, cooperation between Greek and Turkish communities on Cyprus, which was needed to make the constitution work, had ceased to exist. At the same time, Greek extremists who wanted *enosis* (union with Greece) launched a series of attacks on Turkish-Cypriots, killing some and taking others hostage. Under the threat of a Turkish invasion, a cease-fire was established. This was policed initially by British forces from the sovereign base areas and later by the UN Peacekeeping Force in Cyprus (UNFICYP). The next 10 years were marked by a series of incidents of greater and lesser seriousness. The most dangerous of these produced another threat of Turkish invasion in 1967; the resolution of this crisis involved the withdrawal of Greek and Turkish forces in excess of agreed numbers.

In 1974, the Greek-Cypriot National Guard, led by Greek officers, overthrew the government of Cyprus with a view to establishing *enosis*. Turkey called for the resignation of the new regime and the withdrawal of the Greek officers who had led the coup. When this call went unheeded, Turkey invaded Cyprus. Many lives were lost in the fighting, and an even larger number of refugees were created, mainly Greek-Cypriots, as the part of the island under Turkish control was extended. Since then, negotiations have continued, but no decisive breakthrough has been made. Cyprus remains divided along the line established in 1974. This buffer zone continues to be policed by UNFICYP.

In retrospect, none of these interventions was wholly successful. Least successful were the various Greek interventions. If the objective was *enosis*, they manifestly failed. Similarly, the Greek interventions have done nothing to support the interests of Greek-Cypriots. In fact, the Greek intervention led indirectly to the deaths of many Greek-Cypriots and to many others being made homeless. Moreover, they damaged whatever chances existed after 1963 of reestablishing an undivided Cyprus, something that most Greek-Cypriots would probably have preferred to *enosis*. In addition to the other inconveniences it imposes, the division of Cyprus will probably be a major obstacle to its accession to the European Community, another Greek and Greek-Cypriot goal.

The Turkish invasion achieved at least one of Turkey's objectives: the geostrategic goal of avoiding a Greek takeover of Cyprus. A second objective was the protection of the Turkish-Cypriot minority. Success here is harder to evaluate. Many Turkish-Cypriots died in the fighting in 1974, and large numbers were made homeless during the invasion and its aftermath. On the other hand, given the nature of the coup leaders, it is not clear how safe the lives and liberties of Turkish-Cypriots would have been without the Turkish invasion. For many Turkish-Cypriots, and perhaps for some Turks as well, the long-term division of the island is seen as the only credible basis for ensuring the community's security.

The Turkish invasion, however, achieved this goal only in a partial sense: The island remains divided, but the Northern Cypriot state has not been recognized by the international community, a situation that leaves the authorities there, as well as the Turkish-Cypriots, with many impediments. Because other states (excluding Turkey) do not recognize the Northern Cypriot government, they will not negotiate airway agreements with it. As a result, there are no direct flights into Northern Cyprus, something that has hampered efforts to reestablish its once-booming tourist industry. In addition, the legal difficulties surrounding the ownership of land in Northern Cyprus are a deterrent to foreign investors. On a more local level, the economic embargo imposed by the government of Cyprus adds to the north's difficulties. A prosperous future for the Turkish community must be established on the basis of international recognition; this will come only with a settlement that reunifies Cyprus, perhaps in some federal configuration.

It is also hard to characterize the international community's intervention in Cyprus as a complete success. The March 1964 UN Security Council resolution that established the UNFICYP states that "the function of the force should be, in the interest of preserving international peace and security, to use its best efforts to prevent a recurrence of fighting and, as necessary, to contribute to the maintenance and restoration of law and order and a return to normal conditions."[8] In its main task, to prevent a recurrence of the fighting, UNFICYP evidently failed—although it has almost certainly prevented many deaths in smaller incidents. It is possible that, without UNFICYP, the events of 1974 would have taken place much earlier and in an even more bloody form. Nevertheless, the presence of a UN force did not, on its own, prevent a recurrence of fighting. UN forces were able only to patrol dangerous zones and to control access to enclaves. They could not police every inch of Cyprus, nor safeguard its constitution.

The goal of the peacekeeping force is not to settle the Cyprus dispute: this is for the parties themselves and for UN mediators. UNFICYP was, nevertheless, charged with contributing to a return to normal conditions. In fact, it has probably done the opposite. By stabilizing the situation, it has made it possible for everyone to live with a divided Cyprus and has thus removed some of the pressures for a complete settlement. Also, by freezing a particular status quo, UNFICYP has favored one side—in this case, the Turkish-Cypriots who have shown a consistent preference for a divided Cyprus.

UNFICYP has also served a further purpose unstated in the Security Council resolution. This was to lessen the risk of a direct conflict between Greece and Turkey, two North Atlantic Treaty Organization (NATO) allies. In this, the international community was successful, but only just. Although it was not UNFICYP itself that prevented war, it is nevertheless fair to conclude that, without UNFICYP and the active engagement of the international community, the risks of a direct Greek–Turkish clash would have been much greater. On balance, therefore, UNFICYP has a positive record, although it is not a total success. Set against this decision by the international community must be the financial and human costs of an operation that has gone on for nearly 30 years.

THE INDIAN PEACEKEEPING FORCE
IN SRI LANKA

In Sri Lanka, the extreme violence of the 1980s followed a long buildup of tension.[9] The downward slide began with the election in 1956 of S.W.R.D Bandaranaike on a "Sinhala only" platform. It continued with the abandonment of the two-language policy in 1960, the 1972 constitution that gave Buddhism the foremost place in national life, and the formation of the first important Tamil organization in 1973. Discrimination against Tamils in employment and education led to the formation of extremist separatist movements. From 1983 onward, a cycle of guerrilla attacks by Tamil separatists, reprisals by the government or by Sinhala civilians, and further guerrilla attacks brought an increasing level of violence.

India was concerned by the conflict in Sri Lanka for a number of reasons. First, there is a large Tamil population in India. Indeed, many of the Tamils in Sri Lanka were classed as Indians, rather than as Sri Lankans, by Sri Lanka's citizenship law; this had the effect of disenfranchising them. Not surprising, there was sympathy for Tamils in Sri Lanka among Indian Tamils in Tamil Nadu, the Indian state closest to Sri Lanka. Second, the troubles in Sri Lanka brought a large number of Tamil refugees to Tamil Nadu—more than 100,000 in 1983 alone. These refugees included guerrillas who trained in camps in Tamil Nadu, apparently with support from Indian authorities. From time to time, the violence and criminal behavior of the Tamil militants on the mainland—drugs and gunrunning, as well as robbery and murder—brought a crackdown by the government of India. It also increased the pressure on the Indian government to find a solution to Sri Lanka's problems. Finally, India probably saw itself as having geostrategic interests in Sri Lanka. On the one hand, it had no love of the Sri Lankan government, which had allowed Pakistan to use its airports in the 1971 war, nor did India welcome President J.R. Jayewardene's attempts to bring foreign (British or US) forces into Sri Lanka. On the other hand, the Indian government had no interest in seeing a Tamil state established in Sri Lanka, because this might have encouraged Tamil separatism on the mainland.

These complex motives were to prove a handicap during the Indian intervention: Although the Indian government did not mind seeing the Sri Lankan government weakened, it did not wish to support a separatist solution to the conflict. Above all, the Indian government may have believed that, as the major power in the region, it had a right or a responsibility to intervene.

Intervention came when, in 1987, the Liberation Tigers of Tamil Eelam (LTTE) announced that they were taking over the civil administration of the Jaffna Peninsula, where the Tamil population is concentrated. This prompted a military offensive by the Sri Lankan army and a blockade of the Jaffna Peninsula. Both lasted for five months. The blockade, which prevented food and fuel from reaching Jaffna, together with artillery fire and bombing raids for a period of five months, caused grave hardship to the civilian population of Jaffna. In June 1987, Indian ships attempted to take relief supplies to the peninsula, but were turned back. India then made an airdrop of food under military escort, without the agreement of the Sri Lankan government.

Once India had demonstrated that it was prepared to take the law into its own hands, President Jayewardene accepted an accord with India. This provided, inter alia, for military assistance from India to implement the agreement. The accord, which also included political provisions on the status of the Tamils, provided for a cease-fire in which the Tamils would surrender their weapons, and the Sri Lankan army would be confined to its barracks.

Although India sent 7,000 troops to Sri Lanka to implement the cease-fire, this proved difficult. The LTTE did not give up its weapons and continued to launch guerrilla attacks, mainly on other Tamil groups. The Indian peacekeeping force, whose numbers had risen to 20,000, attempted to disarm the LTTE using force. In the process, it killed and wounded a large number of civilians (estimates go as high as 3,000) and itself took a considerable number of casualties. Although it eventually disarmed some LTTE groups, these groups had little difficulty replenishing their armaments, either from hidden supplies or from the international market. The Indian peacekeeping force (IPKF), meanwhile, became increasingly identified with another Tamil group, the Eelam People's Revolutionary Liberation Front (EPRLF).

As the intervention continued, the Indian force came to be resented by almost every group in Sri Lanka. The fact that President Jayewardene did not fulfill one of the key provisions of the accord—holding a referendum on the merger of the two main Tamil provinces—helped to undermine its legitimacy. Even Tamils who were not supporters of the LTTE did not see the IPKF as representing long-term protection from the Sinhalese. The LTTE itself was at war with the IPKF. The Indian presence meant that, in the south, the left-wing Janatha Vimukthi Perumena (JVP) was able to draw on anti-Indian support in its attacks on the government so that it became a more serious threat than before.

A military stalemate continued in the north until May 1989, nearly two years after its initial deployment, when the Sri Lankan government called for the IPKF to withdraw. In a sense, the IPKF became a common enemy around which the Sri Lankan government wished to forge national unity. Although the Sri Lankan government called for an immediate withdrawal of the entire IPKF by the end of July 1989, negotiations were protracted. The process was speeded up when Indian Prime Minister Rajiv Gandhi, who had been responsible for the deployment of the IPKF, lost the Indian election in December 1989. When the Indians ultimately left, they took with them their EPRLF allies, effectively leaving the LTTE in control of the north and in continuing conflict with the Sri Lankan government.

The Indian intervention was a success only in its earliest phase. Had India not been prepared to intervene, there is no telling what would have happened in the siege of Jaffna. Thereafter, it was a failure on almost every count. Far from protecting the Tamils, Indian forces were responsible for many Tamil deaths. They certainly did not bring peace to northern Sri Lanka. Instead of disarming the LTTE, the IPKF left the Tigers stronger and better armed than ever before. Some refugees have returned from the mainland to Sri Lanka, but most are still in Tamil Nadu.

The initial basis of the Indian deployment was flawed: The political agreement reached with the Sri Lankan government was never genuinely accepted by the LTTE. Given the LTTE's political aims, it is improbable that any agreement with the Sri Lankan government would have stuck; deploying troops on such a basis was risky. In all of this, there was a lack of clarity with respect to Indian aims. India sought to protect the Tamils by securing for them some sort of political autonomy. However, at least some of the Tamils wanted rather more. This led to attempts to enforce an agreement that was really not an agreement at all, and India paid a heavy price. In financial terms, Indian costs were estimated to have been $150 million, with the IPKF involving 45,000 troops at one stage. In human terms, most reports suggest that more than 1,000 Indian soldiers were killed in Sri Lanka.[10]

Far from preventing the Sri Lankan troubles from spilling onto the mainland, India's involvement may have achieved the opposite effect, as Rajiv Gandhi's assassination tragically demonstrated. Finally, the operation did little to enhance either India's geostrategic position or its international reputation. Perhaps India's biggest success was that it managed to get out at all. For that, the Sri Lankan government and the Indian general election were responsible.

BANGLADESH

Some 16 years earlier, India intervened with great success in a rather different ethnic conflict. Until 1971, the peculiarity of the Pakistani state was that it was divided geographically, as well as ethnically. Indeed, Pakistan "came into being as a geographical absurdity" with the country physically divided by a thousand miles of Indian territory.[11]

Ever since independence from British rule in 1947, the Bengalis of East Pakistan, which constituted 54 percent of the total population of the country, had been dominated by the Urdu-speaking minority in West Pakistan. Although the Bengalis had played a crucial part in Pakistan's struggle for independence, their subsequent exclusion from all higher positions in the civil and military bureaucracies of the new country led to growing resentment. This was reinforced by a range of discriminatory policies adopted by the West Pakistani elite, including the initial insistence that Urdu should be the only state language, even though less than 1 percent of the Bengali population could speak the language. East Pakistan also suffered economically from its association with West Pakistan. The ruling elite's persistent refusal to accommodate Bengali demands for majority rule and greater autonomy further exacerbated tension between the two halves of the country.

These problems came to a head in 1970 when elections were called. The Awami League, a party based entirely in East Pakistan, won almost all the seats there, sufficient for an absolute majority in the Pakistani national assembly. Its leader, Sheikh Mujib announced a program of radical devolution. Political and military leaders in West Pakistan refused to accept this; they proclaimed a state of emergency in East Pakistan and launched a campaign of military repression there. India suffered a large influx of refugees—more than 10 million; India also offered facilities to Bengali guerrillas. Throughout 1971, the ferocity of both the guerrilla campaign and the Pakistani army's repression in East Pakistan continued.

Although different in scale, the situation in East Pakistan was similar in some respects to Sri Lanka. The Indian response, however, was different. In this case, India placed itself squarely on the side of the democratically elected separatist movement and adopted the straightforward military objective of defeating the Pakistani forces. Although which party attacked first is still in dispute, India's military and political victory over Pakistan is not. In the end, Pakistan was divided, and India achieved all its objectives—geostrategic, humanitarian, and refugee-related. This was accomplished in a short period of time, with the loss of some 1,000 Indian lives.

In retrospect, India is probably disappointed with its geostrategic achievements: The breakup of Pakistan has not prevented it from remaining a thorn in India's side; Pakistan may be weaker, but it is still dangerous. The intractable dispute about Kashmir also continues. Nevertheless, in the terms in which events presented themselves in 1971, India's success seems almost total. However, this is a unique case among ethnic conflicts. The Bengalis represented a subordinate, homogeneous population with a distinct language, history, and culture. Moreover, they had a clearly defined homeland some 1,000 miles away from the dominant ethnic group. Equally important, in their secessionist struggle, they had full political and military support from India. Other cases are much more complicated.

LEBANON

Lebanon has undergone, and is still undergoing, a number of foreign interventions. This chapter will focus on three: the Syrian intervention from 1976 onward, the Israeli intervention in 1982, and the international interventions that followed.[12]

Lebanon's troubles have two origins: the Christian–Muslim divide is ethnic and internal, and the Arab–Israel dispute has forced itself on Lebanon from the outside. This combination has been disastrous. Sporadic troubles in Lebanon developed into a major civil war in 1975. The power-sharing system (Christian president, Sunni prime minister, Shi'a speaker) no longer provided political legitimacy due to ideological differences between the Muslims, who had been attracted by pan-Arab ideas since the 1950s, and the Christians who had not. In addition, there were demographic changes, as the Muslim population grew faster than the Christian. Above all, there was the impact of the Arab–Israeli conflict. This had two effects. First, it sharpened the political division between ethnic groups: Muslims identified with the Palestinian struggle against Israel; Christians wanted to stay out of the conflict. Second, it led to a large influx of Palestinians from Israel (1948) and from Jordan (1970), including the political and military headquarters of the Palestine Liberation Organization (PLO). Beirut lost control of southern Lebanon to the Palestinians and to Israeli proxy forces. A UN force in the south, United Nations Interim Force in Lebanon (UNIFIL), provided some security for local people, but did not prevent sporadic strikes by Israel against Palestinian targets and vice versa.

Syrian intervention in Lebanon was driven by three main motives. First, there were ephemeral reasons connected to support for particular groups in Lebanon and hostility toward others—principally, those backed by Syria's Arab enemies. Second, the Syrian government was conscious that the Lebanese civil war might spill over into Syria, which is itself a far from homogeneous society. The third, and probably most important reason, was geostrategic. On the one hand, Syria had no wish to find Lebanon either under the control of an Israeli-backed Christian government or of radical Muslim groups; either would pose a threat to Syria. On the other hand, it had historic claims on Lebanon and a long-standing goal of making Lebanon a part of a Syrian sphere of influence.

At first, Syria's involvement came in the form of mediation between the main parties in the civil war, the Muslims and the Maronites. When this failed and PLO intervention on the Muslim side threatened to win a victory for a left-wing coalition, Syria answered Christian appeals for help. Syrian moves were carefully calculated and based on a tacit understanding with Israel about zones of influence and deployments (the Red

Line). The effect of the Syrian intervention was to redress the balance in Lebanon in favor of the Christians. Initially, Syrian intervention facilitated Christian repression of the PLO; subsequently, Christian connections with Israel led to a Syrian alliance with the PLO. The Syrian intervention had tacit US support and was legitimized by two Arab summit conferences convened in October 1976 in Riyadh and Cairo.

Since their intervention, the Syrians appear to have achieved two broad objectives. The first was to avoid an all-out war with Israel. It has been prepared to accept considerable losses—notably, the whole of its air force and air defenses in 1982—without making a major response. Its second, and perhaps overriding, objective has been simply to remain in Lebanon, shifting alliances as necessary with different Lebanese factions to consolidate its political influence. After a considerable number of ups and downs, patience and political flexibility seem to have paid off. Syria's special role in Lebanon was recognized in 1989 in the Taif Accord, sponsored by the Arab League. In 1990, it achieved a military victory over anti-Syrian forces led by Michel Aoun, when the Iraqi invasion of Kuwait undercut Iraqi support for Aoun, and Israel was on its best behavior. Although Lebanon remains fragile, one must judge that Syria's objectives—pacification and expanding its regional influence—have been achieved, at least for the moment.

Israel has intervened in Lebanon on many occasions in different ways. Its two major invasions took place in 1978 and 1982. The first of these had relatively little to do with Lebanon's internal troubles. It was a response to the PLO presence in Lebanon established after its expulsion from Jordan. This intervention followed a limited and defensive definition of Israeli interests in Lebanon: to keep the PLO at a safe distance, to avoid conflict with Syria, and to avoid deep involvement in Lebanese politics.

The 1982 intervention also began as an anti-PLO operation. It was, however, different from the 1978 invasion in two crucial respects. First, Israeli objectives were confused. It is generally agreed that the defense minister, Ariel Sharon, had objectives that were more ambitious than those of the full Israeli government. These far-reaching objectives included the complete removal of the PLO from Lebanon and the establishment of a sympathetic government in Beirut. These aspirations ultimately led to a conflict with Syria (which Israel won easily), a much deeper involvement in Lebanese domestic politics, and a much closer association with the Maronite Christians. These objectives were not easily attained. In military terms, the task proved difficult once the PLO retreated to Beirut where it was supported by Syrian forces also trapped there. In political terms, the massive use of Israeli power against Beirut attracted international, including US, revulsion. The result was that, when the PLO finally left Beirut following US-mediated negotiations, they were seen as having made a heroic resistance, rather than having suffered a humiliating defeat. The Israeli action also caused serious political problems domestically and within the Israeli defense forces. In any event, removing the PLO did not remove all threats from southern Lebanon: As the PLO disappeared from view, Hizbollah came to prominence. Israeli difficulties in dealing with the PLO made their second objective—the establishment of a pro-Israeli Christian government in Beirut—even more difficult to attain. Moreover, by aligning themselves with the Maronites, the Israelis found that they had to bear some of the responsibility when the Christian militia massacred refugees in the camps at Sabra and Shatila. Eventually, domestic pressures led to an Israeli withdrawal from Lebanon, which was completed between February and April 1985. Their intervention against the PLO was partly successful, but their intervention in Lebanese politics was almost entirely unsuccessful. The cost to Israel in terms of lives, money, and reputation was considerable. In many ways, the failure in 1982 demonstrated the virtues of the approach followed in 1978: Limited defensive objectives were attainable; attempts to control events within Lebanon were not.

The third intervention in Lebanon, by multinational forces, followed the Israeli intervention. The first multinational force (MFN I) was deployed in August 1982, following a US-negotiated agreement for the withdrawal of the PLO from Beirut. The force consisted of 800 French troops, 800 Americans, and 400 Italians. It was deployed in Beirut to guarantee the safety of PLO members withdrawing by road to Syria and by sea to Tunisia; it was also supposed to protect Palestinians remaining in Beirut and Palestinian civilians in refugee camps. This was a classic, limited peacekeeping operation, based on an agreement among those principally concerned. These tasks were subsequently accomplished, and MFN I withdrew approximately two weeks after it was first deployed.

The third objective—protecting Palestinian civilians in the refugee camps—could be achieved, however, only while MFN I was in Lebanon. Shortly after its withdrawal, however, Christian forces murdered hundreds of civilians in the Sabra and Shatila camps in West Beirut, which was then occupied by Israel. An international outcry followed. Israel was widely blamed, although no Israelis had been directly involved in the slaughter. The United States, which had handed over West Beirut to the Israelis, also felt some responsibility and organized a second and larger multinational force (MFN II). This force was deployed about two weeks after MNF I left the scene. The force initially included 1,500 French troops, 1,400 Americans, and 1,400 (later increased to 2,200) Italians. A

British contingent joined later. This deployment was an emotional response to the massacres, and its objectives were not clearly defined. Explaining the deployment, US President Ronald Reagan said: "We seek the restoration of a strong and stable central government." In accepting the request of the Lebanese cabinet to redeploy and augment the international peacekeeping force in Beirut, Reagan described it as "an interposition force . . . to assist the Lebanese government and armed forces."[13]

The difficulty with this mandate was that, by this time, there was no nationally accepted Lebanese government. The authority that MFN II was supposed to support were merely factions in the Lebanese civil war. Among the multinational forces (which never operated effectively as a single unit), the French had close ties with the Maronites, and the Americans had political links with Israel. Italian forces were deployed in mainly Palestinian areas. British forces, which came from the peacekeeping mission in Cyprus, remained in contact with a number of different groups.

The uneasy balance in Lebanon was disturbed in the summer of 1983 as the Israeli forces began to pull out of Beirut. This led to conflict between the Lebanese armed forces and a loose Muslim coalition, with each side fighting for control of the vacated area. US and French forces gave support to the Lebanese armed forces, with the United States using heavy artillery from its fleet offshore. By this time, parts of the multinational force were clearly identified with Christian factions in the civil war. Both France and the United States suffered for this, losing 58 and 214 lives, respectively, in suicide bombings. The US, British, and Italian contingents withdrew from Lebanon early in 1984. The French withdrew the bulk of their forces, leaving behind a small contingent that was eventually evacuated in 1986.

MFN II accomplished little, if anything. It was deployed on an ambiguous mandate, which made it a peacekeeping force, but also linked it to one side in the conflict. It did not function as a single unified force; indeed, the different force participants sought different objectives. In the end, there was no basis for it to act as a peacekeeping force: There was no peace to keep, and parts of the force were not perceived as neutral. Similarly, MFN II lacked the capacity or resolve to assist the Christian groups with which it became identified. Like the Indian force in Sri Lanka, MFN II had two moments of success: its initial deployment, which was welcomed on all sides, and its withdrawal.

CURRENT CASES
Former Yugoslavia

In 1992, the United Nations launched a major peacekeeping operation in former Yugoslavia: initially, in Croatia and, subsequently, in Bosnia-Herzegovina.

In Croatia, some 14,000 UN troops, including police forces and observers, were deployed in March to monitor a cease-fire agreement reached between Serb and Croat forces following the war of 1991. Specifically, the UN Protection Force (UNPROFOR) has been deployed in four UN-protected areas, coinciding roughly with Serbian-occupied enclaves. The aim has been to provide enough intercommunal peace and security necessary for negotiations on an overall settlement to proceed. Although there has been no large-scale eruption of violence in these areas since the deployment of UNPROFOR, the UN force has not succeeded in establishing its authority in the protected areas. Indeed, a situation of extreme anarchy within the UN zones, with continuing acts of terrorism and ethnic cleansing by Serbian irregulars, has persisted.[14] In a report about the deteriorating situation in Croatia, the UN secretary-general observed in November 1992 that the Security Council might soon have "to make the difficult choice between withdrawing the operation, in the knowledge that this will be likely to lead to a resumption of fighting, or keep it in place, in the knowledge that this may involve the Council in a large and expensive commitment for an indefinite period of time, without any certainty that the mandate of the operation will be fulfilled."[15]

In the meantime, the UNPROFOR mandate has been extended to Bosnia-Herzegovina to provide protective support for the delivery of humanitarian assistance there. This represents a new kind of peacekeeping operation, although the traditional rules of engagement have been maintained. The UN operation in Bosnia has done little or nothing to stop the cycle of ethnic violence and war. As Patrick Moore points out, one of the striking features of the Bosnian conflict is the fact that aid work is being carried out and evidence of war crimes collected in the thick of war.[16] Increasingly, as the war continues, calls are made for the United Nations to sanction military action against the Bosnian Serbs.[17]

Former Soviet Union

Within the former Soviet Union, Russian or Commonwealth of Independent States (CIS) forces have intervened in South Ossetia and Abkhazia in Georgia, Moldova, and Tajikistan. Russian mediation between Armenia and Azerbaijan led to Russian observers being deployed in the Nagorno-Karabakh region in September 1991, but these have since been withdrawn. In South Ossetia, deployment of a trilateral Russian–Georgian–Ossetian force was agreed to by Russian President Boris Yeltsin and Georgian President Eduard Shevardnadze in late June 1992. Russians dominate this force. Against expectations, it has been largely successful in maintaining a cease-fire, although there has been no progress toward a political solution to the overarching conflict. In Abkhazia, a similar agreement in September 1992 has not been implemented; the dispute between Abkhaz separatists and the Tbilisi government has actually escalated, and Russian troops, accused by each side of helping the other, have been deployed to guard some key installations.

In Moldova, Russia's Fourteenth Army was already in place when trouble started between Moldovan, and Dniestrian (mainly, ethnic Russian) forces in March 1992. Although supposedly observing strict neutrality, the support of the Fourteenth Army's leadership for the Dniestrians became increasingly open. For the Moldovans, who saw it as an army of occupation, it was not acceptable as a peacekeeping force. A mixed Russian, Moldovan, and Dniestrian force was subsequently deployed, following an agreement between Presidents Yeltsin and Mircea Snegur in July 1992.[18]

In Tajikistan, the civil war continues, although in November 1992 a parliamentary session for national reconciliation invited the introduction of a CIS peacekeeping force. Although this primarily involves Russian troops already in Tajikistan, Moscow is keen for any force to include more than nominal representatives of the other republics. The parliament of Kyrgyzstan has, however, voted against sending its troops into Tajikistan.

Liberia

Whether the Liberian civil war should be characterized as an ethnic conflict is hard to judge. Its origins were in foreign (Libyan) subversion, rather than ethnic rivalry. It has, however, polarized the country along ethnic lines (Krahn and Mandingo versus Gio and Mano tribes). For neighboring countries, it has brought up to half a million refugees, threats to their own internal stability and to their nationals trapped in Monrovia. La Force Ouest-Africaine d'Interposition (ECOMOG), a West African peacekeeping force of 2,500, arrived in Monrovia on August 24, 1990, with the agreement of Liberian President Samuel Doe and Prince Johnson, the leader of one of the rebel factions, but without the agreement of the other rebel leader, Charles Taylor. ECOMOG forces have been involved in fighting, mostly against Taylor's forces. (President Doe was captured while visiting ECOMOG headquarters and subsequently murdered.) As of January 1993, ECOMOG has secured control of Monrovia, where life is returning to normal, although much of the country remains under the control of Taylor's forces. A political settlement to the conflict still appears distant; agreements on disarming Taylor's forces have not been effective so far.

CHARACTERISTICS OF ETHNIC CONFLICTS

Even the limited number of cases studied here makes one thing clear: All conflicts are different; all interventions are sui generis. It is, nonetheless, worth asking whether there are any features peculiar to ethnic conflicts, as opposed to other kinds of civil war or interstate war. Two points stand out.

First, ethnic conflicts seem to last a long time. Perhaps this is in the nature of things. If the parties to the conflict are defined by some unalterable or nearly unalterable characteristic—such as race, religion, or language—the tension between the parties is likely to be long-lasting.[19] This may create the conditions for lasting conflict as well. Of the cases examined above, only one—Bangladesh—seems to have been fully resolved. Others, although each is at least a decade old, give the impression of being contained, rather than resolved. Ethnic tensions in the former Yugoslavia and the former Soviet Union, reinforced by the experience of brutal and divisive war, may prove even more long-lasting.

A second important characteristic of ethnic conflict is the nature of the parties to the conflict. Interstate warfare is conducted by governments. Civil wars are most often conducted between rival governments. Ethnic conflicts—at least in the cases studied here—seem generally to be between governments and ethnic movements, that is, between a legally recognized authority, on the one hand, and a rather ill-defined and possibly illegal movement, on the other. Each may refuse to accept the other's legitimacy. In the initial stages of ethnic conflict, there is often a siege of different groups within the ethnic community's struggle all seeking to establish themselves as legitimate representatives. This characteristic is not universal because, in some cases, existing arrangements provide a focal point for the leadership of the ethnic movement: In Cyprus, the constitution recognized the existence of a Turkish community; in Bangladesh, geography defined the community. Other cases, such as Lebanon and Sri Lanka, may be more typical. In these cases, groups are unstable, at least at first. Even in situations in which ethnic movements have well-established structures, they are unlikely to be recognized as being on equal footing with a government.

Before turning to military intervention, it is worth noting that the question of recognition is one of some importance and one that gives both leverage and responsibility to the international community. To some extent, the success of an attempt at secession will be in the hands of the international community. In the case of Bangladesh, the willingness of the international community to recognize its separation from Pakistan was a key factor in the success of India's intervention. In Lebanon, Syria has worked hard to secure Arab and international recognition of its special status there. In the former Yugoslavia, the recognition of Croatia and Bosnia-Herzegovina by the European Community and the United States influenced the development of the conflict in important ways.[20]

Questions about diplomatic recognition and the legitimacy of outside intervention play an important part in ethnic conflict. Even those who are not directly involved should not take decisions on these matters lightly.

MOTIVES FOR INTERVENTION

The cases examined above illustrate the wide variety of motives that exist for outside intervention in ethnic conflicts: hegemonic ambitions; concerns about regional stability; ethnic sympathy for oppressed groups; a sense of international responsibility, perhaps allied to some notion of world order or regional order; and humanitarian concerns. In most of the cases considered here, those who have intervened have had mixed motives, often including motives that are both altruistic and self-interested. Nonetheless, it makes sense to distinguish between two broad types of intervention: those in which the dominant motive is one of interest or realpolitik, and those that are primarily of a peacekeeping nature. As indicated above, the practice of peacekeeping has evolved dramatically since 1987: Consideration of outside collective intervention in ethnic conflict requires a distinction to be drawn between "traditional" peacekeeping operations and those that may depart from the consensual and nonforceful pattern of past operations.[21] Increasing international pressure for "coercive" intervention in Bosnia-Herzegovina, and the persistence of conflict in former Soviet Asia and Caucasia, further highlights the importance of making this distinction.[22]

INTERVENTIONS OF INTEREST

One of the lessons suggested by the case studies is that the most successful interventions are those in which the intervening power sees a clear national interest to be at stake. This was the case in the Turkish intervention in Cyprus: Turkish motives may have included both geostrategic considerations and ethnic sympathy. In Lebanon, Syria had long-term geostrategic interests, as well as concerns about regional stability. In Bangladesh, India had well-defined strategic goals. Such motives are not, however, a sufficient condition for success: The Greek intervention in Cyprus demonstrates the obvious point that it does not pay to take on a more powerful adversary. The Israeli intervention in Lebanon shows that, even when backed by military power, interest is not a guarantee of success. Nevertheless, if ethnic conflicts tend to be of long duration, an intervention is more likely to be successful if it can be sustained for a long period. There is no substitute for a solid perception of national interest. In the case of Bangladesh, a prolonged commitment proved unnecessary, but the scale of the Indian effort suggests that India would have been ready for one. In Cyprus, Turkey's willingness to commit troops and resources in large numbers and over a long period has contributed to the success of that intervention. In Lebanon, Syria's patient willingness to remain constant to its objectives, even while shifting tactical alliances and taking considerable losses, has been an essential element in Syria's success. National interest may be helpful in sustaining peacekeeping operations: The fact that many NATO members had a vital Cold War interest in avoiding the conflict between Greece and Turkey, as well as Britain's interest in retaining sovereign base areas, may have played a part in sustaining the Cyprus peacekeeping operation for nearly 30 years.

"Success" as it has been defined in these cases is not necessarily palatable to the international community. Ethnic conflict has been constrained in Cyprus by enforced separation, in Lebanon by the imposition of order from outside (in a fairly brutal fashion) in the form of a *Pax Syriana*. Neither of these methods appeals to democratic idealists. Nevertheless, these are solutions that are within the scope of military power. Armed forces can impose order, usually in a rather arbitrary fashion, and they can be used to separate people. In so far as these kind of "solutions" are envisaged and are backed by a strong interest, intervention has some chance of success.

PEACEKEEPING INTERVENTIONS
Ethnic Conflict and Traditional Peacekeeping

As a distinctive form of third-party intervention involving the deployment of military personnel, traditional peacekeeping operations have been expressly nonthreatening and impartial in character. Governed by the principles of local consent and minimum force, peacekeeping forces have not been empowered to impose solutions on combatants. At present, two operations with an important ethnic dimension are under way: UNIFIL, which was established in 1978, and UNFICYP.

There is something paradoxical about deploying a military force to establish peace. The classical use of military force is to defeat an enemy. Peace may thereby be established, but this is a side effect of a successful war, not the main objective. Nevertheless, there are many cases in which the armed forces of outside powers, in the shape of peacekeeping forces, have contributed to maintaining peace. The most successful cases have been those that fulfill the conditions listed by the UN secretary-general in the proposed guidelines for the UN force set up between Egypt and Israel in 1973: First, it must have, at all times, the full confidence and backing of the Security Council. Second, it must operate with the full cooperation of the parties concerned. Third, it must be able to function as an integrated and efficient military unit.

Legitimation

In practice, the most successful interventions have been conducted under UN authority. This may be a consequence of the UN's experience in the field, but is more likely a function of the UN's ability to confer legitimacy and guarantee neutrality. The importance of legitimizing operations should not be underestimated. Even governments motivated primarily by self-interest are keen to establish the legality of their interventions: Turkey invoked its position as a guarantor power; Syria took pains to obtain Arab endorsement of its position in Lebanon; India mounted a diplomatic campaign to obtain approval of its activity in Bangladesh, while also claiming self-defense as a justification for its actions.

In the case of peacekeeping operations, legitimation is even more important. Peacekeeping operations are increasingly called upon to restore law and order; it would be inconsistent to launch interventions of this type without proper legal authority. Of the cases discussed here, the most successful peacekeeping operation—UNFICYP—had Security Council backing. The unsuccessful cases, the IPKF and MNF II, were both non-UN operations. Both suffered as a result. Without a Security Council resolution, the only way a peacekeeping force can be legitimized is by a request from a government or from a regional organization. Government requests were indeed the legal basis for the interventions by both the IPKF and MFN II. Such justifications mean, however, that peacekeeping forces are likely to be seen as partisan: The government is usually one party to the conflict. Thus, the IPKF became identified with the Sri Lankan government and was considered a legitimate target by the LTTE; MFN II—or at least its French and US components—behaved as an ally of the Lebanese government and suffered the consequences. With regard to regional organizations, it should be noted that the roles of the Conference on Security and Cooperation in Europe and the European Community in the former Yugoslavia and the experience of CIS operations in the former Soviet Union clearly demonstrate the limitations of regional organizations, rather than the United Nations, acting as the legitimizing authorities for peacekeeping operations. In ethnic conflicts, regional organizations, consisting of states bordering the epicenter of conflict, may be particularly ill-suited for military interventions.

The Need for an Agreement

The secretary-general's second condition for intervention—full cooperation by the parties involved—can also present difficulties in the case of ethnic conflicts. One difficulty is that, as argued above, parties, factions, or movements may not be easily identified or recognized. In the recent

Somali peace talks held in Addis Ababa, no less than 11 groups or factions were represented. "Full cooperation" normally implies some kind of agreement among the parties. This may be difficult to establish if the parties are not willing to speak to each other. Even if agreements are reached, they may not stick. Leaders of ethnic movements are not the same as properly constituted authorities. They are more at the mercy of their followers, and reaching agreements with internal enemies or with foreigners may not prove popular. In such circumstances, therefore, agreements are difficult to reach and are likely to be unreliable, even when those who reach them are honest. The failure of countless cease-fire agreements in the former Yugoslavia illustrates the same point.

Sri Lanka and Lebanon also illustrate some of these problems. In Lebanon, MFN I's deployment was not based on a UN resolution, but there was an agreement among recognizable actors that held; MFN I remained in Beirut for no more than two weeks. MFN II, on the other hand, although initially welcomed by all sides, was not based on any agreement among the Lebanese factions. In Sri Lanka, India faced this difficulty: The LTTE was far from committed to the accord that formed the basis for India's intervention.

Peacekeeping intervention in ethnic conflict may be difficult, but that is not to say that success is impossible. There will always be a point, even in ethnic conflict, when two sides find that they have a shared interest in a cease-fire. There may also be times when, either because some shred of decency remains, or because they do not wish altogether to alienate outside opinion, the parties decide to let outsiders perform humanitarian tasks. They may allow this even when it is contrary to their strict military objectives. When they are performing a peacekeeping role, outside intervention forces operate on this margin of agreement and decency, as the International Committee of the Red Cross has operated for many years in interstate conflicts. In ethnic conflicts, the margin is likely to be especially narrow and uncertain; the elements of decency and self-discipline will be more unreliable than in interstate conflicts.

Enforcing Agreements in Ethnic Conflicts?

If agreements are shaky, can outside intervention be used to enforce them? The issue of whether peacekeeping forces should engage in enforcement action if parties to a dispute renege on a settlement (as is currently the case in Bosnia and Cambodia), requires careful consideration. The 1,000 Indian lives lost in Sri Lanka were seeking to impose an agreement. The implication is that, if an agreement needs to be enforced, it is not really agreed. If peace, or some "agreement" is to be enforced in these circumstances, it can be done only by imposing heavy costs or defeat on the other side. This will not be easy, especially in ethnic conflicts. As suggested above, a foreign or multinational intervention force may have objectives defined in terms of peace, justice, or humanitarian goals. There may also be an element of national interest involved. For these goals, outsiders may be prepared to accept some losses and to pay some costs. However, if they find themselves in direct conflict with an ethnic insurgent group, it will almost always be an unequal struggle because the adversary will see itself as fighting for survival. An ethnic group fighting for survival will be willing to pay almost any price and to suffer enormous losses. Having little stake in the status quo, the ethnic group may also be willing to break any rule, convention, or agreement if this will further its cause. For guerrilla movements, survival can provide a justification for almost anything.

This aspect of ethnic conflict places a premium on the formulation of clear and specific objectives for any outside military intervention, be it unilateral or collective. External interventions may succeed when goals are geostrategic and based on well-defined national interests. In such cases, the intervening country will take sides and may be prepared for a long haul (Syria in Lebanon, India in Bangladesh). In a more limited way, outside intervention can succeed when its objectives are to provide humanitarian assistance or to limit the scope of conflict. What does not succeed is a confusion of the two. International forces can operate on the margin of consent obtainable among local actors; they may even work to enlarge that margin. Alternatively, they can seek to *impose* a solution by military means. However, the two are different operations requiring different levels of commitment, different military deployments, and different rules of engagement. Peacekeepers in the Congo deployed thinly for monitoring functions became vulnerable when the UN force started to employ coercion. MFN II forces had neither the agreement necessary for a peacekeeping operation, nor the force levels and commitment necessary for a partisan intervention. Indian forces in Sri Lanka demonstrated the difficulty of coercive peacekeeping.

It follows that it will be difficult to set objectives for a peacekeeping force that is not merely interpository in nature. Success is likely to be limited. A military force cannot by itself establish a constitution, persuade people to live together, and set up a system of government and justice that inspires the trust of all involved ethnic groups. Therefore, it does not make sense to make the objective of this sort of intervention a full political settlement. In addition, it must be recognized, as in the Cyprus case, that a successful intervention may delay a political settlement. It may also prejudice the kind of political settlement obtainable.

Outside intervention is more likely to promote some solutions than others. Foreign forces can keep groups apart more easily than they can bring them together. Thus, it makes sense to set limited objectives for peacekeeping operations: keeping violence and the loss of life within certain bounds. Those intervening from outside will, therefore, probably be prepared to deploy only limited forces. Consequently, a balance must be struck between the degree of stability that a foreign force may bring and the costs that it brings to bear. This will imply a readiness to withdraw when the costs of intervention become unacceptable. In retrospect, successive Indian decisions to reinforce the IPKF, rather than to withdraw it, appear to be strategic misjudgments. However, it is always easy to say with hindsight that governments should intervene early and withdraw early. Such advice is rarely given at the time, and if it were, would rarely be practical in political terms.

With regard to the future of the United Nations in military interventions in ethnic conflicts, there is a more fundamental issue that needs to be addressed. As noted earlier, the legitimacy accorded by the UN is preferable to that provided by governments or regional organizations. Yet, the United Nations has not seriously addressed the question of how it can effectively intervene in intrastate—as opposed to interstate—conflicts. As Sydney Bailey points out: "The Charter was drafted on the assumption that disputes arise between states . . . there is no provision in the Charter by which the Security Council or General Assembly may relate to nonstate agencies such as liberation movements, communal minorities, or political parties."[23] The cases surveyed in this chapter make it clear that any discussion of intervention cannot be divorced from the broader political and administrative order that the intervenor is supposed either to impose or protect. The failure of the United Nations to address this issue is understandable, but it strongly reinforces the cautionary approach to military intervention in ethnic conflicts emphasized above.[24]

There is a dilemma here that many peacekeeping forces may face in ethnic conflicts: What should be done when a peacekeeping operation is established on a basis of a cease-fire or some other kind of agreement (for example, on elections) that fails to stick? (Mutatis mutandis, the same dilemma exists when the premises of a coercive intervention collapse, as in Israel's 1982 intervention in Lebanon.) To withdraw immediately may put at risk the chance of peace; it may also give a cheap victory to those who prefer violence to negotiation. To stay on in an ambiguous role carries all the dangers outlined above. There is no simple solution: Costs and benefits have to be weighed carefully, and goals, as suggested above, have to be judged in relative, rather than absolute, terms. It is striking that, in most of the cases cited above, withdrawal has proved difficult. In some cases, it has seemed like a defeat; in most, it has not taken place at all. Only in Bangladesh and the case of MFN I did the intervening power get out in good order. Bangladesh was a particularly unusual case, and MFN I's withdrawal from Lebanon was quickly followed by massacres. Perhaps the best one can say is that any group intervening in an ethnic conflict should not go in without thinking carefully about the circumstances under which it will get out.

CONCLUSION

Three basic points should be kept in mind when considering outside military intervention in ethnic conflict. First, it is important to have clear short- and long-term political objectives. Equally important, these objectives must be capable of being translated into realizable military goals. Second, the intervention needs to have a credible and sustainable source of legitimacy. The question of legitimacy is particularly important with regard to multinational intervention in ethnic conflict. Although the advantages of the United Nations in terms of universality and impartiality are significant, the organization has not yet addressed the broader implications of its role in intrastate conflict. Third, the intervening force must satisfy operational requirements in terms of logistics, command and control, and training, that will ensure success in the field. This issue is of particular importance in cases in which the intervening force is not engaged in traditional combat operations, but may nonetheless be required to operate in a semipermissive operational environment. Such operations will require a high degree of discipline and political sensitivity. The requirement will be for particularly well-trained and well-led forces. It is by no means clear that all the outside forces in Yugoslavia or Liberia currently meet this requirement.

Ethnic conflicts, experience seems to show, are nasty, brutish, and long. Outside intervention in ethnic conflicts is likely to be particularly uncertain because one may be venturing into places that are not under anybody's control. Outside intervention, whether it springs from motives of interest, ethnic sympathy, or for more idealistic reasons will therefore require clarity of purpose and operation.

Notes

Robert Cooper was, at the time of writing, the Head of Policy Planning Staff in the British Foreign Office. Opinions expressed here, however, are his own and should not be taken as an expression of official government policy.

[1] Anthony Smith defines an ethnic community, or *ethnie*, as a "named collectivity sharing a common myth of origins and descent, a common history, one or more elements of distinctive culture, a common territorial association and a sense of group solidarity." See Anthony Smith, "*Ethnie* and Nation in the Modern World," *Millennium:*

Journal of International Studies, vol. 14, no. 2, Summer 1985. See also Anthony Smith, *The Ethnic Origins of Nations* (Oxford: Basil Blackwell, 1986), pp. 22–41.

[2] For a discussion on the various types of intervention, see Ramses Amer, *The United Nations and Foreign Military Intervention: A Comparative Study of the Application of the Charter* (Uppsala, Sweden: Department of Peacekeeping and Conflict Research, Uppsala University, 1992), pp. 9–15.

[3] See Philip Windsor, "Towards a New World Order?" *The Oxford International Review*, vol. 2, no. 3, Spring 1991, pp. 1–3.

[4] See W.J. Durch and Barry Blechman, *Keeping the Peace: The United Nations in the Emerging World Order* (Washington, D.C.: Henry Stimson Center, 1992), pp. 17–21. See also, B.G. Ramcharan, "The Security Council: The Maturing of International Protection of Human Rights," *The Review* (International Commission of Jurists), no. 48, June 1992, pp. 24–37.

[5] For an excellent account of the implications of the Kurdish crisis for the principle of nonintervention, see James Mayall, "Non-intervention, Self-determination and the 'New World Order'," *International Affairs*, vol. 67, no. 3, July 1991, pp. 421–428.

[6] See "Letter dated November 26, 1992 from the Secretary-General to the Security Council," UN Document S/24868, November 30, 1992.

[7] This section draws in part on J.T.A Koumoulides, ed., *Cyprus in Transition, 1960–1985* (London: Trigraph, 1986).

[8] UN Security Council Resolution 186, March 4, 1964.

[9] For an analysis of the sources of conflict between the Sinhalese and Tamils in Sri Lanka, see Jayantha Perera, "Political Development and Ethnic Conflict in Sri Lanka," *Journal of Refugee Studies*, vol. 5, no. 2, 1992,

pp. 137–148. See also Rajesh Kadian, *India's Sri Lanka Fiasco: Peace Keepers at War* (New Delhi: Vision Books, 1990).

[10] Kadian, *India's Sri Lanka Fiasco,* p. 156; Mahnaz Ispahani, "India's Role in Sri Lanka's Ethnic Conflict," in A. Levite, B. Jentleson, and L. Berman, eds., *Foreign Military Intervention: The Dynamics of Protracted Conflict* (New York: Columbia University Press, 1992), p. 229.

[11] Harun al-Rashid, "Bangladesh: The First Successful Secessionist Movement in the Third World," in R. Premas, S.W.R. de A. Samarasinghe, and A. Anderson, eds., *Secessionist Movements in Comparative Perspective* (London: Pinter Publishers, 1990), p. 87.

[12] For a recent analysis of Syrian and Israeli involvement in Lebanon, see Yossi Olmert, "Syria in Lebanon," and Shai Feldman, "Israel's Involvement in Lebanon: 1975–1985," in Levite, Jentleson, and Berman, *Foreign Military Intervention.*

[13] Yehuda Bar, "The Effectiveness of Multinational Forces in the Middle East," in Abdulaziz bin Khalid Alsudairy, et al., *Five War Zones: The Views of Local Military Leaders* (Washington, D.C.: Pergamon-Brassey's, 1986).

[14] See *Report of Secretary-General Pursuant to Security Council Resolution 762*, UN Document S/24353, July 27, 1992; Security Council Resolution 779, October 6, 1992.

[15] *Further Report of the Secretary-General Pursuant to Security Resolution 743*, UN Document S/24848, November 24, 1992.

[16] Patrick Moore, "The Widening Warfare in the Former Yugoslavia," *Radio Free Europe/Radio Liberty Research Reports* (hereafter as *RFE/RL Research Reports*), vol. 2, no. 1,

January 1993, p. 6.

[17] For an analysis of intervention in Yugoslavia, see James Gow and Lawrence Freedman, "Intervention in a Fragmenting State: The Case of Yugoslavia," in Nigel S. Rodley, ed., *To Loose the Bands of Wickedness: International Intervention in Defence of Human Rights* (London: Brassey's, 1992).

[18] For an account of Russian involvement in CIS peacekeeping, see Suzanne Crow, "The Theory and Practice of Peace-keeping in the Former Soviet Union," *RFE/RL Research Reports*, vol. 1, no. 37, September 18, 1992, pp. 31–36.

[19] On the particular difficulties associated with resolving ethnic conflicts, see Hugh Miall, *The Peacemakers: Peaceful Settlement of Disputes since 1945* (Oxford: Macmillan, 1992), pp. 141–147.

[20] See Misha Glenny, "Bosnia: The Last Chance?" *The New York Review of Books*, January 1993, p. 5.

[21] For an account of "second-generation" multinational operations, see Jarat Chopra and John Mackinlay, "Second Generation Multinational Operations," *The Washington Quarterly*, vol. 15, no. 3, Summer 1992, pp. 113–131. See also Indar J. Rikhye, *Strengthening UN Peace-keeping: New Challenges and Proposals* (Washington, D.C.: US Institute for Peace, 1992).

[22] See, for example, Adrian Hastings, "Suitable Case for Intervention," *The Guardian*, December 17, 1992, p. 17; Leslie H. Gelb, "The Rescue of Bosnia Can No Longer Wait," *International Herald Tribune*, January 11, 1993, p. 8.

[23] Sydney Bailey, "The United Nations and the Termination of Armed Conflict, 1946–1964," *International Affairs,* vol. 58, no 3, Summer 1982, p. 469.

[24] The academic community has also been slow to reassess the role of the United Nations, although some bold, but politically sensitive, ideas are beginning to emerge. Helman and Ratner, for example, have argued the case for UN "conservatorship." See Gerald Helman and Steven Ratner, "Saving Failed States," *Foreign Policy,* no. 89, Winter 1992–1993, pp. 3–20.

Chapter 11

The United Nations and International Security

Adam Roberts

In recent years, there has been a remarkable growth in demands for the services of the United Nations (UN) in the field of international security. The 1991 authorized action in Iraq was quickly followed in 1992 by a fivefold increase in the numbers of troops deployed in UN peacekeeping activities and by an increase in the types of roles they perform. At long last, the United Nations seemed to offer the prospect of moving decisively away from the anarchic reliance on force, largely on a unilateral basis, by individual sovereign states. The United Nations has, and will probably continue to have, a far more central role in security issues than it did during the Cold War.

However, the United Nations' multifaceted role in the security field faces a huge array of problems. Almost every difficulty connected with the preparation, deployment, and use of force has reemerged in a UN context and does not appear to be any easier to address. Excessive demands have been placed on the United Nations, which has been asked to pour the oil of peacekeeping on the troubled waters of a huge number of conflicts, to develop its role in preventing breaches of the peace and to play a central part in defeating aggression and tackling the aftereffects of war. Arms control, too, is embroiled in controversy, with various states— Iraq and North Korea being the clearest examples—challenging what they see as a discriminatory nonproliferation regime. Above all, the increasing role of the United Nations in international security raises two central questions: First, is there any real coherence in the vast array of security activities undertaken by the United Nations? Second, is there a danger that the elemental force of ethnic conflict could defeat the United Nations' efforts?

One pioneering attempt to develop a coherent rationale for UN activities is UN Secretary-General Boutros Boutros-Ghali's 1992 report, *An*

Agenda for Peace.[1] It is admirably clear, courageous, and notably optimistic in tone. It includes useful accounts of the different UN roles in
tackling security questions and strong pleas for better arrangements for
financing UN forces and ensuring their availability. It is especially welcome because the United Nations lacks a strong tradition of reflection and
vigorous debate in regard to its overall performance and direction, not
least in the security field. It is an important symbol of a sea change in its
capacity and willingness to authorize the use of force for international
purposes. It recognizes that traditional peacekeeping operations may need
to be complemented by more forceful measures, including preventive
deployments and peace enforcement. Its publication could not have been
more timely.

An Agenda for Peace was never intended to be a comprehensive
overview of the problems of international order in the post-Cold War
world. Rather, it resulted from a request for an "analysis and recommendations on ways of strengthening and making more efficient within the
framework and provisions of the Charter the capacity of the United
Nations for preventive diplomacy, for peacemaking, and for peacekeeping." This request, made by the first-ever Security Council meeting at the
head-of-state level, held at the end of January 1992, set the tone: one of
"strengthening and making more efficient," rather than exploring problems and questioning traditional prescriptions. The resulting report, not
surprisingly, is most notable for making a number of proposals and
suggestions, addressed to member-states, for enhancing UN capacity to
respond to the challenges of the post-Cold War world.

Boutros-Ghali has viewed *An Agenda for Peace* as the beginning rather
than the end of a debate, and he has supplemented it with various subsequent statements and reports. He added in January 1993: "I plan during
the course of this year to produce a sequel to *An Agenda for Peace*. This
report would attempt to speak to the deeper foundations of international
peace and security. These are rooted in the great issue of development in
all its aspects: economic, social, political, and environmental."[2] There
have been other important contributions to the debate, both from within
the United Nations, as well as from outside.[3]

Since its publication in June 1992, *An Agenda for Peace* has received a
positive but limited response. In the General Assembly debate in autumn
1992, there was no opposition in principle to the proposition that the
United Nations should have an enhanced capacity for preventive diplomacy, peacemaking, and peacekeeping. However, the report's more ambitious proposals for making armed forces available to the United Nations
on a permanent basis, and for more secure financing of peacekeeping
efforts, have so far yielded only limited results.[4] In particular, states seem

more reluctant to transfer control of their armed forces than the report's authors had hoped. This may be partly due to reservations about the United Nations' existing machinery for directing military forces under its control; however, it may also be due to broader doubts about the United Nations' capacity to manage a world torn apart by a huge range of conflicts.

The main argument of this chapter is that *An Agenda for Peace* has serious flaws. Most notably, it ignores some important issues, thus raising doubts as to whether its authors have fully appreciated the wide range of problems the United Nations is asked to address. This article advances the following propositions about the United Nations' post-Cold War role in the field of international security:

1. The United Nations has become seriously overloaded with security issues, for good and enduring reasons. The extent to which it can transfer these responsibilities to regional organizations is debatable.
2. Most conflicts in the contemporary world involve an element of civil war or inter-ethnic struggle. They are different in character from those conflicts, essentially interstate, that the United Nations was established to tackle.
3. There is only limited agreement among the major powers about the basis of international security and only a limited shared interest in ensuring that international norms are effectively implemented.
4. The structure of the Security Council, including the system of five veto-wielding permanent members, is in danger of losing its legitimacy. Although a formal change of membership or powers will be very hard to achieve, changes in the council's procedures and practices may be both desirable and possible.
5. There are some advantages in the practice whereby enforcement has taken the form of authorized military action by groups of states, rather than coming under direct UN command as a literal reading of the UN Charter would suggest.
6. The forms of action used in support of UN positions pose problems. There is a tendency for the United Nations and its member-states to rely on methods of remote control of debatable efficacy, including economic sanctions, and on methods of limited involvement, including peacekeeping and humanitarian operations. There may have to be more willingness to take decisive action, even setting up trustee-type administrations.
7. The application of the laws of war poses special problems for the United Nations, including the proclamation of standards in circumstances in which they are difficult to enforce.

8. Although the United Nations' role is increasing, basic questions about collective security remain. There is no prospect of a general system of collective security supplanting existing strategic arrangements.

These propositions, each discussed in a separate section below, are in no way intended as criticism of the increased emphasis given to the United Nations and its role in the foreign policies of many states. Rather, they constitute a plea for the sober assessment of both the merits and defects of an increased role, as well as for constructive thinking about some of the difficult issues it poses, and a caution against the hasty abandonment of some still-valuable aspects of traditional approaches to international relations.

THE OVERLOAD PROBLEM

The UN Charter confers on the Security Council "primary responsibility for the maintenance of international peace and security"—a phrase echoed in *An Agenda for Peace*.[5] In an era in which the Security Council is at last able to agree on some forms of action, this phrase ceases to be a near-meaningless aspiration and, instead, begins to look like a recipe for infinite obligation. Practices of the past few years confirm this worry. Peacekeeping and other security responsibilities in a wide range of countries are overstretching the resources of the UN Security Council and the UN Secretariat. The capacity of UN bodies and member-states to think effectively about so wide a range of problems, and to manage so many operations, is in doubt. That there is some degree of overload is accepted in the UN Secretariat. Boutros-Ghali has spoken of "the tumult of demands" placed on the United Nations and of a "crisis of expectations."[6] He also said in his letter of November 29, 1992, about Somalia: "The secretariat, already overstretched in managing greatly enlarged peace-keeping commitments, does not at present have the capacity to command and control an enforcement action of the size and urgency required by the present crisis in Somalia."[7]

Reasons for such a heavy demand to deal with wars, civil strife, and other crises are numerous and persuasive. Whatever difficulties the United Nations may face in the coming years, these reasons will not suddenly disappear. Three stand out. First, the impressive record of the United Nations in the years 1987–1992 has raised expectations. The United Nations has contributed to the settlement of numerous regional conflicts, including the Iran–Iraq War, the South African presence in Namibia, the Soviet presence in Afghanistan, and the Vietnamese presence in Cambodia. It provided a framework for the expulsion of Iraq from Kuwait. Second, given a choice, states contemplating the use of force beyond their borders often prefer to do it in a multilateral, especially UN, context. A multilateral approach helps neutralize domestic political opposition, increases the opportunities to acquire useful allies, reassures the international community that operations have limited and legitimate goals, and reduces the risk of large-scale force being used by adversaries or rival powers. Third, the United Nations has some notable advantages over regional organizations in tackling security problems: It is universal; it has a reputation, even if it is now under threat, for impartiality; and it has a more clear set of arrangements for making decisions on security issues than do most regional organizations, including even the North Atlantic Treaty Organization (NATO).

An Agenda for Peace does not address the problem of overload directly. It does, however, imply that one solution to the problem is to put more resources, including troops and money, into the hands of the United Nations on a regular basis.[8] This would reduce the hand-to-mouth element that is a feature of the way the United Nations must run peacekeeping operations. An organization that scarcely possesses a blue beret, yet is in such demand to provide forces, is remarkable even by the standards of the paradox-ridden field of international relations.

Even if dramatically increased resources were available to the United Nations on a permanent basis, it is far from clear whether its most serious problems of overload would be alleviated. If the Security Council had troops permanently available and if it had fewer worries about financing new activities, the running of existing peacekeeping and other military operations would indeed be facilitated. However, because the demand for UN services is elastic if not infinite, there would also be a risk that even more would be asked of the United Nations; the demands on the secretariat might become more, rather than less, serious.

In any case, a major aspect of overload has to do, not with resources, but with the inherently difficult nature of the issues being tackled. There are problems in international relations that are not soluble through the application of resources from outside. One of the challenges facing the UN Security Council is to find some means of dealing with what may become an increasingly urgent concern: states using the United Nations as a "garbage can" into which they throw urgent and difficult matters that they cannot tackle themselves.

The UN overload could have several serious consequences. First, the UN members most involved in paying for and conducting security operations of various kinds may become tired of their heavy responsibilities. Second, states or other entities wishing to take offensive military action may act precipitately to take advantage of the UN's preoccupations elsewhere. Third, a tendency may emerge to ignore certain problems or to pass them to other bodies, which may or may not be capable of handling them; possible examples include conflicts in the former Soviet Union, including in Georgia, Nagorno-Karabakh, and Tajikistan.

Recognizing that the United Nations is seriously overloaded, much thought has been given to the question of cooperation with regional security organizations. *An Agenda for Peace* is particularly interesting for its recognition that there has to be a partnership between regional organizations and the United Nations, not a shuffling of responsibilities between them.[9]

The idea that the United Nations and regional institutions could share responsibility for security seems to be emerging, albeit hesitantly, in Europe. The proliferation of European bodies with responsibilities in the security field is notorious: the Conference on Security and Cooperation in Europe (CSCE), NATO, the European Community (EC), the Western European Union (WEU), and the North Atlantic Cooperation Council (NACC) all play roles of varying importance. Several are developing roles as regional organizations with a close relationship to the United Nations. For NATO, this is not in principle new: The 1949 Treaty of Washington, which led to the creation of NATO, put much emphasis on the United Nations.[10] NATO played an important role in a number of ways in the 1991 Gulf War.[11] However, the connection between NATO and the United Nations has not been adequately articulated. Although the major document on NATO's post-Cold War role, the Rome Declaration of November 1991, contained extensive references to the CSCE, it said little about the United Nations.[12] Subsequently, the crisis in Yugoslavia, and NATO's contribution to United Nations Protection Force (UNPROFOR) II and other UN operations there, forced the Alliance to pay more attention to its actual and possible future contributions to peacekeeping.[13]

Despite such developments, enlarging the international security role of regional organizations is easier said than done. These organizations have a bewildering variety of purposes and memberships, and they often have great difficulty in reaching decisions and in taking action. Many regional bodies are seen as too partial to one side. Moreover, it is often far from self-evident which regional body should have the principal role in addressing a given problem. The United Nations has often encouraged regional bodies to handle crises only to find that important aspects of the problems remained within its own domain.

THE CHANGING CHARACTER OF CONFLICT

Many of the conflicts in the contemporary world have a very different character from those that the United Nations was designed to address.

Above all, those who framed the UN Charter had in mind the problem of international war, waged by well-organized states: This reflected the view, still common today, that aggression and international war constitute the supreme problem of international relations. Although the problem of interstate war has by no means disappeared, for many, civil war—whether internationalized or not—has always represented the deadlier threat. Some of the twentieth century's principal political philosophies have underestimated the significance of ethnicity, however defined, as a powerful political force and source of conflict: This is now changing through the pressure of events.[14]

An Agenda for Peace characterizes the sources of conflict and war in the contemporary world as "pervasive and deep." It refers to "fierce new assertions of nationalism and sovereignty" and says that "the cohesion of states is threatened by brutal ethnic, religious, social, cultural, or linguistic strife." It asserts, in simple form, the proposition that the "deepest causes of conflict" are "economic despair, social injustice, and political oppression." It wisely warns that there are limits beyond which self-determination should not be taken: "If every ethnic, religious, or linguistic group claimed statehood, there would be no limit to fragmentation . . . ."[15] All this constitutes an unexceptionable, but hardly adequate, statement of some of the problems now faced by the United Nations.

There are, of course, more hopeful developments in the world, and it would be wrong to characterize global politics as being exclusively driven by ethnic divisiveness. *An Agenda for Peace* duly notes that authoritarian regimes have given way to more democratic forces, and it points to connections among democracy, human rights, and peace. In subsequent speeches, Boutros-Ghali has continued to put much emphasis on democracy and its significance both for economic development and international peace.[16] It may well be that, in the long run, the United Nations' greatest contribution to international security will lie in actions outside the field of security narrowly defined. Although there are several grounds for caution regarding the proposition that liberal democracies do not make war with each other, in the long run, the United Nations' increased commitment to democracy, if it aids in democratic development around the world, could help reduce the risks of war. In the short term, as has been seen in the successor states of the former Yugoslavia and the former Soviet Union, the elimination of authoritarian regimes and the beginning of democracy can help unleash terrible forces of communal and ethnic conflict.

In the overwhelming majority of UN Security Council operations today, there is a strong element of civil war and communal conflict. For the United Nations, involvement in such conflict is hardly new, as the long-standing and continuing problems of Palestine/Israel and Cyprus bear witness. The collapse of large multinational states and empires almost always causes severe dislocations, including the emergence or reemergence of ethnic, religious, regional, and other animosities. The absence of fully legitimate political systems, traditions, regimes, and state frontiers all increase the likelihood that a narrowly ethnic definition of "nation" prevails. These difficulties are compounded by the fact that, for the most part, the geographical distribution of populations is so messy that the harmonious realization of national self-determination is impossible. Conflict-ridden parts of the former Yugoslavia and the former Soviet Union are merely the two most conspicuous contemporary examples of imperial collapse leading to inter-ethnic war. In both cases, the taboo against changing old "colonial" frontiers has been undermined much more quickly and seriously than occurred in postcolonial states in Africa and elsewhere in the decades following European decolonization.[17]

An Agenda for Peace fails to explore the special problems that beset peacekeeping, humanitarian aid, election-monitoring, and enforcement efforts when they occur in the midst of bitter internal conflicts where there are no front lines; it also fails to address how the United Nations can avoid having impossible burdens thrust upon it. It would be a tragedy if the United Nations, at the point when it has some chance of increasing its role in international relations, were to be damaged by the combined forces of ethnicity and communal hatred. Yet, it is by no means impossible that internal conflicts could drag the United Nations down: Its inability to prevent a resumption of war in Angola following the September 1992 elections is an ominous indicator of this type of hazard.

Internal conflicts, especially those with a communal or ethnic dimension, present special risks for international engagement, whether in the form of mediation, peacekeeping, or forceful military intervention.[18] First, internal conflicts tend to be "nasty, brutish, and long," and they leave communities with deep and enduring mutual suspicions based on traumatic experiences and continuing proximity. Intervention requires a willingness to stay what may be a very long course. Second, internal conflicts are typically conducted under the leadership of nongovernmental or semigovernmental entities, which may see great advantages in the degree of recognition involved in negotiating with UN representatives and yet be unwilling or unable to carry out the terms of agreements. Third, internal conflicts typically involve the use of force directed against the civilian populations, thus becoming especially bitter and posing difficult problems related to the protection of dispersed and vulnerable civilians. Fourth, internal conflicts are often conducted with small weapons: rifles, knives, and the arsonist's match. It is very difficult to control the use of such weaponry by bombing, arms embargoes, or formal methods of arms control. Finally, in cases such as these, there is frequently no territorial *status quo ante* to which to return. Cease-fires and other agreements are vulnerable to the charge that they legitimize the use of force and that they create impossibly complicated "leopard-spot" territorial arrangements, based on ethnic territorial units that are small and separated and, thus, difficult to defend.

The power of communal and ethnic divisions merits a more careful and judicious use of the word "nation" than in most contemporary usage, including at the United Nations.[19] The sentimental assumption that all states are "nations" is built into such terms as "United Nations" and "international." It is also deeply embedded in the American usage. Where possible, it is preferable to use more neutral terms such as "state" or "country," especially when speaking of the majority of states, which are hardly coterminous with a single "nation."

Communal and ethnic conflicts raise awkward issues about the criteria used in recognizing political entities as states and in favoring their admission to the United Nations. When the United Nations admits member-states, it is in fact conferring a particularly important form of recognition, and it is also implicitly underwriting the inviolability of their frontiers. Yet, the United Nations does not appear to be taking sufficient account of traditional criteria for recognition, which include careful consideration of whether a state really exists and coheres as a political and social entity. Many European states also forgot these traditional criteria in some of their recent acts of recognition, many of which did not involve setting up diplomatic missions. If the results of recognition are risky security commitments to purported states that never really attained internal cohesion, public support for UN action may be weakened.[20]

Such conflicts also raise issues about the appropriateness of certain principles derived from interstate relations, including the principle that changing frontiers by force can never be accepted. This principle, which is very important in contemporary international relations, has been frequently reiterated by the international community in connection with the Yugoslav crisis.[21] A successful armed grab for territory on largely ethnic grounds would indeed set a deeply worrying precedent. Yet, it must be asked whether it is wise to express this legal principle so forcefully in circumstances in which existing "frontiers" have no physical existence, in which they lack both logic and legitimacy, in which there are such deep-seated ethnic problems, and in which almost any imaginable outcome will involve recognition of the consequences of frontier violations.

LIMITED HARMONY AMONG THE MAJOR POWERS

An Agenda for Peace recognizes with admirable frankness that the sovereign state is still the fundamental unit in the international system.[22] At the same time, it assumes that member-states, including the major powers, are in substantial agreement with each other on central security issues: "The manifest desire of the membership to work together is a new source of strength in our common endeavor. . . .Even as the issues between states north and south grow more acute, and call for attention at the highest levels of government, the improvement in relations between states east and west affords new possibilities, some already realized, to meet successfully threats to common security."[23]

It is undeniable, and very welcome, that there is more agreement among states about international security issues now than there was during the Cold War. However, there remain fundamental differences of both interest and perception. These may not be enough to prevent the Security Council from reaching decisions on key issues, but they can frustrate efforts to turn decisions into actions in fast-changing situations. *An Agenda for Peace* says virtually nothing about state interest as an explanation of state behavior; what it says about the sources of conflict applies more to postdecolonization problems than to traditional rivalries between great powers.[24] This underestimation of national interest could lead to excessive expectations about the prospects of taking action to enforce the international order.

Differences of interest among states are complemented by differences in perceptions about the fundamental nature of world politics. Depending largely on their different historical experiences, some states view colonial domination and imperialism as the most serious problems in international relations; others see civil war as the most dangerous threat to international security; yet others view aggressive conquest and international war as the central problems.

Such serious differences of perception and interest are, of course, reflected in the proceedings of the UN Security Council. One should not necessarily expect relations among major powers to be good, and there may be perfectly valid reasons why countries perceive major security problems differently. The different perceptions of the permanent five may yet prove serious with respect to Yugoslavia: In particular, Russia's traditional friendship with Serbia is leading powerful political forces in Russia to take a view on sanctions and military policy that is at odds with Western positions. Moreover, China's world view, although undergoing important changes, retains distinctive elements—including a fear of foreign subversion, a strong belief in state sovereignty, and some identification with developing states—which could set it against other Security Council members.

THE PROBLEMATIC STRUCTURE OF
THE SECURITY COUNCIL

An Agenda for Peace says little about the structure of the Security Council, its decision-making procedures, and the system of five permanent veto-wielding members. This is understandable, given the sensitivity about these issues. Yet, if the United Nations is indeed to have an enlarged role in security affairs, its system of decision-making must be seen to be legitimate.

The powers of the Security Council are, in theory, very extensive: "The members of the United Nations agree to accept and carry out the decisions of the Security Council in accordance with the present Charter."[25] In practice, the Security Council cannot impose its will on the membership in the way this statement implies and, despite the absence of any system of formal constitutional challenge, there is no sign of the emergence of a doctrine even hinting at the infallibility of UN Security Council pronouncements. However, these limitations on the power of the Security Council do not mean that states, having successfully retained considerable sovereign powers in security matters, see the existing arrangements as satisfactory.

The criticisms of the composition of the Security Council involve several elements: doubt about preserving unaltered, half a century later, the special position of those countries that were allies in World War II; concern that three of those powers—France, Britain, and the United States—make most of the agenda-setting decisions in running the Security Council; irritation, especially on the part of Germany and Japan, about "taxation without representation"; and frustration that the views of the nonpermanent members of the Security Council, and indeed of the great majority of the 181-strong General Assembly, count for little. These criticisms could become much more serious if events take such a turn that they coincide with a perception that the Security Council has made serious misjudgments on central issues.

There are considerable pressures to alter some of the Charter provisions on membership of the Security Council. A change of the council's composition is by no means impossible: In 1965, by formal amendment of Article 23 of the Charter, the number of nonpermanent members was increased from 6 to 10. There now exist various widely canvassed proposals for further expansion. Japan and Germany have often been identified as possible permanent members of the Security Council, especially in statements by the United States;[26] there have also been signs of flexibility on this in some Russian pronouncements. However, there is bound to be resistance to the idea of increasing the number of vetoes and to any proposal that would give two conspicuously "Western" states the same status as the five, while leaving out Brazil, Egypt, India, Indonesia, Nigeria, and others. More acceptable proposals for Charter amendment might involve the creation of a new category of permanent member, one without a veto; however, here too, the naming of candidates for such membership is very contentious.

On the veto issue, *An Agenda for Peace* implies that its use is largely irrelevant today.[27] A Security Council veto has not been used since May 31, 1990, when the United States voted against a resolution on the Israeli-occupied territories. However, even when not actually used, the veto has a significant effect on the deliberations of the Security Council. It is not hard to imagine future occasions when one of the five members may apply it.

The veto system privileges a group of five states in a way that is bound to be contentious; it is widely perceived as having held the United Nations back from fulfilling its functions in the Cold War years. Yet, the veto has merits as well as faults: It helped to get and keep the major powers within a UN framework when they would otherwise either not have joined in the first place or else deserted it later; it may have saved the United Nations from damaging conflicts with its major members and from involvement in divisive or impossible missions; and it may have contributed to a sense of responsibility and a habit of careful consultation among the permanent five. In short, the veto can be viewed as one of several factors that have made UN decision-making procedures superior to those of its predecessor, the League of Nations, and of many regional organizations.

Modification or abandonment of the veto would be problematic. The procedures governing amendments to the Charter make any change affecting this power particularly difficult, as the consent of the countries concerned would be required. The UN Charter stipulates that all amendments to the Charter must be adopted by two-thirds of the members of the General Assembly and be ratified, in accordance with their respective constitutional processes, by two-thirds of the members, including all of the permanent members of the Security Council.[28] That said, if its decision is to retain legitimacy, the Security Council will eventually have to adapt.

Membership in the magic circle of the permanent five naturally involves heavy costs, as well as privilege. That power has its rewards is indicated by the tenacity with which Britain and France hang on to their position as members of the permanent five. Yet, in some of the more problematic UN operations, it also involves the risk of direct association with failure. Membership also involves an obligation to follow votes in the Security Council with commitments of force in crisis-torn areas. The overextension of Britain and France's capabilities, so familiar in the nineteenth century, appears ready to haunt these countries, albeit in UN colors, as they approach the twenty-first century.

Meanwhile, other states have vetoes of a kind on enforcement actions. First, there is the famous, but largely theoretical, "sixth veto" on the Security Council—the capacity of the Security Council members to defeat a resolution by denying it the nine affirmative votes needed to pass.[29] Second, despite the words of the Charter, states do not have to take part in enforcement or peacekeeping operations if they do not wish. As long as they guard their powers to make decisions about their forces, they are much more than mere pawns of the United Nations.

No formal proposal for a change in the provisions for permanent membership of the Security Council has been tabled. Hopes at UN headquarters that Germany and Japan might be brought in by the United Nations' fiftieth anniversary in 1995 appear unlikely to be fulfilled. The changes currently under way in these two countries to address their constitutional limitations on the use of force tackle only one aspect of the problem; revision of the Charter is still far off.

In the history of the United Nations, much more has been achieved by changes in practice, rather than Charter revision. More thought will have to be given to how the Security Council might develop its procedures and practices: for example, by strengthening the selection of nonpermanent members to reflect their contributions to the United Nations' work and developing more regular Security Council consultation with major states and interested parties. Such changes, although difficult to implement, might go at least some way toward meeting the strong concerns of certain states about being left out of decisions that affect them vitally.[30]

THE PROBLEM OF ORGANIZING ENFORCEMENT ACTIONS

The issue of organizing enforcement actions is central to almost every discussion of the United Nations' future role. It brings out the conflict between "Charter fundamentalists," who would like such actions to be organized precisely in accord with the UN Charter, and those with a "common law" approach, who believe the most important guide is UN practice.

Three times in the UN era, major military action authorized by the United Nations has been under US, not UN, command: in Korea in 1950–1953, Iraq in 1990–1991, and Somalia in 1992–1993. These episodes

suggest the emergence of a system in which the United Nations author-
izes military actions, which are then placed under the control of a state or
group of states. There are important advantages to such an arrangement.
First, it reflects the reality that not all states feel equally involved in every
enforcement action. Moreover, military actions require extremely close
coordination between intelligence-gathering and operations, a smoothly
functioning decision-making machine, and forces with some experience
of working together to perform dangerous and complex tasks. These
things are more likely to be achieved through existing national armed
forces, alliances, and military relationships, than they are within the
structure of a UN command. As habits of cooperation between armed
forces develop, and as the United Nations itself grows, the scope for
action under direct UN command may increase, but this will inevitably be
a slow process.

An Agenda for Peace contains no discussion of the merits and defects
of this system of authorized command. Indeed, the report's treatment of
enforcement actions in general is remarkably unsystematic.[31] The main
proposal that it advances is that the UN Security Council might have
forces available on call as specified in Article 43 of the UN Charter. It
envisages that member-states might "undertake to make armed forces,
assistance and facilities available to the Security Council. . .not only on an
ad hoc basis but on a permanent basis. . . .The ready availability of armed
forces on call could serve, in itself, as a means of deterring breaches of the
peace since a potential aggressor would know that the council had at its
disposal a means of response."[32]

One statement on the use of military forces under UN control can easily
be seen as evidence of a kind of international discrimination underlying
the whole *Agenda for Peace* project: "Forces under Article 43 may
perhaps never be sufficiently large or well enough equipped to deal with a
threat from a major army equipped with sophisticated weapons. They
would be useful, however, in meeting any threat posed by a military force
of a lesser order."[33] This can easily be interpreted as evidence that the
United Nations is ready to use force against Third World countries, but
not against major powers. It appears possible, however, that this statement is merely an implicit admission that when there is a threat from a
major military power, members might have to resort, as in Desert Storm,
to an authorized action, as distinct from direct UN command.

An Agenda for Peace offers no serious discussion of the reasons states
have traditionally been nervous about proposals for making forces permanently available to the United Nations. These reasons include a natural
concern about the command of troops being put into the hands of an
international body that might employ them, risking their lives in an

operation that was distant from home, controversial, and might be mismanaged. States may well prefer a situation in which the provision of military force for UN activities is managed in an ad hoc manner, thereby giving them a greater degree of control over events. Such a view is not surprising. Whether correct or not, states jealously guard their power, including that of deciding the exact circumstances in which their armed forces will or will not be used. Just as the power of national governments needs to be subject to constraints both internal and external, so must the United Nations itself. In principle, some limitations on the United Nations' power may be warranted, although it is doubtful that withholding forces is the most desirable form of constraint.

As a result, permanent large-scale availability of forces to the UN in peacetime, as envisaged in Article 43 and in *An Agenda for Peace*, appears improbable. What may be more realistic is the earmarking, preparation, and training of national military units for possible use in peacekeeping operations. In early 1993, Boutros-Ghali seemed to accept this conclusion when he suggested that force structures for UN peacekeeping missions could be broken down into "standard 'building blocks' of operational capability, such as infantry battalion, medical company, transport company, and observer team." He envisaged, without being very specific, that states could train and maintain such units with a view to a possible UN role and could hold them available to the United Nations on a standby basis.[34] The training of national military forces to operate and cooperate internationally may increase, and the United Nations is negotiating standby agreements with countries willing to provide units for peacekeeping duties on short notice. These are significant developments, even if they fall far short of the Charter vision of forces permanently on call for enforcement actions.

Experience seems to show that mobilizing for collective security only works when one power takes the lead. However, as a result of the effort, that same power may be reluctant to continue assuming the entire burden of collective security. After the Korean War, the United States tried to set up regional alliances to reduce its direct military obligation. After the 1991 Gulf War, the United States was manifestly reluctant to get entangled in Iraq and to underwrite all security arrangements in the area. The desire to limit the degree of US involvement is likely to remain strong under US President Bill Clinton.

The issue of UN versus authorized national command arises in nonenforcement connections as well. As UN-controlled peacekeeping forces become involved in more complex missions, in which neat distinctions between peacekeeping and enforcement are eroded, the adequacy of the United Nations' existing machinery for controlling complex operations in distant countries is increasingly called into question. In 1992, leading figures connected with UN peacekeeping activities in both Somalia and Bosnia-Herzegovina had major disputes with the UN headquarters in New York. The UN special representative for Somalia, Mohammed Sahnoun, resigned on October 26, 1992; the former head of UN forces in Sarajevo, Major-General Lewis MacKenzie, made the memorable if hyperbolic complaint: "Do not get into trouble as a commander in the field after 5 p.m. New York time, or Saturday and Sunday. There is no one to answer the phone."[35] This command-and-control problem has been acknowledged by the secretariat. As UN Under Secretary-General for Political Affairs Marrack Goulding has said:

> ... peacekeeping operations take place under the command and control of the secretary-general, who is responsible to the Security Council. Existing structures in New York have found it increasingly difficult to plan, command, and control the greatly increased peacekeeping activities of recent years. When the Security Council authorized the despatch of additional troops to protect the delivery of humanitarian supplies in Bosnia and Herzegovina, it was decided to take "off the shelf" elements of a NATO headquarters to establish the new command in Bosnia. This has not been an entirely happy experiment. A better solution may lie in greatly strengthening the staff in New York, and especially the military staff, to give it the resources not only to plan new operations, but also to provide the core elements of their headquarters.[36]

A special problem associated with UN-controlled operations is the rigidity of their mandates and rules of engagement. The fact that defining the mission of UN forces has to be subject to international agreement can seriously reduce flexibility in fast-changing situations, leading to criticism from within and from outside.

Could the UN Military Staff Committee, if life were breathed into it, usefully take on the role of coordinating major military actions under the Security Council? The idea that such a disparate international committee might be in charge of military operations has attracted little interest; the Military Staff Committee is only touched on incidentally in *An Agenda for Peace*.[37] For the foreseeable future, there is no point in thinking of the Military Staff Committee as a commanding body for major military actions. However, there may be more modest tasks that it or some other body could and should perform, including developing the rules of engagement, harmonizing the laws-of-war rules as they affect multilateral forces, and tendering military advice on a wide range of issues.

Meanwhile, in respect to both Somalia and Yugoslavia, there is evidence that the United Nations is seeking to develop ad hoc systems of command and control, containing important elements from both troop-contributing countries and the UN headquarters. In Somalia, when the United Nations takes over from the US-led force, the secretary-general will, for the first time, have command and control of an enforcement action under Chapter VII of the Charter. In a parallel move, the United Nations is creating a new command-and-control center, intended to be a 24-hour-a-day "war room" to keep the UN headquarters in New York linked day and night with all peacekeeping operations around the world.[38] This move may be an effective response to one aspect of the criticism of how the United Nations has managed peacekeeping operations, but it is far from certain that it will be enough to induce the countries involved to entrust to the United Nations the running of a larger, riskier, more complex, or faster-moving enforcement action than that in Somalia.

PROBLEMATIC FORMS OF ACTION

The main forms of action taken to carry out Security Council mandates are deeply problematic. *An Agenda for Peace*, while courageously pointing out both the need for UN action and the dangers facing UN personnel, nowhere considers whether the array of methods generally used under UN auspices is adequate for the types of conflicts in which the United Nations is involved.

For the most part, actions taken under UN auspices have involved either methods that seek to control events in a country from afar (economic sanctions, arms embargoes, air exclusion zones, attempts to broker cease-fires) or involve a limited military presence with the consent of the parties (peacekeeping, observer, and humanitarian activities). Such methods, generally low risk, but also low in coercive or protective power, may sometimes work or at least may be one factor assisting in the solution of a crisis. They are undoubtedly reinforced by the UN's reputation. However, the overall record of such methods is patchy, bringing to mind the Chinese proverb quoted by Zhou En-lai in 1971: "Distant waters do not quench fire."[39] In the former Yugoslavia in 1992–1993, the combination of such methods had the tragic effect of denying many, mainly Bosnian Muslims, both weapons for defense and military protection by outside forces.

One reason for the tendency to use low-risk methods is that the countries that have had a principal role in carrying out UN Security Council mandates have been understandably reluctant to embark on actions that involve a strong probability of casualties and failure. This may be inevitable in a system of collective security, in which countries get involved in distant lands for interests that are international as much as national. However, the United Nations may face—indeed, it may already be facing—some problems that require a more committed and forceful presence if there is to be a chance of tackling them effectively.

Air power, with all its known limitations, could be viewed in this context as one, often low-risk, means of implementing Security Council decisions. According to the little-noted Article 45 of the UN Charter, members are required to "hold immediately available national air force contingents for combined international enforcement action." The use of air power in Desert Storm played a key role in minimizing coalition casualties. Since the 1991 war, there has been a fairly consistent pattern by the West of using air power against Iraq, while shrinking from major (and risky) reliance on land forces.

Sanctions and embargoes of various kinds have had a larger part in UN practice and are the most conspicuous example of low-risk methods that have had limited success. The Charter provides for sanctions as one response to a threat to the peace and views them as more than mere prologue to the use of force. There is a need for tough thinking within the United Nations about whether the extensive use of sanctions has lived up to the expectations generated by the Charter. The only aspect of economic sanctions discussed in *An Agenda for Peace* is the special economic problems they may create for certain states.[40] This is hardly the central issue.

Economic sanctions raise five other major problems that need more careful discussion than they have had at the United Nations or elsewhere. First, economic sanctions may be ineffective because there are always some countries or companies that do not take part. It is far from clear what actions can be taken against those who break sanctions. Second, sanctions, even if 100 percent effective in stopping all trade, may still be 0 percent effective in bringing about a desired change of policy in the target state. Third, in the target states, sanctions are more likely to hurt the innocent before the guilty. Fourth, sanctions may, like some forms of strategic bombing, have the perverse effect of making the inhabitants of a country more dependent on their government. Finally, the timing and mode of making the transition from economic sanctions to military action can be intensely controversial: witness the debates on this matter in the 1990–1991 Gulf crisis.

In short, economic sanctions are a blunt instrument. Their record has not been improved by their application against Iraq since August 1990 and against Serbia and Montenegro since May 1992. Nonetheless, they have value in some crises as a declaration of intent or as an expression of solidarity among the sanctioning states. Moveover, they can sometimes be effective when used in a discriminate way or regarding an issue about which the target state can be flexible.

More thought is needed on measures short of military force that can be employed in particular crises. The sanction provisions of the UN Charter should not be allowed to become a straitjacket, forcing the Security Council into a Pavlovian reaction and preventing creative thought about a range of other methods that might be appropriate to a particular situation. In Europe, for example, the CSCE process, particularly the 1975 Helsinki Final Act, did much to assist peaceful change in Eastern Europe, culminating in the events of 1989. Here, a form of constructive engagement— particular to a given situation and ultimately assisting change to emerge from within the societies in question—was more important than sanctions.

Many crises, including communal and ethnic ones, lead to calls for direct UN military involvement in defending humanitarian aid convoys, in cease-fire enforcement without full consent, or in the protection of threatened populations. *An Agenda for Peace* foreshadows a much more active UN role, not least in the area of peacekeeping, which it defines as "the deployment of a United Nations presence in the field, hitherto with the consent of all the parties concerned."[41] The innocent-sounding word "hitherto" has caused great controversy, but it is only realistic to proceed on the assumption that some UN actions, particularly in situations of a collapse of state authority, may have to take place without the consent of all parties. What is more worrying is that these and other actions may be actively opposed. Experience suggests that active opposition is particularly likely in deep-seated communal and ethnic conflicts, especially from those who see their interests or dignity threatened or who condemn the United Nations for not taking action that appears self-evident to them. The issue of the safety of UN personnel is discussed in *An Agenda for Peace*, but only in general terms.[42]

A special risk arises in a situation in which simultaneous but different kinds of action are needed. There are obvious hazards, for example, in having peacekeeping troops and humanitarian relief workers in a country at the same time that UN military action is being taken. The fate of the US-led multinational force in Lebanon in the early 1980s is a warning of the terrible risks peacekeepers face when they become associated with, or involved in, controversial policies and military actions, and then become a target for retaliation. In the wars in Yugoslavia—especially in discussions in 1992–1993 regarding the enforcement of air exclusion zones— some states, including France and Britain, expressed reservations about the United Nations having a dual (peacekeeping and military) role in the same conflict. Within the United Nations, the practice thus far has been to try to avoid charging peacekeepers with direct military functions and to look to other bodies to carry out the latter.

Some crises may require not just the placing of large numbers of troops in hostile territory, but also the establishment of a trustee-type administration to replace the system of government that has broken down. The admirable anticolonial instincts of both the United Nations and the United States, and the postcolonial weariness of European countries, have contributed to a reluctance to develop such a role. Yet, the logic of involvement in fractured societies in which state institutions have collapsed may sometimes point in the direction of what British Foreign Minister Douglas Hurd has called "painting a country blue."[43] The responsibilities laid down for the UN Transitional Authority in Cambodia (UNTAC) in the 1991 Paris Agreements on Cambodia are one example of a trend toward more direct (in this case, awkwardly shared) involvement in governmental functions.[44] Such action may be needed, but is bound to breed local opposition. The United Nations and its members will have to be prepared to stay on in some very rough situations if they move in this direction.

APPLICATION OF LAWS OF WAR
TO UN ACTIONS

Are international forces acting on behalf of the international community subject to the same rules of restraint as ordinary belligerents in an interstate war? *An Agenda for Peace* avoids the subject entirely—an example of the way in which laws-of-war matters, actively pursued in many parts of the UN system, are treated fitfully in those parts of the United Nations most directly involved in the management of international security.

There is little serious dissent from the proposition that the laws of war or *jus in bello* (also referred to, especially in international organizations, as international humanitarian law) do apply to forces in collective security actions, whether involved in peacekeeping or combat. However, the application of such rules presents special problems in large, ad hoc multinational coalitions typical of collective security actions. First, different partners may have different national standards and be bound by different treaties. Second, the perceived legitimacy of an operation, and the maintenance of coalition unity, may depend on a public perception that warlike actions will be restrained in certain ways. Third, rules based on an assumption that neutrality requires impartiality may conflict with the obligations of all states, including neutrals, to support the principles, purposes, and actions of the United Nations. Fourth, economic sanctions, which often hurt the innocent along with the guilty, may conflict with certain underlying principles of the laws of war. Fifth, the tricky issue of war crime trials can arise both in large coalition actions against a state and in ethnic conflicts characterized by outrages against civilians.

The UN Security Council might usefully devote more consistent attention than it has in the past to the laws of war. The United Nations risks developing a bad reputation if the Security Council (in regard to Iraq in 1990–1991 and Somalia and Yugoslavia in 1992–1993) passes resolutions containing warnings about violations of international humanitarian law and then fails to follow up with effective action. In February 1993, the UN Security Council passed a resolution on the establishment of a tribunal for war crimes committed in the former Yugoslavia, but there is no prospect that another Nuremberg tribunal will follow: The United Nations does not have the power to arrest, which the Allies had in occupied Axis countries in 1945; indeed, it has already found itself sponsoring peace negotiations with some of the very people likely to be wanted for war crimes. There is no sign yet that any of the UN forces in the former Yugoslavia will have their mandates changed to allow them to seize suspected war criminals. The impotence of the United Nations and of the major powers in this regard has been exposed.

PROSPECTS FOR COLLECTIVE SECURITY

Is it possible to say that out of the rubble of the Cold War a system of collective security is emerging? The term "collective security" appears in *An Agenda for Peace*, but is not extensively discussed there.[45]

The term "collective security" normally refers to a system in which each state in the system accepts that the security of one is the concern of all and agrees to join in a collective response to aggression. In this sense, it is distinct from collective defense or alliance systems, in which groups of states ally with each other, principally against possible external threats.

"Collective security" proposals have been in circulation since the beginning of the modern states system and were indeed aired at the negotiations that led to the 1648 Peace of Westphalia. The attractive theory of collective security, when tested against some basic questions, often reveals some fundamental flaws.[46]

Whose collective security? There is always a risk that a collective security system will be seen as protecting only certain countries or interests or as privileging certain principles at the expense of others. Some countries may, for whatever reason, feel excluded from its benefits or threatened by it. The anxieties expressed by some countries in the developing world regarding the concept of a "New World Order," while they have not yet crystallized into definite opposition to any specific UN action, are evidence of concern on this point.

Can there be consistent responses to security problems? Although the UN system is the first truly global international system and although it involves the subscription of virtually all countries in the world to a common set of principles, it is not yet evident that the same principles and practices could or should be applied consistently to different problems, countries, and regions. Difficulties can arise both from the consistent application of principles to situations that are fundamentally different and from the inconsistent application of principles. It is also not yet apparent that collective security can operate as effectively for East Timor or Tibet as for Kuwait. The widespread perception that Israel has successfully defied UN Security Council resolutions while other states have not, although arguably facile in certain respects, illustrates the explosiveness of emerging accusations of "double standards" at the United Nations. The political price of apparent inconsistency could be high.

Against which types of threat is a system of collective security intended to operate? There is no agreement that collective security should apply equally to the following: massive aggression and annexation; cross-border incursions; environmental despoliation; acts of terrorism; human rights violations within a state; communal and ethnic conflict; and the collapse of state structures under assault from internal opposition. In 1990–1991, many people argued that it was the particularly flagrant nature of the Iraqi invasion, occupation, and annexation of Kuwait that justified the coalition's response; even then, the international military response was far from unanimous. The fact that this argument was so widely used underlines the point that in cases in which aggression is not so blatant, it might be much harder to secure an international military response: A state caught up in such a conflict might have to look after its own interests. Since 1991, inspired partly by the establishment of "safe havens" in northern Iraq and partly by a trend of opinion, admittedly far from universal, in favor of democracy, there has been some increased advocacy, not least in France and the United States, of a right of intervention in states even in the absence of a formal invitation. This remains a deeply contentious issue and serves as a useful reminder that the ends toward which collective security efforts might be directed are not fixed.

How collective does enforcement have to be? Is complete unanimity impossible to attain, especially in the case of military action? Is there still space for some states to be neutral? In practice, there has never been, on the global level, a truly "collective" case (let alone system) of collective security. In the Gulf crisis of 1990–1991, the key UN Security Council resolution avoided the call for all states to take military action. Instead, it merely authorized "member-states cooperating with the government of Kuwait" to use "all necessary means" to implement relevant UN resolutions.[47] This implied that it was still legitimate for a state to have a status of neutrality or nonbelligerency in this conflict. It marked an interesting and realistic interpretation of some optimistic provisions in Chapter VII of the UN Charter.

How can a system of collective security actively deter a particular threat to a particular country? In the wake of the 1991 Gulf War, there was much discussion as to possible means by which, in the future, invasions could be deterred before disaster struck. This idea, which had been proposed earlier by former Soviet President Mikhail Gorbachev, was echoed in proposals for "preventive deployment" in *An Agenda for Peace*.[48] Following a unanimous Security Council decision of December 11, 1992, the idea was implemented by the United Nations for the first time in Macedonia. Ironically, a state that until April 1993 remained a nonmember was thus receiving protection from a state, Yugoslavia, that was still, for most practical purposes, a UN member. Despite remarkable progress, the idea of "preventive deployment" is fraught with difficulty. There is the risk that large numbers of states would request it, that it would be insufficient to discourage aggression, and that it might be used by a government as an alternative to providing for its own defense. It should not, however, be taken for granted that military deployments are absolutely essential. There may also be some residual deterrent value in the lessons of Korea (1950–1953) and Kuwait (1990–1991): Twice, under UN auspices, the United States has led coalitions that have gone to the defense of invaded states to which the United States was not bound by formal alliance commitments and in which it had no troops deployed at the time. This curious fact may not be entirely lost on would-be aggressors. Yet, there are bound to be cases in which some kinds of preventive UN deployments, of which Macedonia is a harbinger, are considered necessary.

Who pays for collective security? The question of burden-sharing in international security matters is notoriously complex, as shown by the experience of NATO, of UN peacekeeping, and of the US-led operations in the 1990–1991 Gulf crisis. In 1992, the annual cost of UN peacekeeping activities was the highest ever—about $2.8 billion. Unpaid contributions toward UN peacekeeping operations in September 1992 stood at $844 million, but by the beginning of 1993, this figure was reduced to about $670 million.[49] States have responded well to the increased costs of peacekeeping. However, if more UN peacekeeping (or other) operations go badly, there could be added difficulty in securing payment. Even if they do not, there are problems to be addressed. During the US presidential campaign, Bill Clinton, while indicating that he would act on payment of the US debt to the United Nations, repeatedly called for new agreements for sharing the costs of maintaining peace and suggested that the US apportionment of UN peacekeeping costs be reduced from 30.4 percent to 25 percent.[50] The extraordinary paradox of the country most deeply involved in military support for an international organization being simultaneously its major (although steadily repaying) defaulter is yet one more illustration of the gulf between the theory of collective security and its practice.[51] However, future payment difficulties may come from states not involved in, or critical of, Security Council decisions.

What is the place of disarmament and arms control in a system of collective security? Most proposals for collective security call for lower levels of armaments, consistent with the needs of internal security and international obligations. As was widely noted, there was little discussion of disarmament and arms control in *An Agenda for Peace*. The secretary-general subsequently issued a report on the subject, in which he identified his central priority: "First, it is my strong feeling that the time has come for the practical integration of disarmament and arms regulation issues into the broader structure of the international peace and security agenda." He also proposed changes in the UN disarmament negotiating machinery and a "greater Security Council involvement in disarmament matters, and in particular, the enforcement of nonproliferation."[52] Within the UN system generally, the end of the Cold War has resulted in a less propagandistic approach to these matters, and this has been reflected in the output of the UN Office for Disarmament Affairs.[53] However, the United Nations has yet to work out a coherent philosophy to guide its efforts in the field of disarmament and arms control in the post-Cold War era. "Arms control" is still seen by many as a suspect, meliorist concept. Attempts to develop guidelines for conventional arms transfers have many sharp critics, including China. The rationale for arms reductions, for control of arms transfers, and for nuclear nonproliferation efforts, all still need to be carefully examined and refined. This is especially important in view of the common fears that existing arms control arrangements are discriminatory—fears that could be exacerbated if the Security Council assumes a more central role in nonproliferation matters.

CONCLUSION

In recent years, the United Nations' role in security affairs has grown enormously, not only in scope, but also in type of activity and in complexity. In early 1993, Boutros-Ghali commented that "precedents are created in reality before theories gain consensus"; Goulding said that UN peacekeeping had been through a period of "forced development."[54] Can there be a coherent rationale for all this?

For all its limitations, *An Agenda for Peace* contains a vision of what the United Nations' international security role might be. Although acknowledging that the United Nations will coexist with sovereign states for the foreseeable future, it suggests a full agenda for the United Nations—one that may well involve it deeply in wars, whether civil or international. In one of its few direct references to warfare, *An Agenda for Peace* confirms the strong moral sense of the UN's obligation to intervene: ". . . armed conflicts today, as they have throughout history, continue to bring fear and horror to humanity, requiring our urgent involvement to try to prevent, contain, and bring them to an end."[55]

This vision is defective in numerous respects. It makes too little allowance for the real differences of perspective among states and for their narrow and often competing interests. It contains little recognition of the sheer difficulty of some conflicts in which the United Nations is invited to intervene, and it fails to acknowledge the reluctance of states to get deeply involved in dangerous situations far from home. On the basis of harsh experiences, from Angola to the former Yugoslavia, from Kurdistan to Cambodia, the United Nations may have to learn to temper the zeal that characterizes *An Agenda for Peace* with an element of caution about entering into commitments. This is hard for a global organization. Boutros-Ghali has shown his awareness of the problem, especially in his open questioning as to "whether conditions yet exist for successful peacekeeping in what was Yugoslavia."[56] What Goulding has said in respect of peacekeeping may apply more generally in the field of international security:

> . . . on the one hand, the secretary-general has to try to ensure that peacekeepers are not deployed in conditions where failure is likely; on the other hand, he has to avoid appearing so cautious as to create doubts about the real usefulness of the United Nations or provide a pretext for member-states to return to the bad old ways of unilateral military action.
>
> This is not a responsibility which the secretary-general should be asked to bear alone. The power of decision in these matters rests with the Security Council. It is important that the members of the council should, if necessary, stand up to the clamor of domestic or regional pressures and take care to satisfy themselves in advance that conditions do really exist for a proposed peacekeeping operation to succeed.[57]

The United Nations and its member-states may indeed have to learn, as many empires before them, that distant control of strife-torn provinces is hazardous, and there is a high price to pay for attempting to bring about peace in such places. Running the world from New York may yet prove even more troublesome than was running large parts of it from Rome, London, Paris, and Moscow.

Although there is a much more cooperative approach to security today, a system of true collective security is not yet in place. Indeed, collective security may properly be considered, not as a general system of international security, but rather as a form of action that is mobilized occasionally—and imperfectly. Its most common use may be in response to especially glaring aggressive actions by military powers of the second rank. Multilateral, if not complete collective, action under UN auspices has an increasing role, and it draws on national and alliance efforts in numerous ways, but it is not a substitute for such efforts.

The possibility that has been opened up in the past few years is not of a completely new system of collective security, nor of an entirely new agenda, nor indeed of peace other than in the limited form of a possible reduction of major interstate conflicts. Rather, it is of a coexistence of unilateral, alliance-based, and UN-based uses of force in almost the entire gamut of circumstances in which force has traditionally been deployed. In this context, many problems can be addressed more satisfactorily than before, and there have been significant developments in the multilateral training and use of armed forces. However, some conflicts, especially communal ones, look resistant to treatment.

Acknowledgments

The author would like to thank various colleagues in Oxford for help in the preparation of this chapter, particularly Andrew Hurrell and Martin Ceadel for seminar papers on the concept of collective security; Benedict Kingsbury and Rosemary Foot for comments on drafts of the present text; and the various contributors to Roberts and Kingsbury's *United Nations, Divided World* (Oxford: Oxford University Press, revised edition, *forthcoming*). An earlier version of this chapter was presented in January 1993 to the House of Commons Foreign Affairs Committee in connection with its inquiry on the expanding role of the United Nations.

Notes

1 Boutros Boutros-Ghali, *An Agenda for Peace: Preventive Diplomacy, Peace-making, and Peacekeeping,* UN Doc. A/47/277, June 17, 1992. (Also published as a booklet by the UN's Department of Public Information, New York, 1992.)

2 Boutros Boutros-Ghali, Statement on the Future of Collective Security, New York University, January 22, 1993, UN Department of Public Information Press Release SG/SM/4920, February 2, 1993, p. 7.

3 For a particularly thoughtful subsequent survey, see UN Under Secretary-General for Political Affairs Marrack Goulding, "The Evolution of United Nations Peacekeeping," Cyril Foster Lecture at the University of Oxford, March 4, 1993, to be published in *International Affairs,* vol. 69, no. 3, July 1993. (References are to the lecture text as delivered.)

4 The increased financial demands of peacekeeping (to which members responded positively in 1992), and the

remaining problem of arrears, are outlined in Ibid., p. 12.

[5] UN Charter, Article 24; Boutros-Ghali, *An Agenda for Peace,* especially in paragraph 64.

[6] Boutros Boutros-Ghali, *Report on the Work of the Organization, 1992,* UN Doc. A/47/1, September 1992, paragraph 44. (Also published as a booklet by the UN's Department of Public Information, New York, 1992.)

[7] Letter from Secretary-General Boutros Boutros-Ghali to the president of the National Security Council, November 29, 1992, UN Doc. S/24868, November 30, 1992, p. 6.

[8] Boutros-Ghali, *An Agenda for Peace,* paragraphs 51–54, 69–73. The question of additional military resources being put directly at the United Nations' disposal is discussed further in Section 5.

[9] Ibid., paragraphs 60–65.

[10] The North Atlantic Treaty, Washington, D.C., April 4, 1949, Preamble and Articles 1, 5, 7.

[11] See Jonathan T. Howe, "NATO and the Gulf Crisis," *Survival,* vol. 33, no. 3, May–June 1991, pp. 246–259.

[12] The Rome Declaration on Peace and Cooperation, issued by the Heads of State and Government participating in the meeting of the North Atlantic Council, Rome, November 7–8, 1981, contains one passing reference to the United Nations in paragraph 42: "Allies could, further, be called upon to contribute to global stability and peace by providing forces for United Nations missions." See *NATO Review,* vol. 39, no. 6, December 1991, pp. 19–32.

[13] See the brief paragraph 13 on the United Nations in the communiqué of the ministerial meeting of the North Atlantic Council, Oslo, June 4, 1992, in *NATO Review,* vol. 40, no. 3, June 1992, pp. 30–32. See also the extensive references to UN peacekeeping in the communiqué and in the statement on former Yugoslavia, issued by the North Atlantic Council, Brussels, December 17, 1992, in *NATO Review,* vol. 40, no. 6, December 1992, pp. 28–32.

[14] On the importance of ethnic issues in today's world, the underestimation of them in much US and Marxist thinking, and the limits of the doctrine of national self-determination, see Senator Daniel Patrick Moynihan, *Pandaemonium: Ethnicity in International Politics* (Oxford: Oxford University Press, 1993).

[15] Boutros-Ghali, *An Agenda for Peace,* paragraphs 5, 11, 15, 17.

[16] Ibid., paragraphs 9, 81–82. Boutros-Ghali discussed democratization in his speeches to the Boston World Affairs Council on March 16, 1993, and to the American Publishers Association in Washington D.C., March 25, 1993.

[17] For a lucid discussion of the causes of ethnic conflicts in the post-Soviet and post-Yugoslav states, and of their security aspects, see especially Jack Snyder, "Nationalism and the Crisis of the Post-Soviet State," chapter 5 in this volume, and Barry Posen, "The Security Dilemma and Ethnic Conflict," chapter 6 in this volume.

[18] See especially Jenonne Walker, "International Mediation of Ethnic Conflict," chapter 9 in this volume; on the same issue, see Posen, Ibid.

[19] For use of the term "nation" to refer to member-states, see Boutros-Ghali, *An Agenda for Peace,* paragraphs 3, 32. However, the report does use "state" or "country" more frequently.

[20] On the traditional criteria as applied to emerging states, the best study remains James R. Crawford, *The Creation of States in International Law* (Oxford: Oxford University Press, 1979).

[21] See, for example, the Declaration of September 3, 1991, of the CSCE states; Security Council Resolution 713 of September 25, 1991, and numerous

subsequent Security Council resolutions; the Statement on the Situation in Yugoslavia, issued by the North Atlantic Council, Rome, November 7–8, 1991, paragraph 2; Statement of Principles adopted on August 26, 1992, by the London Conference on the Former Socialist Federal Republic of Yugoslavia, paragraph ii.

[22] Boutros-Ghali, *An Agenda for Peace,* paragraphs 2, 10, 17, 19, 30.

[23] Ibid., paragraphs 6, 8.

[24] Ibid., especially paragraphs 5, 8, 11–13.

[25] UN Charter, Article 25.

[26] Bill Clinton said while campaigning for the presidency: "Japan and Germany should be made permanent members of the UN Security Council." See Bill Clinton, Address to Foreign Policy Association, New York, April 1, 1992; Bill Clinton, "A New Covenant for American Security," *Harvard International Review,* vol. 14, no. 4, Summer 1992. The US Secretary of State Warren Christopher said on January 25, 1993, that it was time for "some reorganization of the UN Security Council to bring it into keeping with modern realities," and he noted that during the election campaign, Clinton had raised the issue of giving Germany and Japan permanent membership of the Security Council.

[27] Boutros-Ghali, *An Agenda for Peace,* paragraphs 14, 15.

[28] UN Charter, Article 108.

[29] Ibid., Article 27.

[30] A 20-strong "Chapter VII Consultation Committee" of the General Assembly, to keep an open line between the Security Council and the General Assembly, is proposed by W. Michael Reisman, "The Constitutional Crisis in the United Nations," *American Journal of International Law,* vol. 87, no. 1, January 1993, p. 98.

[31] Boutros-Ghali, *An Agenda for Peace,* paragraphs 41–44.

[32] Ibid., paragraph 43. On preventive

deployments, see Section 8.

[33] Ibid.

[34] Boutros-Ghali, Statement on the Future of Collective Security, p. 3. He repeated the "building blocks" idea in his speech in Washington, D.C., on March 25, 1993.

[35] Simon Jones, "General MacKenzie Slams UN's Nine-to-Fivers," *The Independent,* January 31, 1993.

[36] Goulding, "The Evolution of UN Peacekeeping," p. 15.

[37] Boutros-Ghali, *An Agenda for Peace,* paragraph 43.

[38] Paul Lewis, "UN Is Developing Control Center to Coordinate Growing Peacekeeping Role," *New York Times,* March 28, 1993, p. 10.

[39] Zhou En-lai, interview with Dara Janekovic, *Vjesnik,* August 28, 1971.

[40] Boutros-Ghali, *An Agenda for Peace,* paragraph 41.

[41] Ibid., paragraph 20.

[42] Ibid., paragraphs 66–68.

[43] Goulding, "The Evolution of UN Peacekeeping," p. 11.

[44] Text of the Paris Agreements of October 23, 1991, on a Comprehensive Political Settlement of the Cambodia Conflict, UN Doc. A/46/608-S/23177, October 30, 1991.

[45] Boutros-Ghali, *An Agenda for Peace,* paragraphs 42, 63.

[46] For an excellent enumeration of issues relating to collective security systems, see Andrew Hurrell, "Collective Security and International Order Revisited," *International Relations,* vol. 11, no. 1, April 1992.

[47] Security Council Resolution 678, November 29, 1990.

[48] Boutros-Ghali, *An Agenda for Peace,* paragraphs 28–32.

[49] Goulding, "The Evolution of UN Peacekeeping," p. 12; Boutros-Ghali, *Report of the Work of the Organization, 1992,* paragraphs 18, 46.

[50] Clinton, "A New Covenant"; Bill Clinton, Statement to UNA–USA,

October 9, 1992.

[51] As of September 30, 1992, the United States still owed nearly $525 million to the UN regular budget, of which roughly half was delayed payment for 1992. It also owed $129 million in peacekeeping dues. The total, roughly $654 million, was about 44 percent of all money owed by all 179 member-states on that date. See *Great Decisions 1993* (New York: Foreign Policy Association, 1993), p. 21. By the end of 1992, the United States—continuing its policy of paying its dues almost in full and its arrears in annual installments—had reduced its arrears to the regular budget to about $240 million.

[52] Boutros Boutros-Ghali, *New Dimensions of Arms Regulation and Disarmament in the Post-Cold War Era: Report of the Secretary-General on the Occa-sion of Disarmament Week, October 27, 1992,* UN Doc. A/C.1/47/7, October 1992, paragraphs 4, 43–44.

[53] See John Simpson, "Disarmament, Arms Control, and the UN of the 1990s," Paper presented at British International Studies Association Annual Conference, Swansea, December 14–16, 1992.

[54] Boutros-Ghali, Statement on the Future of Collective Security, p. 7; Goulding, "The Evolution of UN Peacekeeping," p. 2.

[55] Boutros-Ghali, *An Agenda for Peace,* paragraph 13.

[56] Boutros Boutros-Ghali, "Empowering the United Nations," *Foreign Affairs,* vol. 72, no. 5, Winter 1992–1993, p. 91.

[57] Goulding, "The Evolution of UN Peacekeeping," p. 17.

Chapter 12

Managing the Politics of Parochialism
John Chipman

Regional stability in most areas of the world today suffers from an overindulgence in the domestic and international politics of parochialism. There has developed, in effect, a new imperialism of parochialism, in which conflicts over territory are frequently ethnic in motivation. If ideology—the politics of intellectual dogmas—plays a less prominent part in determining potentially violent struggles within and between states, ethnicity and nationalism—the politics of cultural particularisms—have come to take center stage in many theaters of military conflict. Moreover, even where ideological struggles occur, they are often trumped by ethnic differences or provincial solidarities. The civil war in Tajikistan of 1992–1993 was less a battle between Islamicists and communists, as so often portrayed, and more a regional competition— often based on the complex politics of clan affiliation— between Khojent and Kulab, on the one hand, and Garm and Pamir, on the other.

Although some political ideologies can dampen ethnic conflict in different ways—communism by denying or manipulating, often forcibly, the principle of nationality; liberal democracy by protecting individual or group rights to a degree that usually makes the assertion of ethnic political programs less urgent—the tendency for people to organize around ethnic affiliations is now nearly always nascent. Different ethnic or national groups can live intermingled or side by side for many years, and yet when certain individual, political, social, economic, linguistic, religious, or even environmental rights cannot be defended or advanced through any other instrument, ethnic conflicts emerge. They may also surface when others force people to see themselves as capable of political expression only through violence best organized ethnically. Ethnicity may once have been the primordial repository of cultural definition, but it has now become the ultimate resort of the politically desperate.

The defense and advance of ethnic claims is a dramatic corollary of the ease with which popular passions can be harnessed and the difficulties leaders have in disassociating political victories from issues of identity. The nineteenth century certainly witnessed many examples of militant nationalism: Giuseppe Mazzini was the most famous preacher of the idea of national liberation and recommended it to everybody until commentators in midcentury, after the nationalists had checkmated each other in 1848, complained of "nationalism as the curse of Europe."[1] However, ethnic conflict has been most prominent in the twentieth century (as states that emerged after decolonization were betrayed by what was false within) and most powerful at the century's end (as older states have proved unable to arbitrate ethnic passions). Ethnic liberation and irredentism are again claimed on the basis of ancient historical rights. It is worth recalling in this context that earlier conflicts taking a territorial form often did not necessarily lead to the promotion of cultural or nationalistic goals in conquered territory. When Louis XIV annexed Alsace, he did not ban the German language; it was only in 1768 that attempts were made to establish schools in which French might be taught. Even in the nationalist nineteenth century, one writer wryly and prophetically noted that "the political ethnomaniacs, to be consistent, ought to propose the annexation of Alsace to some German state."[2]

Admittedly, much military conflict today is unrelated to specific ethnic designs. Still, it is in the twentieth century that popular passions and political projects have most persistently fused to create the genre of dispute known as ethnic conflict. Earlier periods saw the defense of national honor at the *state* level, but in the twentieth century, with the increase in popular participation in politics, citizens feel capable of interpreting national honor and rising up against their leaders if they betray that honor. In this lie elements of a democratic paradox, for if "jingoism is the form of patriotism specially invented by democracies," it is equally true that democracies can limit the extent and power of ethnic disputes.[3]

The prevalence of ethnic conflict today has created a security question, but one more comprehensive than in previous periods in which ethnic or national hatred was prominent. There are three reasons for this. First, peoples have at their disposal the right to self-determination, which can both provide the animus and give dramatic form to claims for greater freedom and respect. The increased codification of international law relating to human rights and the predilection of the international community to act for their observance are also relatively new features that affect both causes and outcomes of ethnic conflict. The right to self-determination and the practice of humanitarian intervention are in part contradicted by the principle of territorial integrity, which places constraints on the creation of new subjects of international law (states) and the principle of state sovereignty, which normally limits outside interference in local affairs. This conflict of principles becomes a primary dilemma for conflict managers.

Second, the capacities of ethnic groups to receive assistance from abroad turn domestic disputes into international issues. The commutability of ethnic conflicts is often stated as the reason outsiders should act to force early containment. Ethnic conflicts themselves may not "spill over" as automatically as milk from a broken jug, but the effects of ethnic conflict, particularly in refugee flows, are often regional and rarely only domestic. The existence of an ethnic conflict in one state can also mean that neighboring states may find themselves harboring, intentionally or otherwise, terrorists or freedom fighters from another state, which naturally affects interstate relations.

Third, the flow of information and the effect of television mean, especially for the great powers who retain power projection capacities, that public opinion might support the deployment of force for preventive diplomacy, humanitarian aid, peacekeeping, or pacification, even without the national interests of the "expeditionary state" being remotely engaged. This impels states to become involved in the parochial quarrels of others. Leaders may know that their citizens will not support heavy casualties where no great strategic interest is at stake, but often the demand "to do something" cannot be refuted by reasoned argument. The political settlement of ethnic disputes thus affects, first, a more activist international community at the level of principle; second, local states, which see their regional security compromised, even if only indirectly; and, finally, distant states, which may come under domestic pressure to become directly involved, despite the absence of a nationally defined political aim.

The difficulties of solving ethnic conflicts are intimately related to their special twentieth century features. Indeed, it is best to begin by asserting that once ethnic conflict has broken out, there can be no happy solutions. All ethnic conflict is testimony to some prior failure of political arrangements that somehow once acted as a prophylactic to the organization of competition around ethnic claims. It is equally true that some ethnic conflicts liberate people from repressive or otherwise inappropriate political arrangements, but this does not make finding new and fair ones easy. Furthermore, ethnic conflicts become both more violent, and more difficult to solve, as political calculations give way to the naked assertion of will.

The French intellectual Julien Benda noted in the 1920s "how commonly men let themselves be killed on account of some wound to their pride, and how infrequently for some infraction of their interest."[4] The more passionate ethnic conflict becomes, the more those previously outside the fray must choose a position within it. One of the great cruelties of ethnic conflict is that everyone is automatically labeled a combatant—by the identity they possess—even if they are not. Thus, ethnic conflicts in their extreme can become total conflicts. They turn everyone into participants and so give every individual—not only organized groups, parties, factions, or alliances—a personal stake in the outcome. This fact, above all others, is what makes the resolution of ethnic conflict different from other types of conflict resolution. To work, it must satisfy great numbers of politically engaged individuals who must learn again the primacy of political calculation over the repeated assertion of absolutist hopes of "glory" or "historical retribution." When national or ethnic feelings can be expressed as interests, they tend to be subject to negotiation; when they are seen to be little more than the exercise of pride, they become uncompromising in their essence. It is this truism that governs everything about ethnic conflict, from its possible causes to its potential solutions.

Ethnic conflict has become a universal security dilemma. This is so precisely at the time when the international community is claiming through both the United Nations (UN) and certain regional organizations a greater *droit de regard* over the efficacy and security implications of domestic political arrangements. A consistent failure to manage ethnic conflicts could contribute to the reversal of this trend and, in itself, frustrate efforts to build regional security more on the basis of enforceable norms of acceptable behavior and less on balance-of-power arrangements with no inherent moral content. All ethnic conflicts may be different, just as, pace Tolstoy, all unhappy families are unhappy in their own way, but general guidelines of principle and policy should be available to negotiators of political settlements. There are no magic potions to remove the taste, once acquired, of ethnic dispute, and there are too few cases of successful ethnic conflict management on which to build optimism. Yet, in an age of parochialism, the international community must do what it can to deter nationally and ethnically based groups (either in government or in opposition) from establishing dictatorships of nationality and undermining the prospects for genuine democracy in multiethnic territories.

A new intrusiveness of the international community is necessary if ethnic conflicts are to be resolved. The fair application of the moral, political, and legal criteria to ethnic conflict often requires outside parties to act. However, as this chapter intends to show, two features of ethnic conflict management need to be borne in mind by diplomats and politicians who engage themselves in finding solutions. First, initial solutions to potential conflicts within states often have destabilizing external consequences. Second, and as a result, "single solutions" are rarely enough: Several answers need to be found simultaneously and regionally to ethnic strife that may, in the first instance, affect a small area in a single state.

THE MORAL, POLITICAL, AND LEGAL CONTEXT
OF ETHNIC CONFLICT RESOLUTION

At the root of all ethnic conflict are competing answers to the following question: Should everything be done to fit the state to the people, or is it best to fit the people to the state?[5] Even liberals have traditionally fought about this dilemma. Lord Acton argued that "the coexistence of several nations under the same state is a test as well as the best security of its freedom."[6] He felt that multinational states were, in effect, the best guarantor of liberty and that "a state that is incompetent to satisfy different races condemns itself."[7] According to this conception, the quality of government is all important. In contrast, John Stuart Mill felt that it was "in general, a necessary condition of free institutions that the boundaries of governments should in the main coincide with those of nationalities."[8] This view states that both freedom and stability are best assured when the nation is coextensive with the state—as rare a feature in the contemporary state system as it was in Mill's time. It constitutes the pure version of the nationality principle in politics.

Modern liberals have tended to take a pragmatic stand, as exemplified by Michael Walzer's assertion that "the moral standing of any particular state depends upon the reality of the common life it protects and the extent to which the sacrifices required by that protection are willingly accepted and thought worthwhile. If no common life exists, or if the state doesn't protect the common life that does exist, its own defense may have no moral justification."[9] This view implicitly encapsulates the idea that popular sovereignty is elemental in the forging of the state and that the test of a state's success consists in proof of a notional "social contract" being honored between the state and its inhabitants.

All of these notions are confused in the modern principle of self-determination, itself a product of liberal (and specifically) Wilsonian thinking. Lawyers have disagreed as to its current status in international law, while political analysts, although acknowledging its power as a rallying cry, wonder whether its traditional application is not seriously flawed.[10] The principle of self-determination had its intellectual origins in the nineteenth century and received a political impetus at the Versailles peace conference, where it became the vehicle for the redivision of Europe and the continental dismemberment of the defeated empires.[11] However, this principle did not rise to become a rule of international law at the time the UN Charter was drafted and does not feature in the 1948 Universal Declaration of Human Rights. In the context of the accelerated trend toward decolonization, the principle of self-determination was converted into a "right" with the adoption by the UN General Assembly in 1960 of the Declaration on the Granting of Independence to Colonial

Countries and Peoples. That declaration refers to the right of peoples to self-determination and their consequent right to determine their political status.

Independence (from colonial domination) is explicitly stated not to be conditional on any perceived adequacy of political, economic, social, or educational preparedness. The same declaration also reinforces the principle of territorial integrity by recalling that any attempt aimed at the partial or total disruption of national unity or territorial integrity is incompatible with the purposes and principles of the United Nations. Later UN declarations have done little to clarify exactly when the "right" to self-determination is applicable (especially outside colonial situations) and when the ultimate result of the assertion of the "right" need be independence. Indeed, when India ratified the 1966 International Covenant on Civil and Political Rights, it explicitly stated that, in its view, the right to self-determination applied only to peoples under foreign domination and not to sovereign independent states or to a section of a people or a nation.

State practice suggests that many agree with this view, and indeed many regional organizations appear to place primary value on the maintenance of territorial integrity. The most celebrated example of this is the commitment to territorial integrity in the Charter of the Organization of African Unity (OAU), reinforced by the resolution passed at the 1964 Cairo OAU Summit at which member-states pledged "to respect the borders existing on their achievement of political independence." The effect over time has been to establish a rule of regional customary law by which the territorial status quo is accepted.[12] In fact, the normative power of the OAU doctrine is such that the expected confirmed secessions of Eritrea and possibly Somaliland will probably be the exceptions that will prove the rule, rather than precursors of a flood of frontier litigation and state fragmentation.[13] Nevertheless, it will be important for both Africans and outsiders, given the fractionating tendencies in so many other African states, to maintain the view that self-determination should take place within existing states rather than through their destruction. If there are too many exceptions to this rule, regional order (and the rule itself) would collapse.

The balance of legal opinion suggests that neither in the instruments of the United Nations, nor in customary international law as a whole, does there exist any legal right to independence, by means of the right to self-determination for any noncolonial people or for a minority within an existing state. In a formal sense, the international community recognizes the right to self-determination probably in only two senses: freedom from a former colonial power and the independence of an entire state's population from foreign intervention or influence.[14] Politically, however, the right to self-determination has considerable support, and most groups who seek to have it implemented try to argue that they need freedom from some form of "colonial" domination or that they have been deprived of their homeland by some prior aggression. Neither a lawyer nor a politician could credibly argue that, except for the few formal colonial situations that still remain, there are no cases in which the right to self-determination should lead to independent statehood. There are specific cases in which the historical, legal, and political background is such that the appropriate application of the principle of self-determination can only lead to the creation of a state. This may be the case for the Palestinians (whose right to self-determination is not merely generally, but specifically, recognized by UN resolutions), even if the state they intend to create eventually enters into federal arrangements with some of its neighbors. There may be other cases in which the creation of a new state is the best political and legal answer to the moral and security questions raised by ethnic or national instability. However, in the wake of the ethnomania that has broken out since 1990, it is necessary to bear in mind not only the formal limitations to the right to self-determination as summarized above, but also its ultimate purpose, as well as the security consequences of investing the principle with greater specificity than it currently enjoys.

The case of Yugoslavia has recently added weight to the view that territorial integrity is a particularly prized feature of public international law and of practical politics. The Arbitration Commission set up by the European Community (EC) in 1991 in the context of its Conference for Peace in Yugoslavia made several rulings on borders and the applicability of the principle of self-determination. In December 1991, it found that Yugoslavia was in the process of dissolution and that the republics needed to settle among themselves, in keeping with international law, such issues of state succession that might arise, while paying particular attention to human and minority rights. It also said that it was up to the republics that wished to work together to form a new association.[15] By January 1992, when asked to rule on whether the internal frontiers between Croatia and Slovenia, on the one hand, and between Serbia and Bosnia-Herzegovina, on the other, could be considered international frontiers under international law, it decided that the external frontiers of the republics deserved protection in international law. (None had at this stage received formal diplomatic recognition by EC states.) In effect, the commission proposed extending the cover of Article 2(4) of the UN Charter concerning the territorial integrity and political independence of member-states to the republics, arguing that the former boundaries acquired the character of borders protected by international law according to the principle of *uti possidetis*, initially recognized in the settlement of decolonization issues in Africa and Latin America.[16] Having relied on the principle of *uti possidetis*, the commission essentially found that the population of entities established as territorially defined administrative units of a federal nature could benefit from a collective right to self-determination leading to independence if certain procedures were followed, including the holding of a referendum. This right did not apply in the same sense to minorities within such defined territorial units, however. Thus, the minority Serb populations in Croatia or Bosnia-Herzegovina could "obtain recognition of the nationality of their choice with all the rights and obligations deriving therefrom in relation to all states concerned."[17]

The right to self-determination in relation to these minorities was not seen as a people's right to independence, but as a human right of minorities and groups. In the commission's view, common consent of the relevant states was needed for the exercise of the right to self-determination to lead to a change of borders. It was best, therefore, to see the right to self-determination with respect to minorities who were inhabitants of already existing territorial entities (federal states), as part of the body of human rights law. Reorganizing people of a common ethnic group into territorial units matching their geographical distribution was ruled out.[18] The application of these principles as defined by the commission also meant that self-determination—leading to independent statehood—was not deemed applicable to territorially defined enclaves within former federal entities where a minority formed a local majority. Thus, the Serbs in Krajina could not demand statehood, nor could the Albanians in Kosovo, despite the fact that preexisting structures of autonomous government remained.[19]

Policies pursued in Yugoslavia suggest that achieving independent statehood on the basis of a right to self-determination is highly dependent on the preexisting juridical status of the borders that the group claiming a right to independence wish to be their own. In practical terms, the aim of self-determination must be for individuals alone and in identifiable groups to achieve a high degree of political, cultural, and economic freedom within a specific territory. Peoples who suffer from colonial domination or illegal annexation clearly have no such capacity and, therefore, can seek within the constraints of international law to establish their own independent state to guarantee these freedoms. However, it does not follow that when ethnic or minority groups are suppressed within a given state, the international community has an obligation to accept their statehood on coherent expression of its demand because of the principle of self-determination. This is not merely because, as is so often argued, the ethnic patchwork of states means that the expansion of the principle of self-determination to guarantee statehood to groups who claimed it would result in the near-endless creation of petty states. It is also because the creation of a new state may not end the disputes that gave rise to the group's demand and because the new state itself may not respect the minorities newly found within it.

Morally, a secession from an existing state may be permissible when numerous conditions are met, including the following: the group in the seceding territory has consistently experienced an infringement of its rights or its culture, and there is no practicable way, short of secession, that those rights can be preserved; the seceding group is able to compensate innocent third parties (where appropriate) for any losses they might suffer; the purpose of the secession is not to establish an illiberal state that would merely provoke new injustices; and the sum of the injustices avoided and the rights of people protected and advanced is deemed politically significant enough to grant title to territory that was previously held by others.[20] Furthermore, the case of Yugoslavia shows that people are allowed to secede from a colonial context, but they cannot do so by changing internal frontiers. Of course, where the constitution of a state allows for the independence of its constituent parts (as was the case of the Soviet Union), some or all of these questions might not arise in a formal sense, and equally where secession or partition takes place by negotiation, as in the case of the Czech and Slovak Republics, the international community is bound to accept the results. Finally, when confederal states collapse in the political sense, recognition of the formally constituent parts may, as a practical matter, not be based so much on any perceived right to self-determination, but on interpretation of the laws of state succession.

In general, the international community is and should remain very reluctant to sacrifice the principle of territorial integrity to the principle of self-determination, especially given that the latter, widely defined, can usually be satisfied by political acts short of the creation of a new state. Moreover, there are often security issues that arise when new subjects of international law appear, and the international community has a right to consider the effects of new state creation as much as it might pass judgment on the legitimacy in practical, moral, or legal grounds of the case made for new entrants to the club of states.

What makes this position more sustainable now is the international community's tendency to be more intrusive in the affairs of states to ensure that human, group, or minority rights are respected. The rise of a limited right of humanitarian intervention and the existence in certain areas, particularly the Conference on Security and Cooperation in Europe

(CSCE) region, of more activist supervision of the manner in which states treat their own citizens suggest that there may be modest ways in which the international community can protect from the outside what states fail to protect from the inside.[21] The achievements in this area remain modest. In Europe, where the relevant organizations have tried to deepen minority rights "legislation," member-states have reflected very different philosophical approaches to this issue. Even among Western powers, assorted views exist on the priority attached to individual liberty, as opposed to specific minority or group rights. This has severely limited the creation of enforceable norms in this area.[22] Still, it is certainly becoming less acceptable for governments to claim that the territory they control has greater rights than the people they suppress, thus insulating themselves from outside complaint or sanction through sometimes cynical recourse to the protection "sovereignty" provides them. The interdependence of international affairs has given outsiders a *locus standi* to act and comment on the international implications of policies, initially only domestic, in both origin and purpose. The sovereignty so many seek in the form of states for themselves is now very different from the sovereignty states enjoyed in the great period of nationalism in the nineteenth century.

The problem is that the international community and regional organizations are inconsistent in the degree to which they involve themselves in the internal affairs of others, even when they have decided on norms whose breach entitles intervention. They also rarely demonstrate the "staying power" necessary to bring ethnic conflicts to a satisfactory and durable settlement. Having tinkered diplomatically or even militarily with some of the initial problems, outsiders often lose interest. Local combatants know that patience is a strategic asset: If they keep a low profile when outsiders are around, they will be able to fight again when the outsiders leave. For this reason, few are willing to rely on the limited protection international legislation on domestic governance affords. Certainly, once conflict has broken out, such political and legal instruments on human and minority rights are unlikely to carry weight. Thus, the Serbs in Krajina during 1992–1993 were clearly more interested in a UN military presence, no matter how flimsy, than in Croatian political assurances with respect to their minority rights, no matter how they might be internationally guaranteed.

THE INTERNATIONAL EFFECTS OF
ETHNIC CONFLICT MANAGEMENT

In the first instance, most ethnic conflicts are managed internally. In some cases, brutal policies of assimilation are pursued that contain revolts against the political center, but only lay the seeds of future complaint. In other cases, new provinces are created in multiethnic states to give groups a greater sense of local power and to divert conflict from the center. Central authorities sometimes try to buy allegiance by increasing development assistance to areas in which particular ethnic groups are dominant or by including particular ethnic groups in major government positions. From time to time, even without pressure from outside agencies, minorities are given special rights—including self-government—to alleviate their inherent sense of weakness. Occasionally, independence movements are successful and escape relatively peacefully from their former states. However, rarely are "solutions" to ethnic conflict "containable" to the initiating state. They often have external effects. This fact is insufficiently appreciated by the international community, which until recently has taken as axiomatic that what happens inside states only concerns insiders. Because ethnic groups cut across borders and the effects of domestic ethnic violence are regional, it follows that domestic solutions to ethnic conflict can pacify regional relationships, as well as excite concerns in local states.

The appearance of new states that define themselves in ethnic terms will concern neighboring states that have ethnic minority populations of the same group—and may sometimes inspire countermeasures. For example, the independence of Azerbaijan was immediately of concern to Iran, which has a large Azeri population. Once President Abulfez Elchibey began to speak more generally of his interest in the Azeri "nation," including inhabitants of what he termed southern Azerbaijan (by which he meant the north of Iran), Tehran felt threatened. The decision by Iran to change the name of its East Azerbaijan province with its capital as Tabriz to Central Azerbaijan and to establish a (new) second province called East Azerbaijan with its capital as Ardebil can be read as an attempt by the Iranian leadership to make the Azeri part of Iran less amenable to influence from Baku.[23] By having two Azeri provincial leaderships in two capitals, Tehran is potentially more able to ensure that a bloc Azeri population cannot be mobilized against it.[24]

Similarly, the appearance of an independent Kazakhstan has worried the Chinese leadership; Kazakh and Uigur populations in Xinxiang Province can now develop links with their kith and kin in Kazakhstan. Some of the peoples in Xinxiang already have a measure of formal autonomy, and it is unlikely that the Chinese leadership will make constitutional changes to preempt political activity. There have, however, been increased deployments of security forces in the area, and any excessive political activity is likely to be met more with force than with structural changes in political arrangements. The increased discussion in the Chinese official press about the dangers of the "politics of splittism" implies that the Chinese government fears that the existence of independent states on the former Soviet frontier might lead groups in Xinxiang (and elsewhere) to identify themselves along specific ethnic lines, rather than see themselves simply as "non-Han." This is particularly true of China's Muslim population.

In this context, it is worth recalling that, although nations can and do from time to time form states (despite the low number of nation-states), it is also the case that the existence of states can preserve or even invent nations. When the frontiers between Kyrgystan and Uzbekistan were initially drawn, there were people who did not know whether they were Kirgiz or Uzbek.[25] Some 70 years later, they now "know" who they are and to whom they are similar. Thus, one of the more salient political and security consequences of the creation of national homelands is the appearance of "exiles" to whose appeal neighboring "host states" are naturally sensitive.

Indeed, neighboring states will always be concerned when the result of a political solution is the granting of rights or political powers to ethnic groups or regions that they deny to their own people of similar stock. India, for example, while supporting the Tamil cause in Sri Lanka, would be concerned by a Sri Lankan settlement along federal lines that resulted in Colombo giving more power to provinces in which Tamils were dominant than the Indians give to their various states, including Tamil Nadu. Similarly, as the Tuareg in North and West Africa are a nomadic people who live in six states, agreements between a government and "its" Tuareg rebels are closely watched by others. The agreement in April 1992 between Mali and the four Tuareg rebel organizations active in that country included provisions for decentralized administration in three northern regions.[26] Actual autonomy might have been seen as a slippery slope to secession and might have encouraged the drive toward the establishment of a federation cutting across state frontiers, for which some Tuareg have called. Again, denial of such autonomy may lead to a result that the central government in Mali (and elsewhere) fear.

Sometimes states are forced to accept (and even facilitate) new political arrangements in neighboring states, which provide greater rights for minorities, even though it immediately affects their own politics. Thus, Turkey, a coalition partner during the Gulf War that received large numbers of refugees from Iraq, now finds itself concerned about the level of autonomy that the Kurdish population has received in northern Iraq. The protection provided by the international community to the Kurdish population in northern Iraq, and the self-government they now enjoy in the 36,000 square miles they control, highlights Turkey's policy toward its own Kurdish population, a policy that only recently allowed Kurds to use their own language. The fact that Kurds live in a number of other countries in the region renders it less likely, as it always has done, that a Kurdish state would be formally recognized in northern Iraq. However, to prevent the Kurdish issue from becoming regionally destabilizing, minority rights or levels of self-government would have to be similar in all the countries in which they reside. Otherwise, the anomaly of their position in Iraq, delicate and insecure as it is, compared particularly to their position in Turkey, so closely allied to the West, will keep tensions high.

Neighboring countries that share between them two major ethnic groups, but in which each have a different majority, can suffer from the circular effects of ethnic-based opposition to central government and the responses of the ruling group. A classic African case is Rwanda and Burundi: In the former, the Hutu tribe is dominant, and the Tutsi is in the minority; while in Burundi, the Tutsi govern a Hutu minority. The Palipehutu rebel group in Burundi, which has wanted to overthrow the Burundi government, has been accused of being supported by Rwanda. At the same time, the authorities in Rwanda, who have been opposed by the primarily Tutsi Rwanda Patriotic Front, accuse Burundi of providing Tutsi mercenaries to support the opposition against Rwanda's government. Massacres of the minority in one country have sometimes been followed by killings of the minority in the other. A bilateral agreement between the two countries in June 1992—in which each pledged to deny support to the other's opposition groups—is inherently fragile because it is so easy for suspicions to be raised.

This points to the absolute need for employing confidence-building measures as instruments of ethnic conflict resolution and for greater attention to be given to the ways in which domestic policies on minorities can affect nationalist sentiments in neighboring states. A good example is where the partition of a federal state magnifies the presence and vulnerability of a minority, leading the minority to demand the same sort of self-government that its "host state" has only recently achieved itself. Thus, the independence of Slovakia has provoked fears for the roughly 600,000 Hungarians in the new state, nearly all of them living next to the frontier with Hungary. Prime Minister Vladimir Meciar in Slovakia has expressed the traditional fear that if he were to give in to Hungarian demands for more autonomy, this would only be a first step toward secession and eventual annexation by Budapest.[27] It is also fair to say that the treatment of Hungarians in Slovakia has traditionally been very good.

Yet, a reluctance to provide for some devolution might not only stoke secessionist desires in Slovakia, but also inflame nationalist forces within Hungary that, since January 1993, have gained in strength. Even the Hungarian prime minister, Jozsef Antall, a moderate on these issues, has spoken of himself as leader of all 15 million Hungarians, although only 10.4 million live in Hungary, and has formally endorsed the demand of the Hungarian minority in Vojvodina for autonomy, thus also giving added succor to Hungarians in Romania and Slovakia. In turn, these proclamations, made in part to outflank more extreme domestic elements, have provoked concerns in the region that the arrangements of the 1920 Treaty of Trianon might be overturned and that there might be a need for the Serbs, Slovaks, and Romanians collectively to forestall Hungarian desires for even more dramatic border reforms.

Were minority rights issues to lead to this sort of regional alliance-building, more direct involvement of regional organizations would be necessary. This would be so if only because matters of ethnicity touch at the core of perceptions of national purpose and identity, and bilateral negotiations between two states on rights to be accorded ethnic groups are more détente-consuming than détente-producing. The reality so often is that the "structure" of the negotiations can appear asymmetric, with one side simply demanding recognition of minority rights for "their" people with little to offer besides calmed nerves. The creation of the state of Slovakia, which has heightened Hungarian concern, also provides an auspicious opportunity because of the need to establish new constitutional and other arrangements, for the new state to implement changes that later would be more difficult to undertake. Historically, arrangements for regional autonomy or special group rights are most likely to take hold when they are part of general changes in the political arena. The democratization of Spain, for example, provided the occasion for the establishment of regional autonomy for the Basques, Catalans, and Galicians.[28] If pressure were put on the new Slovakia from non-Hungarian sources, a regional ethnic domino might peaceably be lifted from the table.

As the previous example demonstrated, certain countries possess an ethnic mix so representative of regional rivalries that their domestic politics are nearly indistinguishable from regional quarrels. This also makes them subject to the effects of a neighbor's internal policies. Where this is particularly intense, the convention of minority rights or even partial self-government is not enough. Every group in the state needs equal measures of self-government for reasons of both internal and regional security. Thus, in Afghanistan, for example, the conclusion of the civil war is complicated by the fact that the new states of Central Asia are now developing national foreign policies based on ethnic or clan alliances, while both Iran and Pakistan have links with certain groups. The war in Tajikistan has created a considerable flow of refugees into Afghanistan, confusing the security situation there. Inside Afghanistan, Tajiks and Uzbeks (in uneasy alliance) control areas in the north, while

Hazaris of the Shi'a faith hold sway over areas in the west, and the Pashtuns hold areas in the east and south. Most of the guerrilla leaders appear content to establish for themselves sufficient local power to keep control of areas in which their group is prominent, but none would easily accept the power of another at the center. The formal partition of Afghanistan would make the emerging states vulnerable to their larger neighbors and lead to clan rivalries within the new states, creating disputes among the new majorities and minorities. The effective autonomy that competitors for power in Afghanistan have garnered for themselves following the ousting of the communist leadership is probably the most stable situation that can reasonably be hoped for. None of the leaders want their areas absorbed by neighbors, while a unitary state would imply the domination of one ethnic group over all others. Thus, creating a confederation of autonomous states might be the only way of both holding Afghanistan together and keeping its warlords in some uncertain peace. Multiethnic states led at the center by groups that are seen to be little more than ethnically organized factions are inherently unstable.

An insistence on creating a unitary state (to celebrate a national resurgence) in regions in which federal structures have both a historical and a present relevance can be seriously destabilizing. From a geopolitical point of view, one of the most mismanaged cases of domestic ethnic conflict resolution lies in the Caucasus. Leaders of the Georgian state have, at least since 1990, emphasized the need to develop a Georgian national identity within a unitary state. This has often taken place at the expense of minorities, whose representation in parliament, political and cultural autonomy, and even status as citizens has been challenged. The consequent military conflicts in South Ossetia and Abkhazia have involved Russian forces, whose leaders see wider Russian security concerns in the north Caucasus at stake. Although the Russians are accused by some in Tbilisi of imperialism, they are closely watched by those in the seven north Caucasian republics within the Russian Federation who themselves identify and show solidarity with the South Ossetians and Abkhazians and expect Russia to act in their support. A Russian failure to stem perceived Georgian aggression might increase the secessionist desires of the Caucasians within the Russian Federation, many of whom have informally gathered in the Caucasian Mountain Peoples Congress, which includes representatives from Abkhazia and South Ossetia.

The complexity of the Caucasian situation has some in Russia wondering whether the putative security advantage that control over the Caucasus confers should be given up in favor of a contraction of the Russian Federation, leaving the Caucasians to sort out their own fate. This, however, might only lead to further unraveling of the multiethnic Russian

Federation; Tatars, Bashkirs, and others would reexamine the value of their place within Russia. The difficulty for Russia of applying force and a divide-and-rule policy in the Caucasus is self-evident, although the renunciation of this ancient strategy could well lead to a considerable proliferation of new states with very uncertain relationships with each other. Because many of the Caucasians within the Russian Federation have, in recognition of their own internal ethnic diversity, appeared to accept the federal principle as a useful political arrangement, it is proper to ask how the Georgians might come to terms with the presence of North Caucasians on their territory. If the maintenance of a unitary Georgian state were to lead to the atomization of the Caucasus, the political and economic security of most would be damaged.

Russians within their own federation have concluded treaties with groups demanding more autonomy; were Georgia to complete similar treaties with its own North Caucasian peoples and allow them informally to construct agreements with their brethren in the Russian Federation, the basis for regional political cooperation in the Caucasus might be established. This might preempt political collapse in the area. In any event, this is a case in which a domestic conflict cannot be solved except in a regional context and in which any domestically proposed solution to the conflict would require the cooperation of regional states to succeed. Newly independent states are most sensitive to this implied veto power of neighbors, not least when it involves the former "colonial power." Although states should have a general right to organize their internal politics without external interference, the fact that such arrangements so often have external consequences means that the fair treatment of groups who also live in other states is something on which outsiders can fairly comment.

That said, the extraterritorial defense of "nationals" living in other states cannot be accepted as a regular feature of regional or international politics. Ethnic conflict resolution is thus made awkward by the delicate equilibrium that must be maintained between respect for a state's right to order its internal political structures and appreciation for the sometimes malign regional implications of domestic decisions. Because badly managed domestic conflicts almost always have regional consequences and because even successful arrangements for the people immediately concerned can result in (often unintended) distress for peoples living in other states, the international community often needs to become involved. Unfortunately, political solutions to ethnic conflicts have a kinetic quality: With each new arrangement proposed, others that formerly worked become unstuck. Durable solutions require the type of comprehensive approach that can rarely be undertaken by outsiders, who have both short attention spans and limited powers of (or political will for) enforcement. Unless preventive diplomacy becomes a more regular feature of ethnic conflict management by the international community, the international system is bound to be confronted with numerous ethnic conflicts with international repercussions of varying importance, the general solution of which requires the agreement and acquiescence of many regional states.

ETHNIC CONFLICT RESOLUTION AND THE INTERNATIONAL COMMUNITY

Once the international community is brought into ethnic conflict resolution, the shape of the problem and of the possible outcomes changes. Whereas a government would seek to resolve conflict in a manner consistent with its own often sectarian interests, or on the basis of certain principles carefully selected to favor those interests, the international community will tend to apply principles derived from international practice and law without much regard for the advantage they might confer on particular parties. Although a government's primary concern in conflict management will be domestic order (not necessarily justice), the international community needs to consider both justice and the implications of a settlement for regional and international peace and security.

Traditional interpretations of international law can sometimes be superseded by issues of international public policy thought important in the particular case. Outsiders will consider the use of force in a variety of ways that are different from national governments, and the choice by outsiders to deploy force to preserve a cease-fire, provide humanitarian assistance, or enforce a settlement changes the pace of internal politico-military developments, can alter the strategic objectives of the participants, and usually affects the balance of military power between combatants. Finally, the involvement of the international community, if it is able to sustain its activities through to the full implementation of a settlement, normally modifies the political alignments and the structure of the state in which it becomes engaged. As a rule, there will be a determination when the United Nations is involved to ensure free and fair elections and the institutionalization of democratic systems with appropriate guarantees of human and group rights. Often, the forced demilitarization of certain areas or the negotiated merging of rebel armed forces with those of the state against which it was fighting materially affects the possibilities of future armed conflict. None of this is to suggest that the activity of the international community—often involving the engagement of the great powers and particularly the permanent members of the UN Security Council—is always either impeccably objective, wise, or sufficiently intensive to assure success.

Regional organizations carry within them many regional rivalries—which is one reason they exist and contribute to peace and security—and, thus, when they enter into conflict resolution are at least partly hostage to these internal tensions. The early defense of the activities of the European Community in the case of Yugoslavia was that by its existence, the European Community had at least performed the modest task of preventing its member-states from open and direct support of the internal combatants in the decomposing state. Sarajevo in 1992, it was commonly asserted, did not resemble Sarajevo in 1914, precisely because the EC member-states had refrained from the temptation of alliance-building. However, certain national predispositions did influence EC diplomacy, not least on the crucial issue of whether and in what circumstances there should be diplomatic recognition of the successor states. In Liberia, the effort of the Economic Community of West African States (ECOWAS) to establish peace conferences and to engage a "peacekeeping force" was perceived by many as an extension of Nigerian foreign and security policy. This force has been fighting the rebel group led by Charles Taylor (suspected of being helped by Libya) in defense of the interim President Amos Sawyer, whom it supports. Sawyer's control of the country, even with the assistance of the military force of ECOWAS, barely extends beyond the capital, and Charles Taylor's control of most of the country has been credible enough that foreign companies have dealt directly with him. An international effort to solve the conflict in such circumstances would have difficulty recognizing the authority of the president approved by the relevant regional organization in light of the power wielded and territory controlled by his principal opponent.

When the United Nations comes in to assist in ethnic diplomacy first undertaken by a regional organization (as in Yugoslavia) or to take over (as some suggested in 1992 should have been done in Liberia), it necessarily inherits certain political decisions, even legal undertakings, which it will have difficulty reversing, even though justice or the interests of regional peace and security might compel a change. The United Nations cannot easily change the fact that as part of an incomplete process of ethnic conflict resolution, certain states will have been recognized or leaders placed in power whose authority derives more from regional diplomacy than local support and power. This leads to a fundamentally important point about the international community's involvement in ethnic conflict resolution. When its work is sequential to the work of a regional organization, its activity is heavily shaped by previous diplomatic decisions. Similarly, its own diplomacy will be contingent on an analysis of the nature of the war it seeks to end, as much as on the interests and positions of the parties per se. Although solutions to ethnic conflicts involving the international community are, in part, shaped by international, moral, political, and legal principles in the abstract, it is also true that negotiators are guided by the specific principles that need to be asserted as a consequence of the manner in which the given conflict was fought. The desire to deter others from engaging in unprincipled behavior weighs heavily on conflict managers, as does the wish to condemn certain political practices.

Thus, because the Serbs had indulged in what became known as "ethnic cleansing" in Bosnia-Herzegovina, international mediators felt they could not reach the same end by negotiation. In the comprehensive peace plan put forward by the UN and EC negotiators on Yugoslavia, the creation of three ethnically homogeneous provinces for the Serbs, Muslims, and Croats was excluded so as not to reward aggression or give credence to the political aim "ethnic cleansing" was meant to serve. The intentional creation of nine heterogeneous provinces with a single dominant group (plus Sarajevo as a tenth multiethnic province) was thus a moral imperative even though the evidence of the war itself was that the Serbian, Croat, and Muslim communities were not happy intermingling. Similarly, the goal of frustrating the creation of a "Greater Serbia" required that there be no territorial link between the predominantly Serbian provinces in the proposed confederation or between them and Serbia proper or Serbian communities elsewhere in the former Yugoslavia. (The same of course applied mutatis mutandis to predominantly Croat provinces.) This was done in the knowledge that few of the combatant Serbs (and not many combatant Croats) in Bosnia-Herzegovina had wished to pay unique or any homage to the state that the international community had recognized and whose independence it was committed to preserving. Thus, the clash between principles and realpolitik in the case of Bosnia-Herzegovina had tragically become considerable by the time a peace plan could be presented.

The UN–EC peace plan was an excellent product of the "grand settlement" school of ethnic conflict management (of which the Lebanese National Pact of 1943 might be seen as the classic model), but it was subject to one great deficiency, for which the mediators themselves cannot bear fault. Essential to the initial success of the Lebanese National Pact was that it entailed a promise on the part of the Maronite Christians to recognize the Arab character of Lebanon and to forego assistance from any European power, in return for which Sunni Muslims foreswore allegiance to a "greater Syria," pledging instead their loyalty to Lebanon.[29] While the UN–EC plan addressed the governance of the various provinces, the form of central government's legislature, the manner in which the presidency would rotate, and many other constitutional issues—applying all the lessons on the need for equality and reciprocal concessions that previous conflict managers have argued essential—the principal *political* promise was missing. That is, without a clear public and credible pledge by the Serbs that they would give up plans for a Greater Serbia and pay homage to the state of Bosnia-Herzegovina, by the Croats likewise publicly to abandon hopes of any formal link to Croatia, and by the Muslims to assure the secular nature of the state they wished to be their homeland, mutual suspicions on these scores could easily continue and frustrate a durable peace. The international community can do many things in ethnic conflict management, but one thing it cannot do is force an oath of fealty to a state many of the inhabitants believe is artificial. Without that promise, structural arrangements for the state itself are without foundation.

If the international community is powerless to create loyalties to states, it is equally weak in creating normal political activity in a state all the inhabitants agree is theirs, but in which they have colluded in destroying. In extreme cases, ethnic conflicts can become so great that they render a state a nonstate, create a type of *terra nullius*, in which there may still be recognized frontiers, but everything inside is anarchy. Ulysses in William Shakespeare's *Troilus and Cressida* described such a state, in which "everything includes itself in power, /Power into will, will into appetite; / and appetite, an universal wolf, /So doubly seconded with will and power, /must make perforce an universal prey, /And last eat up himself." Troy, he concludes, "in our weakness stands, not in her strength." By late 1992, Somalia had become such a state, and when the peacemakers begin their work following the US-led pacification exercise of early 1993, their task will be not only to bring an end to clan conflict, but also to build the state, with institutions capable of channeling and controlling future divisions. This is the necessary, although perhaps impossible, aim. Previous leaders in Somalia have failed; the international community does not have much practice in this area. It is difficult for states to be toward their inhabitants what urns are to ashes. Once the body politic has died, it is hard for institutions alone to preserve it or give it life. Where peacemaking involves politics-creation, the international community is not well equipped to help.

In some respects, therefore, ethnic conflict management by the international community may have the defects of its virtues. An attempt to create peace on the basis of international principles that cannot easily be compromised may result in impracticable results. The United Nations is a club of states and, as such, must seek to maintain peace among states that now so often requires the maintenance of a just peace within states. This is an area in which the international community has previously feared to tread, but in which it must now more regularly move. Yet, it does not follow from this that the United Nations can engage in state-building or politics-creation within states. These are genuinely the jobs (and duties) of citizens. The good offices of the United Nations are sometimes necessary to bring parties together and mediate the essentials of a political compromise as it has done frequently. However, the "management takeover" of ethnically fractured states is an enterprise best avoided except in very particular cases in which it is the only method of effective preventive diplomacy.

Such cases may emerge when new states are recognized before their time. In light of the instabilities that can be caused by the emergence of new states consequent on ethnically based disorder, it is clear that elaborate tests must be established for diplomatic recognition. In the case of Yugoslavia, states were recognized in a short-cut attempt at war termination. However, some of the recognized states did not have control over their territory or effective establishment of a political community, which are two of the main criteria traditionally used to determine whether a state exists de facto.[30] The European Community also adopted a series of moral and public policy criteria for recognition, although states were recognized with insufficient evidence that even these criteria were met. Although states were admitted into the international system in unstable conditions during the period of decolonization, this was part of a decision of international "public policy" to end colonial rule. Some of the imperial states also argued, with varying levels of conviction and truth, that the states so recognized had been prepared for self-government. In the postcolonial era, it will be important for the international community to adopt a circumspect attitude toward new claimants to statehood, unless there are overwhelming reasons of justice and order to accept secession or other collective claims for statehood.

As a practical matter, there may be cases of state collapse that lead to the emergence of premature states—that is, states that do not satisfy the normal criteria of statehood. In such circumstances, as an instrument of preventive diplomacy, it may be necessary for the United Nations to act in an incubating role. Civilian monitors, with some military elements, might be deployed to a new state to supervise the creation of a government and the implementation of policies regarding minority rights or international commitments in the field of arms control, which would rightly condition full diplomatic recognition.

Too often, states have achieved full entry into relevant international fora on the basis of written promises, the implementation of which is incomplete. For example, Croatia was admitted to the International Monetary Fund (IMF) before it was clear that its policy toward the minority

Serb population met the standards initially requested of it. In cases such as these, an "incubating" authority could report to the United Nations on the practical steps governments have taken to meet international norms. An international presence on the territory of the new states would be temporary and for a period would qualify the level of sovereignty the new states enjoyed, but it would have the advantage of assuring a measure of domestic peace and reassuring neighbors who might be nervous about the intentions of the new state. In a very limited sense, this is what the United Nations did in deploying peacekeepers to Macedonia at the beginning of 1993, although for the "incubation" to be effective, more intrusive monitoring of a state's domestic policies would be necessary. Had CSCE monitors been sent to Slovakia to report on the rights of Hungarian minorities immediately after independence, some of the more dramatic statements of the two sides might not have been made. A CSCE report might have allowed for a more objective appraisal of the claims and counterclaims of the immediately implicated parties. The CSCE's High Commissioner for National Minorities must also act, for similar reasons, in the case of Russian minorities outside Russia. More intensive activity of this kind would often be welcomed by the host state because it might consider that the claims of outside states, with respect to minorities in their country, were polemical and ill informed.

Clearly, the international community should, in the first instance, avoid admitting unstable entities into statehood. When recognition of new states is politically unavoidable, but in practice premature, the international community should consider the need for incubation. Incubation need not mean the creation of a "transitional authority" (as the United Nations has attempted in Cambodia), but rather close supervision. Incubation policies would need to be distinguished carefully and completely from the mandatory system of the League of Nations. Because mandates were, in effect, zones of influence often administered by agents of the mandatory power, their relinquishment often had less to do with the perceived fitness of a territory to enter into statehood and more to do with strategic considerations: Britain gave up the Iraqi mandate for its own reasons and the Palestinian mandate after rebellion, while France surrendered its Syrian and Lebanese mandate because of British pressure at a time of French weakness.[31] Whether the "incubating authority" is the United Nations or a regional organization, its sole purpose would be to ensure that commitments given by a state were actually implemented, rather than merely stated and then ignored, and to ensure that the state's domestic and regional policies corresponded to regional norms. This would be confidence-building as preventive diplomacy, an instrument of conflict management for whose use the political will might not always be present, but one that might need to be part of the armory of regional security organizations and of the United Nations in the future. If the United Nations follows through with the recommendations made by the president of the Security Council in its report of January 1993 to increase consultations with regional organizations, the manner in which states emerging from partition are carefully supervised in their early periods of independence might be a worthy subject for discussion.

CONCLUSION: THE PROBLEM OF MARRYING SOLUTIONS TO PROBLEMS

Ethnic conflict resolution in multiethnic states involves two different approaches, either of which can be considerably disorienting not only for domestic, but also for regional politics. The first is major territorial reform, which is disruptive of the state system and may merely turn civil conflict into international tension. This can take the form of secession of a group from a state or the partition of a state, thus creating two entirely new entities. There are occasions when such forms of state creation are just and necessary, but they almost always produce, at least in the short term, some disorder. The second approach involves structural and distributive solutions that, more often than not, depend on the application and acceptance of a political philosophy that is foreign to the combatants. These solutions include political restructuring, such as the establishment of greater political, linguistic, or educational autonomy in geographically defined areas; the addition or subtraction of provinces in a state; and the creation of a confederation from a unitary state, or vice versa. Another option is simply more active implementation of group or minority rights safeguards, and this might extend to a formal system of distributing power by guaranteeing ethnic groups positions at the political center or the institution of electoral reforms that have the same effect.

Grand settlements are sometimes developed that incorporate elements of all of these conflict resolution techniques. It must be added for the sake of completeness that ethnic conflict is sometimes managed through imperial rule and that today there persist cases, such as that of the island of Mayotte, where the inhabitants prefer a measure of external control to attachment to a neighbor (in this case, Comoros). International institutions have also approved of "transitional authorities"—trusts or mandates in the past—and may in the future adopt analogous intrusive practices to secure ethnic settlements through a transitional period.

Although this is the acknowledged "menu" of "solutions" to ethnic conflicts, attempts by academics or policymakers to identify exactly what "solutions" are applicable to what precise cases have failed. So much is contingent on the circumstances of individual cases and the particular regional implications of different types of solutions. Indeed, the error more often lies in thinking that "one solution is enough" and that the application of a single diplomatic effort to a particular situation is sufficient to bring peace and security to the area. This is the principal fallacy of ethnic conflict resolution. In fact, there are few, if any, instances in which selective choice from the menu is possible; more often, the whole menu needs to be applied, various elements in different places, but more or less simultaneously. There are two general reasons for this.

First, politically, the attenuation of ethnic conflicts lies in convincing the parties involved of a reality that all groups instinctively recognize, but to which few give open and coherent expression: All people desire local freedoms and rights, but they also want and need some higher "court of appeal" to mediate failures to compromise at lower levels. This is the essence of all social contracts to which many aspire: recognition and rights at all levels of human interaction, in return for the performance of commensurate duties. Ideally, both people's freedoms and their forms of redress have to be at different tiers of political interaction: the community, the province, the state, and even, regionally and internationally, through the activity of their leaders in international fora. This is the relevance for international peace and security of human and minority or group rights protection at the substate level, as well as guarantees for the territorial integrity of states within the system.

Second, in an age of ethnonationalism, ethnic conflicts are commutable, but so are the effects of their management. Thus, all ethnic conflict resolution must take into account the local consequences and regional implications of a particular outcome, as well its effects for international public policy. This is difficult because ethnic conflict is about details. The participants in ethnic conflicts fight about the details of history, but also of rules as applied to them, of laws from which they should be exempt, of particular rights of which they have been deprived, of special status they should enjoy: the details of past injustices and of future guarantees. Ethnic warriors fight general principles with specificities: Governments exempt themselves from applying human rights to terrorist groups; rebel leaders seize territory to prevent genocide. Because detail is everything, it follows that in any ethnic conflict, the combatants will tend to distinguish their conflict from all others and especially from those whose form of solution they find inapplicable to themselves. Equally, they willingly draw analogies to political situations thought similar and to principles of international law or public policy from which they should benefit.

It follows from both these points that ethnic conflict management requires both a comprehensive and a tailor-made approach. At least where the international community is involved, this requires a balanced appreciation of how the results of domestic conflict management may, while satisfying those immediately affected, cause difficulties elsewhere, which might require preemptive attention. There is a fine line between the containment of ethnic conflict and its exacerbation. Ending military conflicts is certainly a primary aim of peacemakers, and they should not sacrifice the establishment of a local peace merely for fear of creating an awkward precedent or worrying perhaps paranoid neighbors. While facilitating or approving local plans, they also need to keep the larger regional picture in mind. Thus, recognizing a new state might mean insisting on minority rights or autonomy provisions in the new entity, temporarily deploying forces for confidence-building along new borders, providing observers for elections, supervising the merging of rebel forces with the state army, and warning others about extraterritorial defense of their "nationals." This will often require the intrusive supervision of the implementation of certain political programs and internal reforms.

Because good ethnic conflict management requires a wide and sustained approach, it is inevitable that the international community must make hard judgments about priorities, for not all issues can be treated properly by it at the same time. This is the most compelling reason why regional organizations need to develop some credible and autonomous capacities that remain compatible with UN practices. Sadly, few show any promise in this area. Rarely have regional organizations either developed a set of coherent norms with which states should abide in their relations with their citizens or the means to enforce such norms. Both are needed if conflict resolution is to take place locally.

The outside world will not be able to impose a cosmopolitan diktat that will crush the politics of parochialism, nor can it ignore the injustice that takes place for the sole aim of maintaining a narrow vision of the state. To the extent that the international community becomes involved in the resolution of ethnic conflict, it will invariably need to impart the benefits of channeling ethnic competition through different means of political competition. This will be a delicate political mission. Self-government in ethnically divided societies can only take place with the institution of democratic processes, yet so often the first act of forces liberated by the introduction of democracy is to seek some permanent escape from the state they see as having oppressed them. The maintenance of territorial integrity requires the people who inhabit the territory to believe that its frontiers represent no threat to their liberties. Regimes and governments who see themselves as custodians of the state must appreciate this reality in developing the state's institutions. This is the counsel of perfection conflict managers must somehow turn into practical policy.

Solutions to ethnic conflict will be facilitated to the degree that regional organizations in the latter part of the twentieth century feel able to intrude in the internal affairs of states for the benefit of regional stability. Managing the international politics of parochialism means finding new legal bases for benign political intervention. It means, above all, not letting ethnic conflicts fester for too long. Neither domestic solutions nor ones negotiated through often asymmetric bilateral arrangements are sure to endure. Thus, the international community often needs to get involved—as incubator, as mediator, as confidence-builder, and, sometimes, as enforcer. When it does get engaged in making peace, however, it must take a comprehensive approach. There are no quick fixes. Unfortunately, the "single solution" is usually the enemy of the permanent and the ally of the next conflict in the making.

Notes

[1] See the discussion in Michael Howard, *War and the Liberal Conscience* (Oxford: Oxford University Press, 1981), pp. 49–50.

[2] The *Oxford English Dictionary* has an entry for the word "ethnomaniac" and cites the quoted statement on Alsace made in 1863.

[3] See Julien Benda, *The Treason of the Intellectuals* (New York: W.W. Norton and Co., 1969; originally published in 1928), p. 15.

[4] Ibid.

[5] Malcolm Yapp, "The Legacy of Empire in Western Asia," *Journal of Asian Affairs,* October 1992, p. 270.

[6] John Emerich Edward Dalberg-Acton (First Baron Acton), *Essays on Freedom and Power* (Boston, Mass.: The Beacon Press, 1948), p. 185.

[7] Ibid., p. 193.

[8] From John Stuart Mill, *Considerations on Representative Government*, quoted in Acton, *Essays on Freedom and Power*, p. 181.

[9] Michael Walzer, *Just and Unjust Wars: A Moral Argument with Historical Illustrations* (New York: Pelican Books, 1980), p. 54.

[10] A forceful polemic against self-determination can be found in Amitai Etzioni, "The Evils of Self-Determination," *Foreign Policy*, no. 89, Winter 1992–1993, pp. 21–35.

[11] This discussion draws heavily on the analysis in Hurst Hannam, *Autonomy, Sovereignty, and Self Determination: The Accommodation of Conflicting Rights* (Philadelphia, Penn.: University of Pennsylvania Press, 1990), pp. 27–50.

[12] See the excellent discussion in Crawford Young, "Self-Determination, Territorial Integrity, and the African State System," in Francis M. Deng and I. William Zartman, eds., *Conflict Resolution in Africa* (Washington, D.C.: The Brookings Institution, 1991), p. 328.

[13] Ibid., p. 346.

[14] This is Hannam's conclusion, *Autonomy, Sovereignty, and Self-Determination*, p. 49.

[15] Marc Weller, "The International Response to the Dissolution of the Socialist Federal Republic of Yugoslavia," *American Journal of International Law*, vol. 86, no. 3, July 1992, p. 589.

[16] Ibid., pp. 589–590.

[17] The words of the commission as quoted in Weller, "International Response," p. 592.

18 Ibid.
19 Ibid., p. 606.
20 See Allen Buchanan, *Secession: The Morality of Political Divorce from Fort Sumter to Lithuania and Quebec* (Boulder, Colo.: Westview Press, 1991), especially p. 153.
21 The best short discussion of the political and legal developments in this field is in Christopher Greenwood, "Is There a Right of Humanitarian Intervention?" *The World Today*, vol. 49, no. 2, February 1993, pp. 34–40.
22 Author interview with an official of the Foreign and Commonwealth Office, London. In discussions within the CSCE, differences among the United Kingdom, United States, and France on this issue have sometimes been pronounced.
23 See British Broadcasting Corporation, *Summary of World Broadcasts*, ME/1586 A/10, January 14, 1993.
24 It may be worth noting that Azeris were involved in both the revolution and subsequent government, but this may not allay the fear in the minds of some that the Azeris now look more to Baku.

25 Yapp, "Legacy of Empire," p. 268.
26 See *Le Monde,* April 14, 1992.
27 See Sylvie Kauffman, "Un Entretien avec le Premier Ministre Slovaque," *Le Monde,* July 7, 1992, and the discussion in Amaya Bloch-Lainé, *L'Europe Centrale en Quête de Sécurité,* Les Cahiers du CREST No. 9 (Paris: CREST, January 1993), pp. 19–20.
28 This point is made by Donald L. Horowitz, *Ethnic Groups in Conflict* (Los Angeles, Calif.: University of California Press, 1985), p. 623.
29 Ibid., p. 582.
30 There is no place here to dwell on the importance of recognition as a determinant of whether a state exists in fact. States can exist without diplomatic recognition, and puppet states can be "recognized" as an act of aggression. See Ian Brownlie, *Principles of Public International Law* (Oxford: Oxford University Press, 1979), pp. 89–109.
31 See the excellent discussion in Elie Kedourie, *Nationalism,* 3rd ed. (London: Hutchinson and Co., 1979), pp. 135–138.

Bibliography

Alexander, Yonah, and Robert A. Friedlander, eds. *Self-Determination: National, Regional, and Global Dimensions.* Boulder, Colo.: Westview Press, 1980.

Amer, Ramses. *The United Nations and Foreign Military Intervention: A Comparative Study of the Application of the Charter.* Uppsala, Sweden: Department of Peacekeeping and Conflict Research, University of Uppsala, 1992.

Anderson, Benedict. *Imagined Communities: Reflections on the Origins and Spread of Nationalism.* London: Verso, 1983.

Armstrong, John A. *Nations Before Nationalism.* Chapel Hill, N.C.: University of North Carolina Press, 1982.

Banton, Michael. *Racial and Ethnic Competition.* Cambridge: Cambridge University Press, 1983.

Barber, Benjamin R. "Jihad vs. McWorld," *The Atlantic Monthly,* vol. 269, no. 3, March 1992, pp. 53–65.

Barth, Fredrik, ed. *Ethnic Groups and Boundaries: The Social Organization of Culture Differences.* London: Allen and Unwin, 1969.

Bell, Wendell, and Walter E. Freeman, eds. *Ethnicity and Nation-Building: Comparative, International, and Historical Perspectives.* Beverley Hills, Calif.: Sage Publications, 1984.

Birch, Anthony H. *Nationalism and National Integration.* London: Unwin Hyman, 1989.

Boutros-Ghali, Boutros. *An Agenda for Peace.* New York: United Nations, 1992.

Brass, Paul, ed. *Ethnic Groups and the State.* London: Croom Helm, 1985.

Bremmer, Ian, and Ray Taras, eds. *Nations and Politics in the Soviet Successor States.* Cambridge: Cambridge University Press, 1993.

Breuilly, John. *Nationalism and the State.* Manchester: Manchester University Press, 1982.

Brown, David. "Ethnic Revival: Perspectives on State and Society," *Third World Quarterly,* vol. 11, no. 4, October 1989, pp. 1–17.

Brown, J.F. *Nationalism, Democracy and Security in the Balkans.* Aldershot, England: Dartmouth Publishing Company, Ltd., 1992.

Brzezinski, Zbigniew. "Post-Communist Nationalism," *Foreign Affairs*, vol. 68, no. 5, Winter 1989–1990, pp. 1–25.

Buchanan, Allen. *Secession: The Morality of Political Divorce from Fort Sumter to Lithuania and Quebec.* Boulder, Colo.: Westview Press, 1991.

Buchheit, Lee C. *Secession: The Legitimacy of Self-Determination.* New Haven, Conn.: Yale University Press, 1978.

Bull, Hedley. *The Anarchical Society: A Study of Order in World Politics.* London: Macmillan, 1977.

Buzan, Barry. *People, States and Fear: The National Security Problem in International Relations.* Brighton, England: Harvester Wheatsheaf, 1983.

Camilleri, Joseph A., and Jim Falk. *The End of Sovereignty? The Politics of a Shrinking and Fragmenting World.* Aldershot, England: Edward Elgar, 1992.

Chaliand, Gérard, ed. *Minority Peoples in the Age of Nation-States.* London: Pluto, 1989.

Cobban, Alfred. *The Nation State and National Self-Determination.* New York: Thomas Crowell, 1969.

Cohen, Stephen P. "U.S. Security in a Separatist Season," *Bulletin of the Atomic Scientists*, vol. 48, no. 6, July–August 1992, pp. 28–32.

Connor, Walker. "The Politics of Ethnonationalism," *Journal of International Affairs,* vol. 27, no. 1, 1973, pp. 1–21.

Crawford, James R. *The Creation of States in International Law.* Oxford: Oxford University Press, 1979.

Deutsch, Karl W. *Nationalism and Its Alternatives.* New York: Alfred A. Knopf, 1969.

————. *Nationalism and Social Communication.* Cambridge, Mass.: MIT Press, 1966 edition.

Donnelly, Jack. *Universal Human Rights in Theory and Practice.* Ithaca, N.Y.: Cornell University Press, 1989.

Durch, William J., and Barry Blechman. *Keeping the Peace: The United Nations in the Emerging World Order.* Washington, D.C.: Henry Stimson Center, 1992.

Enloe, Cynthia H. *Ethnic Conflict and Political Development.* Boston: Little, Brown, 1973.

Esman, Milton J., ed. *Ethnic Conflict in the Western World.* Ithaca, N.Y.: Cornell University Press, 1977.

————. "Ethnic Politics and Economic Power," *Comparative Politics,* vol. 19, no. 4, July 1987, pp. 395–418.

Etzioni, Amitai. "The Evils of Self-Determination," *Foreign Policy*, no. 89, Winter 1992–1993, pp. 21-35.

Ganguly, Sumit. "Ethno-Religious Conflict in South Asia," *Survival*, vol. 35, no. 2, Summer 1993, pp. 88–109.

Gelfand, Donald E., and Russell D. Lee, eds. *Ethnic Conflicts and Power: A Cross-National Perspective.* New York: Wiley, 1973.

Gellner, Ernest. *Nations and Nationalism*. Ithaca, N.Y.: Cornell University Press, 1983.

Glazer, Nathan. *Ethnic Dilemmas, 1964–1982*. Cambridge, Mass.: Harvard University Press, 1983.

Glazer, Nathan, and Daniel Moynihan, eds. *Ethnicity: Theory and Experience*. Cambridge, Mass.: Harvard University Press, 1975.

Goldwin, Robert A., Art Kaufman, and William A. Schambra, eds. *Forging Unity Out of Diversity: The Approaches of Eight Nations*. Washington, D.C.: American Enterprise Institute, 1989.

Greenfeld, Liah. *Nationalism: Five Roads to Modernity*. Cambridge, Mass.: Harvard University Press, 1992.

Greenwood, Christopher. "Is There a Right of Humanitarian Intervention?" *The World Today*, vol. 49, no. 2, February 1993, pp. 34–40.

Haas, Ernest, B. *Beyond the Nation-State: Functionalism and International Organization*. Palo Alto, Calif.: Stanford University Press, 1964.

Halperin, Morton H., and David J. Scheffer. *Self-Determination in the New World Order*. Washington, D.C.: Carnegie Endowment for International Peace, 1992.

Hannam, Hurst. *Autonomy, Sovereignty, and Self-Determination: The Accommodation of Conflicting Rights*. Philadelphia, Penn.: University of Pennsylvania Press, 1990.

Hayes, Carlton J.H. *The Historical Evolution of Nationalism*. New York: Macmillan, 1948.

Helman, Gerald, and Steven Ratner. "Saving Failed States," *Foreign Policy*, no. 89, Winter 1992–1993, pp. 3–20.

Henze, Paul B. *Ethnic Dynamics and Dilemmas of the Russian Republic*. Santa Monica, Calif.: Rand Corporation Note N-3219-USDP, 1991.

Heraclides, Alexis. "Secessionist Minorities and External Involvement," *International Organization,* vol. 44, no. 3, Summer 1990, pp. 341–378.

—————. *The Self-Determination of Minorities in International Politics*. London: Frank Cass, 1991.

Hinsley, F.H. *Nationalism and the International System*. London: Hodder and Stoughton, 1973.

Hobsbawm, Eric J. *Nations and Nationalism since 1980*. Cambridge: Cambridge University Press, 1990.

Hopf, Ted. "Managing Soviet Disintegration: A Demand for Behavioral Regimes," *International Security*, vol. 17, no. 1,Summer 1992, pp. 44–75.

Horowitz, Donald L. *Ethnic Groups in Conflict*. Berkeley, Calif.: University of California Press, 1985.

Huntington, Samuel P. *Political Order in Changing Societies*. New Haven, Conn.: Yale University Press, 1968.

—————. *The Third Wave: Democratization in the Late Twentieth Century*. Norman, Okla.: University of Oklahoma Press, 1991.

Jackson, Robert H. *Quasi-States: Sovereignty, International Relations, and the Third World*. Cambridge: Cambridge University Press, 1990.

Jervis, Robert. "Cooperation under the Security Dilemma," *World Politics*, vol. 30, no. 2, January 1978, pp. 167–213.

———. *Perception and Misperception in International Politics*. Princeton, N.J.: Princeton University Press, 1976.

Kedourie, Elie. *Nationalism*. London: Hutchinson, 1985 edition.

Kellas, James G. *The Politics of Nationalism and Ethnicity*. London: Macmillan, 1991.

Kennedy, Paul. "The Decline of Nationalistic History in the West, 1900–1970," *Journal of Contemporary History*, vol. 8, no. 1, January 1973, pp. 77–100.

Kohn, Hans. *The Idea of Nationalism*. New York: Macmillan, 1961.

———. *Nationalism: Its Meaning and History*. Princeton, N.J.: Van Nostrand, 1965.

Mair, L.P. *The Protection of Minorities: The Working and Scope of the Minorities Treaties Under the League of Nations*. London: Christophers, 1928.

Mayall, James. *Nationalism and International Society*. Cambridge: Cambridge University Press, 1990.

———. "Non-Intervention, Self-Determination, and the 'New World Order'," *International Affairs*, vol. 67, no. 3, July 1991, pp. 421–429.

Maynes, Charles William. "Containing Ethnic Conflict," *Foreign Policy*, no. 90, Spring 1993, pp. 3–21.

McNeill, William H. *Polyethnicity and National Unity in World History*. Toronto: University of Toronto Press, 1986.

Mellor, Roy E.H. *Nation, State, and Territory: A Political Geography*. London: Routledge, 1989.

Miall, Hugh. *The Peacemakers: Peaceful Settlement of Disputes since 1945*. Oxford: Macmillan, 1992.

Montville, Joseph V., ed. *Conflict and Peacekeeping in Multiethnic Societies*. Lexington, Mass.: Lexington Books, 1990.

Motyl, Alexander, ed. *Thinking Theoretically about Soviet Nationalities*. New York: Columbia University Press, 1992.

Moynihan, Daniel Patrick. *Pandaemonium: Ethnicity in International Politics*. Oxford: Oxford University Press, 1993.

Nahaylo, Bohdan, and Victor Swoboda. *Soviet Disunion: A History of the Nationalities Problem in the USSR*. New York: Free Press, 1989.

O'Donnell, Guillermo, Phillippe Schmitter, and Laurence Whitehead, eds. *Transitions from Authoritarian Rule*. Baltimore, Md.: Johns Hopkins University Press, 1986.

Premas, Ralph R., S.W.R. de A. Samarasinghe, and Alan B. Anderson, eds. *Secessionist Movements in Comparative Perspective*. London: Pinter, 1990.

Ra'anan, Uri. *Ethnic Resurgence in Modern Democratic States*. New York: Pergamon Press, 1980.

Ra'anan, Uri, Maria Mesner, Keith Armes, and Kate Martin, eds. *State and Nation in Multi-Ethnic Societies: The Breakup of Multinational States.* Manchester: Manchester University Press, 1991.

Rodley, Nigel S., ed. *To Loose the Bands of Wickedness: International Intervention in Defence of Human Rights.* London: Brassey's, 1992.

Ronen, Dov. *The Quest for Self-Determination.* New Haven, Conn.: Yale University Press, 1979.

Rothschild, Joseph. *Ethnopolitics: A Conceptual Framework.* New York: Columbia University Press, 1981.

Rustow, Dankwart. *A World of Nations.* Washington D.C.: Brookings Institution, 1967.

Ryan, Stephen. *Ethnic Conflict and International Relations.* Brookfield, Vt.: Dartmouth Publishing Co., 1990.

Schelling, Thomas C. *Arms and Influence.* New Haven, Conn.: Yale University Press, 1966.

Seton-Watson, Hugh. *Nationalism, Old and New.* Sydney: Sydney University Press, 1965.

————. *Nations and States.* London: Methuen, 1977.

Shafer, Boyd C. *Faces of Nationalism: New Realities and Old Myths.* New York: Harcourt Brace Jovanovich, 1972.

Sheffer, Gabriel, ed. *Modern Diasporas in International Politics.* London: Croom Helm, 1986.

Shiel, Frederick L, ed. *Ethnic Separatism and World Politics.* Lanham, Md.: University Press of America, 1984.

Smith, Anthony D. *The Ethnic Origins of Nations.* New York: Basil Blackwell Ltd., 1986.

————. *The Ethnic Revival in the Modern World.* New York: Cambridge University Press, 1981.

————. *National Identity.* London: Penguin Books, 1991.

————. "National Identity and the Idea of European Unity," *International Affairs,* vol. 68, no. 1, January 1992, pp. 55–76.

————. *State and Nation in the Third World.* New York: St. Martin's Press, 1983.

————. *Theories of Nationalism.* New York: Holmes and Meier, 1983.

Smith, Graham, ed. *The Nationalities Question in the Soviet Union.* London: Longman, 1990.

Smith, Mark. *The Soviet Fault Line: Ethnic Insecurity and Territorial Dispute in the Former USSR.* London: Royal United Services Institute for Defence Studies, 1991.

Snyder, Jack. "Nationalism and Instability in the Former SovietEmpire," *Arms Control,* vol. 12, no. 3, December 1991, pp. 6–16.

Snyder, Lewis L. *Global Mini-Nationalisms: Autonomy or Independence.* Westport, Conn.: Greenwood Press, 1982.

————. *The New Nationalism.* Ithaca, N.Y.: Cornell University Press, 1968.

—————. *Varieties of Nationalism: A Comparative Study*. Hinsdale, Ill.: Dryden, 1976.

Stack, John F., Jr. *Ethnic Identities in a Transnational World.* Westport, Conn.: Greenwood Press, 1981.

—————. *The Primordial Challenge: Ethnicity in the Contemporary World.* Westport, Conn: Greenwood Press, 1986.

Suhrke, Astri, and Leila G. Noble, eds. *Ethnic Conflict in International Relations.* New York: Praeger Publishers, 1977.

Tilly, Charles, ed. *Coercion, Capital, and European States.* Cambridge: Basil Blackwell, 1990.

—————, ed. *The Formation of National States in Western Europe.* Princeton, N.J.: Princeton University Press, 1975.

Toland, Judith D., ed. *Ethnicity and the State.* New Brunswick, N.J.: Transaction Press, 1993.

Van Evera, Stephen. "Managing the Eastern Crisis: Preventing War in the Former Soviet Empire," *Security Studies*, vol. 1, no. 3, Spring 1992, pp. 361–382.

Waltz, Kenneth N. *Man, the State and War: A Theoretical Analysis.* New York: Columbia University Press, 1959.

—————. *Theory of International Politics.* Reading, Mass.: Addison Wesley, 1979.

Watson, Michael, ed. *Contemporary Minority Nationalism.* London: Routledge, 1990.

Weiner, Myron. "Peoples and States in a New Ethnic Order?" *Third World Quarterly*, vol. 13, no. 2, 1992, pp. 317–333.

Williams, Colin H. *National Separatism.* Cardiff: University of Wales Press, 1982.

Zametica, John. *The Yugoslav Conflict*, Adelphi Paper 270. London: Brassey's for the IISS, 1992.

Index